CONTEMPORARY INDUSTRIAL RELATIONS: A CRITICAL ANALYSIS

EDITED BY IAN BEARDWELL

Oxford University Press

*This book has been printed digitally and produced in a standard specification
in order to ensure its continuing availability*

OXFORD
UNIVERSITY PRESS

Great Clarendon Street, Oxford OX2 6DP

Oxford University Press is a department of the University of Oxford.
It furthers the University's objective of excellence in research, scholarship,
and education by publishing worldwide in

Oxford New York

Auckland Bangkok Buenos Aires Cape Town Chennai
Dar es Salaam Delhi Hong Kong Istanbul Karachi Kolkata
Kuala Lumpur Madrid Melbourne Mexico City Mumbai Nairobi
São Paulo Shanghai Singapore Taipei Tokyo Toronto

with an associated company in Berlin

Published in the United States
by Oxford University Press Inc., New York

ISBN 0-19-877388-9

PREFACE

In recent years industrial relations in Britain has been at the centre of a series of competing prescriptions and analyses concerning its substance and its future. The legislative reforms of the 1980s have tied unions into a complex web of controls which impose heavy obligations and penalties on many forms of previously lawful action; the labour-market has undergone major restructuring as product markets have come under heavy international competition; management as a function has been afforded greater discretion at a time when managers as individuals have lost a great deal of their security and status; new manufacturing processes from economies such as Japan have combined with an emphasis on quality and the customer to impose new disciplines on work organization; the public sector has been exposed to the presumed benefits of competitive tendering and wholesale privatization.

Across a wide range of industrial relations activity there has been adaption and innovation as the prescriptions for change have flowed in. There can have been few decades in which so much has happened to, and in the name of, industrial relations reform in so active and fundamental a manner.

The questions which are posed by this agenda go to the heart of the collectivized employment relationship in Britain. The decline in union membership, the erosion of collectively determined pay, the growth of the non-union organization, all attest to the shift in priorities in British industrial relations. Assumptions concerning the desire to act collectively on the part of employees are now actively questioned. The support of the State in sustaining a collective industrial relations process is now no longer automatically taken for granted, regardless of political party. In these circumstances, it seems appropriate to bring together a series of analyses which seek to explore these themes in a systematic and extended manner.

The contributions which follow exemplify the range of high quality industrial relations analysis which is being undertaken in British universities at the present time. Each of the contributors has written on a topic on which they have both an expertise and an argument to present; in this sense there is no single ideological or analytical stance that has bound the contributors. What does come through from the range of material presented here is the strength of the analysis being offered and a proper scepticism in dealing with the popular myths of contemporary industrial relations.

The book opens with a discussion by the Editor on the theme of the 'New Industrial Relations', in which the difficulties of establishing what is happening are located in a broader discussion concerning the collapse of the old orthodoxy of 'voluntarism'. David Guest and Kim Hoque examine the issue of whether HRM and trade-unionism are compatible in the specific circumstances of greenfield sites; they argue that single union deals are compatible but that multi-unionism is not and pose the question as to why any employer might want to recognize a union at a new establishment. Stephen Dunn and David Metcalf examine the impact of the law since 1979 to establish whether it played so vital a part in the reshaping of trade unions in circumstances where market conditions had weakened them already. Peter Nolan argues that linkages between industrial relations and economic performance in the 1980s were tenuous and that the basic weaknesses of the British economy remain, despite considerable Government effort to reform trade unions. Ian Clark analyses the role of the State in industrial relations and argues that one consequence of the State's actions in the post-war period has been the relegation of industrial relations to the status of an input problem to the management of the economy to which subsequent reform has failed to find a satisfactory answer. Ed Heery argues that unions have experienced two significant waves of innovation over the past three decades, which have represented a sharp break with pre-existing approaches to members, union government, and union management. Tim Claydon develops further his original and innovative study of derecognition and examines how far and in what ways derecognition has continued in Britain. Rachel Bailey analyses the impact of the profound changes to employment, bargaining, and management in the public sector. David Grant uses a case study to critically examine one of the most important aspects of recent industrial relations, the impact of Japanization.

I am particularly grateful to all the contributors for having written at a time of competing pressures and for their forbearance while the book was put together editorially. As Editor I remain responsible for the final product, but I have been wholly dependent upon the goodwill and high quality of my fellow contributors' chapters which have permitted the book to be accepted by the Delegates of the Oxford University Press. In that respect I have been fortunate in working with David Musson of OUP who has been an unfailing source of support and encouragement as the project unfolded. My final thanks must go to a range of professional colleagues within BUIRA who discussed many of these issues with me, and, in particular, to my Departmental colleagues Ian Clark, Tim Claydon, Damien O'Doherty, Sue Marlow, and Julie Storey who have variously commented on conference papers and other drafts and discussed many of the themes that formed my own ideas for the book.

I.B.

Department of Human Resource Management
De Montfort University
July 1995

CONTENTS

LIST OF FIGURES

LIST OF TABLES

LIST OF ACRONYMS

AA	Automobile Association
ACAS	Advisory, Conciliation, and Arbitration Service
AEEU	Amalgamated Engineering and Electrical Union
AEU	Amalgamated Engineering Union
AFL	American Federation of Labor
AJEI	Anglo-Japanese Economic Institute
APEX	Association of Professional, Executive, Clerical, and Computer Staff
APT and C	Local government Administrative, Professional, Technical and Clerical [staff]
ASTMS	Association of Scientific, Technical, and Managerial Staff
ATL	Association of Teachers and Lecturers
AUCL	Association of University and College Lecturers
AUT	Association of University Teachers
BGSU	Barclay's Group Staff Union
BIFU	Bank, Insurance, and Finance Union
BR	British Rail
BS	British Steel
BUIRA	British Universities' Industrial Relations Association
CBI	Confederation of British Industry
CCT	Compulsory Competitive Tendering
CEP	Centre for Economic Performance (LSE)
CIO	Confederation of Industrial Organizations
CLIRS	Company Level Industrial Relations Survey (followed by no. of survey if appropriate)
COHSE	Confederation of Health Service Employees
CPSA	Civil and Public Services Association
CROTUM	Commissioner for the Rights of Trade Union Members
DEC	Digital Equipment Corporation
DFE	Department of Education
EETPU	Electrical, Electronic, Telecommunications, and Plumbing Union
EFTA	European Free Trade Association
EMC	Executive Management Committee
ESRC	Economic and Social Research Council
FLARE	Fair Laws and Rights in Employment (a GMB campaign)
GCHQ	Government Communications Headquarters

GMB	General Municipal and Boilermakers' Union
GMWU	General and Municipal Workers' Union
HMSO	Her Majesty's Stationery Office
IBM	International Business Machines
ICI	Imperial Chemical Industries
IDS	Incomes Data Services
IFS	Institute of Fiscal Studies
IPM	Institute of Personnel Management
IPMS	Institute of Professional and Managerial Staff
IRS	Industrial Relations Services
IRSF	Inland Revenue Staff Federation
IRRR	*Industrial Relations Review and Report*
ISTC	Iron and Steel Trades Confederation
LEA	Local Education Authority
LGU	Ladies' Golf Union
LSE	London School of Economics and Political Science
MBA	Master of Business Administration
MIT	Massachusetts Institute of Technology
MORI	Market and Opinion Research International
MSF	Manufacturing, Science, and Finance Union
NALGO	National and Local Government Officers' Association
NATFHE	National Association of Teachers in Further and Higher Education
NCU	National Communications Union
NGA	National Graphical Association
NHS	National Health Service
NIESR	National Institute of Economic and Social Research
NJAC	National Joint Advisory Council
NUPE	National Union of Public Employees
NUT	National Union of Teachers
OECD	Organization for Economic Cooperation and Development
PAT	Professional Association of Teachers
PO	Post Office
P&O	Peninsular and Oriental Shipping Company
PSI	Policy Studies Institute
RCN	Royal College of Nursing
RMT	National Union of Rail, Maritime, and Transport Workers
ROPA	Registration of Procedural Agreements
SERTUC	South East Regional Trades Union Congress Women's Committee
STRB	School Teachers' Review Body
TGWU	Transport and General Workers' Union
TQM	Total Quality Management
TSSA	Transport Salaried Staffs Association
TUC	Trade Union Congress

TULRA	Trade Union and Labour Relations Act
TUPE	Transfer of Undertakings (Protection of Employment) legislation
UCATT	Union of Construction, Allied Trades, and Technicians
UNISON	Name given to merged NUPE, NALGO, and COHSE
USDAW	Union of Shop, Distributive, and Allied Workers
WIRS	Workplace Industrial Relations Survey (followed by no. of survey where appropriate)

NOTES ON CONTRIBUTORS

RACHEL BAILEY, Lecturer in Industrial Relations, London School of Economics

IAN BEARDWELL, Professor of Industrial Relations, De Montfort University.

IAN CLARK, Principal Lecturer in Industrial Relations, De Montfort University.

TIM CLAYDON, Principal Lecturer in Industrial Relations, De Montfort University.

STEPHEN DUNN, Senior Lecturer in Industrial Relations, London School of Economics.

DAVID GRANT, Lecturer in Industrial Relations, King's College, London.

DAVID GUEST, Professor of Occupational Psychology, Birkbeck College, London.

EDMUND HEERY, Professor of Human Resource Management, Cardiff Business School.

KIM HOQUE, Research Officer, Centre for Economic Performance, London School of Economics.

DAVID METCALF, Professor of Industrial Relations and Deputy Director, Centre for Economic Performance, London School of Economics.

PETER NOLAN, Montague Burton Professor of Industrial Relations, University of Leeds.

1

'HOW DO WE KNOW HOW IT REALLY IS?' AN ANALYSIS OF THE NEW INDUSTRIAL RELATIONS

Ian Beardwell

1. Introduction

The question which provides the title for this chapter is the question which the historian E. H. Carr posed for himself in the 1961 Trevelyan Lectures at Cambridge (Carr 1961); it is also the dilemma facing contemporary industrial relations analysis in seeking to explain the nature of the 'new industrial relations' debate in Britain.

Carr's question is as relevant to the concerns of industrial relations analysts today as it was to historians thirty-four years ago because of its focus on establishing what constitutes meaningful analysis of complex events. The questions of whether new patterns of industrial relations are emerging and, if they are, their relationship with what went before, are as in need of systematic analysis as Carr suggested was the case for historians in deciding what constituted historically significant facts. Thus any attempt to elucidate whether Britain has a 'new industrial relations' that is significantly different from past practice has to take into account both the nature of the debate about the 'new' and to reflect on what it was about the 'old' that permitted the former to prevail over the latter. The purpose of this chapter is to set out some of the principal areas of this debate and to examine whether the 'new industrial relations' thesis is sufficiently embedded in the UK context for it to be viewed as a sustainable feature of the British employment relationship.

I am particularly grateful to my colleague Ian Clark for his comments on an earlier draft of this chapter and for the opportunity to read some of his doctoral work which I have been able to take into account.

2. The Scope and Content of the 'New Industrial Relations'

The initial British concern with new developments in industrial relations drew heavily from two important, but quite distinct, sources (Beardwell 1992*a*). The first referred to the emergence in the United States of a pattern of non-institutional, non-union (and often non-collectivized) employee relations in which the sustaining rhetoric was not to be found in the language of bargaining, but in the language of commitment and attachment to organizational goals. Within the context of the American experience of the long-run decline in unionization and the weakening impact of collective bargaining, US management developed a mix of measures which, under the generic title of 'human resource management', offered up a means of managing industrial relations that drew heavily upon an agenda that paid little, if any, regard for pluralist conceptions of the employment relationship (Kochan *et al.* 1986). To some extent echoes of this argument found their way into some British analyses of the decline of unionization and its implications for a non-unionized workforce (Bassett 1986).

The second source was indigenous and derived from the reforms of the Conservative Governments across the decade of the 1980s. The driving force behind the legislative changes was the Governments' concern with the role and power of unions in the British economy. Thus reform of industrial relations was couched in very narrow terms concerned almost exclusively with defining, prescribing, and proscribing a range of union activities in order to achieve a set of policy objectives for the British economy; these objectives were more usually expressed in terms of 'flexibility' and 'competitiveness' rather than 'new industrial relations', but the implication of these reforms was that, once achieved, British industrial relations would be 'better' and that benefits would flow into the economy as a consequence.

The difficulty with both of these sources is that neither is sufficiently strong enough in its own terms to explain the pattern of profound change that has overtaken the collectively bargained employment relationship in the UK. The undeniable impact of human resource management-based employment strategies is still not so widely applied in Britain for it to have established itself as the predominant mode (Millward *et al.* 1992). Equally, the intensive focus of legislative reform on union issues has not provided any wider basis on which to construct the employment relationship (Kessler and Bayliss 1992). Taken together, these two influences on the nature of industrial relations provide little by way of a systematic or articulated explanation of what has happened to industrial relations in Britain, although there is some analysis which argues that the implications of some of these shifts in collectivism and human resource management might constitute a new format for employee relations in certain specific contexts (Guest and Hoque 1993).

From the standpoint of the mid-1990s a third source of analytical material can now be added. WIRS3 (1992), CLIRS2 (1993), and the analysis of the 'new industrial relations' in terms of WIRS3 by Millward (1993) all provide valuable insights into illuminating the opening question of this chapter. The extent to which survey data can establish what is happening to industrial relations has become a live issue (McCarthy 1994; Millward and Hawes 1995). What can be said is that WIRS3 has established the scale of the decline of the old order of industrial relations infrastructure in Britain in circumstances where no large-scale replacement has yet emerged to replace it.

Thus the difficulty in assessing the extent and significance of new patterns of industrial relations is that no single source element holds the explanatory key. Indeed, it would be wrong to look towards one set of phenomena that provided just such an answer. If there is a criticism to be made of the work of Kochan *et al.* (1986) in this respect, it is that a new and extensive model of American industrial relations is presented, just as Columbus was able to present the discovery of America as a continent with a viable climate, welcoming inhabitants, and a sustaining habitat. Fully formed new industrial relations processes are rarely to hand and the reality of Columbus's initial discovery lay as much with subsequent explorers' experiences of alligators, deserts, and harsh winters as his own landfall on America's temperate eastern seaboard.

As far as the debate in Britain is concerned, there is a vital element that has to be taken into account which involves explaining how the reformist zeal of the late 1960s and early 1970s did not produce a pattern of industrial relations that was itself new and sustainable in the medium term. In order to do that it is necessary to examine how the traditional concerns of industrial relations were supplanted by new agendas and how the process of reform, stimulated by Donovan, failed to address the shift towards new patterns of managing the employment relationship.

3. Historic and Contemporary Concerns of Industrial Relations

A critical part of the analysis of whether the UK has a new employee relations lies in the central concerns that industrial relations has presented historically, and comparing them with contemporary circumstances. The argument here is that British industrial relations has historically and traditionally been con-cerned, and sometimes obsessed, with the general issue of the location and role of collective bargaining in a market economy: in its most acute form this emphasis has focused on the trade union as the agent of collective bargaining requiring better management by means of more comprehensive or tougher public policy interventions by government. This has given rise to a series of questions which are to do with the space that unions occupy within the employment relationship, the extent of their influence, and the legitimacy of their role. The strength of this prevailing concern sustained a particular form of industrial relations in Britain from the mid-nineteenth century through to the late 1970s and provided the impetus for the Conservative labour law reforms of the 1980s.

The essential element in this form of industrial relations was either containment or legitimization within what grew to be the framework of 'voluntarism', which might best be described as 'collective *laissez faire*', on the part of government. The important point about this central concern with the trade union was that it was unresolved within that construction of industrial relations. The general strength of unions as collective agencies on behalf of employees ensured that the union and voluntary collective bargaining remained as the central elements that had to be addressed and readdressed at regular intervals. The industrial relations legislation of the 1980s could be viewed as part of that process. Although it would not be a sympathetic analysis of the role of trade unions, and would not accord with the analysis that saw the reforms as part of a general weakening of legitimate trade union actions, there is a relationship between the argument over the positioning of unions in the economy and what the legislation set out to achieve. Thus, rather than being viewed as an abrupt break with past philosophies of the legal regulation of industrial relations, recent legal interventions have had a rich and fertile ground in which to root. The point about the reforms of the past decade is not so much their atypicality, and their destruction of the voluntarist pattern, as their direct connection with this central historical concern with the location of the union and the role of collective bargaining in a late twentieth-century economy.

Purcell (1993) has provided a critical analysis of this process in terms of 'The End of Institutional Industrial Relations'; I wish to examine some of the principal components of Purcell's argument because they encapsulate a number of the issues that go to the heart of the debate about the future of British industrial relations. The starting-point for this examination is the concept of 'institution' as applied to the British experience of the employment relationship. Purcell accepts the broad definition of 'institution' offered by Ferner and Hyman (1992) as including the results of collective agreements and their coverage of wide ranges of employees, unionized or not. Thus the participants, processes, and outcomes of collective bargaining in the UK came to be seen as an institutional framework at least as distinctive as that which appeared under different legal systems in other market economies. To this extent, the voluntarism which Kahn-Freund (1954) suggested characterized the British approach to the regulation of collective bargaining was itself raised to the status of an institutional component to the point of becoming perhaps the defining institution for 1960s analyses of industrial relations (Flanders 1967; Donovan 1968); within the framework of voluntarism formal institutional participants such as unions, employers' associations, and government played their roles, alongside what might be termed the 'neo-institutionalism' of stewards, managers, and plant bargaining. Thus what Flanders termed the 'system'—drawing from Dunlop (1955)—was in fact constructed from a wide-ranging but unstable set of actors, formal organizations, processes, and outcomes which, together, coexisted in an alliance that could be described as the institutional context of British industrial relations, which was sometimes turbulent and at other times quiescent but which was always volatile.

Purcell describes the four components of this institutional framework as comprising, first, legal support for union membership and the extension of union influence beyond collective agreements; secondly, legal immunity for trade unions both for disputes in general and secondary actions in particular; thirdly, an acceptance of collective bargaining; and, fourthly, the legitimization of union influence in tripartite institutions and in public sector employment. The extent to which these four pillars have become eroded and weakened marks the extent to which: 'We are seeing the progressive collapse of the system of industrial relations marked especially by the end of institutional mechanisms created over the past 100 years to bring order and stability to industrial relations' (Purcell 1993: 10). The point at issue is whether there ever was an institutional framework in Britain that could have provided the stability that Purcell alludes to, and, if there was, why it proved so curiously susceptible to overturn in the 1980s when, by Purcell's own admission: 'None of these, by themselves, would necessarily lead to a collapse of the industrial relations system since there has been no direct attack on the rights to collective bargaining, the freedom to join trade unions or the ability of employers to recognize trade unions for collective bargaining purposes' (1993: 9). The causes of this paradox lie much deeper than Purcell suggests, so that his analysis, while correct in its description of the contemporary fate of industrial relations, does not address further structural weaknesses that have characterized the British experience.

4. The Non-Institutionalization of British Industrial Relations

The argument under review has stressed the context of institutionalism and its demise over the past decade. However, there is an alternative case to be examined, the premiss of which is that British industrial relations was never institutionalized but was perennially unstable because it was either un- or under-institutionalized. Thus the institutional failure noted by Purcell goes back over thirty years to the reforms of the 1960s rather than ten years to the 1980s. With each successive phase of post-war industrial relations developments, among them extensive unionization, wider collective bargaining coverage, the growth of informal trade union organization, and the diversification of wage payment methods, the four components of institutionalism which Purcell has noted encountered great difficulty in adapting and accommodating to the extent of change occurring. Faced with this large agenda policy-makers sought to create a new institutional framework in order to contain these developments; this can best be seen in considering the concept of voluntarism. Instead of being seen primarily as a means of enabling certain industrial relations processes to operate in the particular circumstances of the UK's economic and legal contexts, it became elevated into an institution in its own right. This elevation was enshrined not only in the recommendations of Donovan, but provided the rationale for a wide range of industrial relations reform—to include the Labour Government's 'In Place of Strife' (1969), the work of the Commission on Industrial Relations (1969–74), the Conservative Government's Industrial Relations Act (1972), the Labour Government's Trade Union and Labour Relations Acts (1974/6) and Employment Protection Act (1975), and the creation of ACAS (1974). Thus voluntarism moved from being a socio-legal analytical construct of the 1950s to a key institutional feature in post-1960s industrial relations analysis which a wide variety of reformers and analysts invoked in order to legitimate their recommendations for reform. The concept of the voluntarist system came to be the descriptor of the late-1960s institutionalization of British industrial relations, containing within it the two ill-defined and imprecise terms of voluntarism and system which were used to explain away a divergent range of British practice and prescription.

An example of this desire to create a new institutional framework for the processes of industrial relations was the attempt to include procedural reform in the neo-institutional net being woven for the post-Donovan world. The extreme was perhaps reached in the ROPA set up by the Department of Employment and Productivity in the wake of the Royal Commission Report, with copies of procedures submitted being held by both the CBI and the TUC on a tripartite basis. The registration of agreements was supposed to stimulate procedural reform and to provide a record of how far unions and managements had taken the process of devising new institutions in a voluntarist world. Whether this formalization and collation of agreements helped or hindered industrial relations thereafter must remain a matter for conjecture.

Thus, so far from providing a reformulated basis for industrial relations, the attempts of the late 1960s and early 1970s to create a neo-institutional framework based around loosely defined constructs left industrial relations susceptible to an excess of expectation as to what could be achieved or improved under voluntarism. When voluntarism cracked in the late 1970s it was under the unrealistic combination of employee pressure for free collective bargaining, Government pressure for union maintenance of incomes policy, and union expectations that the Government could engineer better economic circumstances. None of the neo-institutional framework constructed in the decade following Donovan could provide a means to avert that crisis.

5. The Location of the 'New Industrial Relations'

If the institutional framework described by Purcell was in reality weaker than might have been supposed at the end of the 1970s, it provided rich ground for the emergence of different approaches to managing the employment relationship. With the withdrawal from collective *laissez faire* by the Government, the edifice of post-Donovan neo-institutionalism became highly vulnerable. But the collapse of institutionalized industrial relations owed as much to shifts in sentiment about the relevance of some of the key institutions for many employees and managers as it does to changes in public policy or legal reform. Expressed in this way, the predominant concern of employee relations is no longer about the role of collective bargaining, and the union as its agent, as about securing employee assent and expressing managerial commitment to achieving that assent. Collective bargaining may play a role in that process, and union membership may not be excluded either, but neither are now the primary means by which the employment relationship is expressed. My argument here is that, perhaps for the first time in a century, it is possible to reconstruct the central problem of industrial relations as being not so much the role of the trade union in the market economy as the role of the individual within the employment relationship, and in this way recast the framework of industrial relations so that the traditional collectivism we have been accustomed to is greatly reduced.

Within this framework a new and different conception of employee relations can be perceived. We have customarily regarded the individual employee as in some way incomplete without collective representation, and linked the debate about the location of the union to the importance of the individual achieving such representation. In this model of industrial relations the individual is seen as a victim who must be assisted in overcoming the problem of non-representation by the extension of collective bargaining and union recognition aided by statutory support where appropriate, as in various sections of the 1971 and 1975 legislation, for example. It was this process which the reformism of the post-Donovan era sought to provide by the institutionalization of recognition as State policy. The argument here is that if the contemporary concern of industrial relations is not with the location of the union, but with the location of the individual within the employment relationship in the market economy, then the model moves from portraying the individual as a victim to portraying the individual as an accomplice with management in an indifference to traditional industrial relations values and as less susceptible to the collectivism of representation which has been the unions' strength hitherto (Beardwell 1992*b*).

This is a fairly fundamental shift in the conception of industrial relations in Britain, and sets out the debate about the new industrial relations in a different manner from the more usual interest in changes in detailed collective bargaining procedures. What is at issue is not so much whether we have more or less collective pay, or more or less single-table bargaining, or a greater or lesser number of single union deals, important though all of those issues are in looking at the working of industrial relations, but rather what it is that provides the prevailing ethic of employee relations at a given time. Hitherto, collective bargaining has provided just such a rationale for much of the collective British employment relationship, but with its scope now much reduced other rationales take on a new significance. The idea that individualism might provide a sustaining ethic for the new industrial relations has its supporters but as Kessler and Purcell show (1995) individualism and collectivism are not mutually exclusive categories but are separate components of the same employment relationship. If there are new rationales which address the employment relationship then we face the possibility, at least, that they are not derived from the language and culture of industrial relations as they have been in the past but are provided by other, wider influences.

Storey (1995) points out that it has not been the traditional industrial relations reform model which has contributed to this process of reshaping employee relations, but the language of restructuring and organizational redesign. Thus the new industrial relations can be seen to be composed of a number of elements, by no means all of them systematically linked into what might be termed Kochan's model of a 'new continent' of employee relations. Some of the individualism of employment can also be powerfully expressed as the individualism of the consumer; some of the collectivism once generated by collective bargaining can be expressed as company solidarity in the face of intense competition; some of the values engendered by unions can be refocused towards quality and customer care. This is not to say that any of these new formulations carries a more worthwhile ethic than those that they might have replaced, rather that industrial relations has been slow to recognize and adapt to the external language of markets, competition, and change and the language of reorganization has captured the high ground. This, taken together with the data on union membership, recognition, and collective bargaining, means that the British pattern of industrial relations is working in a different way and that the recent trend in strikes is a clear manifestation of that process. Our new employee relations is emerging, somewhat painfully but nevertheless discernibly, not only from the processes of the old but, perhaps more significantly, from the influences and pressures originating from the concerns of product markets, organizational change, and international competition rather than our twenty-five-year emphasis on the internal workings of procedures and processes associated with collective bargaining.

6. Conclusion

The extent to which Britain is experiencing a new employee relations is a little more susceptible to analysis thanks mainly to more and better information.

But it is a mistake to suppose that if we pore over the data enough we shall discern the moment when the new has arrived. It is important to recall the lesson that E. H. Carr gave in that set of lectures in Cambridge in 1961 entitled 'What is History?'. The shock of the lectures came from the fact that Carr argued that the traditional view of what constituted history was open to a fundamental flaw: so far from historians working in a world typified by a core of facts around which a welter of opinions revolved and where their professional job was to evaluate opinion in the light of these facts, Carr argued that the real problem for historians was that there was a core of opinions surrounded by a constellation of factual material which the historian drew upon at peril. The extent to which the historian was successful in this endeavour marked the extent to which other analysts accepted or rejected constructions produced in this way. In reflecting on the new industrial relations there is much to be drawn on from Carr's historiography which the subsequent chapters in this book well amplify.

REFERENCES

Bassett, P. (1986), *Strike Free* (London: Macmillan).

Beardwell (1992*a*), 'The New Industrial Relations', *HRMJ* 2/2: 1–7.

—— (1992*b*), 'Recasting the Relationship', Paper given at BAM Conference, Bradford.

Carr, E. H. (1961), *What is History* (Harmondsworth: Pelican).

Lord Donovan (1968), *Royal Commission Report* (London: HMSO).

Dunlop (1955), *Industrial Relations Systems* (Southern Illinois (UP) (1971 edn).

Ferner, T., and Hyman, R. (1992), *Industrial Relations in the New Europe* (Oxford: Blackwell).

Flanders, A. (1967), *Collective Bargaining* (London: Faber).

Guest, D., and Hoque, K. (1993), 'Are Greenfield Sites Better at Human Resource Management?' (Centre for Economic Performance Working Paper, 435; London: LSE).

Kahn-Freund, O. (1954), 'The Legal Framework' in A. Flanders and H.A. Clegg (eds.), *The System of Industrial Relations in Great Britain* (Oxford: Blackwell).

Kessler, I. and Purcell, J. (1995), 'Individualism and Collectivism' in P. Edwards, *Industrial Relations* (Oxford: Blackwell).

Kessler, S. and Bayliss, F. (1992), *Contemporary British Industrial Relations* (Basingstoke: Macmillan).

Kochan, T. *et al.* (1986), *The Transformation of American Industrial Relations* (New York: Basic Books).

McCarthy, W. (1994), 'Of Hats and Cattle: Or the Limits of Macro-Survey Research in Industrial Relations', *Industrial Relations Journal,* 25/4 (Dec), 315–22.

Marginson, P. *et al.* (1994), The Second Company Level Industrial Relations Survey, IRRU, Warwick University.

Millward, N., *et al.* (1992), *Workplace Industrial Relations in Transition* (Aldershot: Dartmouth).

—— (1993), *The New Industrial Relations?* (London: PSI).

—— and Hawes, W. (1995), 'Hats, Cattle and IR Research: A Comment on McCarthy', *Industrial Relations Journal* 26/1 (Mar.) 69–73.

Purcell, J. (1993), 'The End of Institutional Industrial Relations', *Political Quarterly*, 64/1: 6–23.

Storey, J. (1995) *Human Resource Management: A Critical Text* (London: Routledge).

2

HUMAN RESOURCE MANAGEMENT AND THE NEW INDUSTRIAL RELATIONS

David Guest and Kim Hoque

1. Introduction

'Human resource management' and the 'new industrial relations', like most terms in the field of management and organization, originated in the United States. Those using the terms were not doing so with a concern for precision; nor were they proposing any tight distinction between them. Rather, they were seeking to convey to a predominantly management audience a sense of innovation and change. There appear to be no compelling reasons why we should therefore seek to impose artificial boundaries of our own. However, 'human resource management' generally conjures up an image of a high technology non-union environment while the use of the term 'industrial relations' inevitably implies that trade unions or some other form of work-force representation are involved. In considering human resource management and the new industrial relations, it is on this absence or presence of a trade union and its consequences for policy, practice, and performance that we will concentrate.

The 1981 *Newsweek* article which perhaps more than anything else proclaimed 'The New Industrial Relations' in the USA suggested that it had arrived almost unnoticed, and until then unannounced, accelerating the demise of the traditional adversarial industrial relations and its replacement by a new collaborative system. In keeping with the spirit of the times (Guest 1990), the article went on to claim that the influences on the new approach came not from Japan or from any European system of codetermination but from a uniquely American tradition with its roots in the work of Mayo, Maslow, and McGregor.

In the kind of system outlined in the *Newsweek* article, the role of trade unions was rather blurred. The work of Kochan, Katz, and McKersie (1986) presented a positive view of the trade union contribution by focusing on cases where successful union–management collaboration had resulted in significant change. They celebrated the 'new' by entitling their book *The Transformation of American Industrial Relations*. What they showed was the possibility of bringing about marked improvements through management–union cooperation. What they could not do was indicate if this yielded better performanace than non-union arrangements.

Alongside the debate on the new industrial relations, human resource management was emerging in the 1980s in the United States as a possible solution to the challenge of an increasingly competitive national and international industrial environment. Although the concept had been around for some time, often as an alternative to the rather jaded image of personnel management, it was given a major boost by the rediscovery of the human side of enterprise in Peters and Waterman's (1982) *In Search of Excellence*. In this book, trade unions scarcely merited a mention; unlike the debate on the new industrial relations, it relegated unions to a minor historical role. Certainly we are left with the impression that they played no significant part in any 'excellent' companies.

As human resource management gained prominence in the United States, it was possible to discern three main strands of work. The first, captured in the work of writers like Tichy, Fombrun, and Devanna (1984), Miles and Snow (1984) and Schuler (1989), was primarily concerned with the relationship between business strategy and human resource management strategy. This implies that the key issue in human resource management is the question of strategic choice and recognition of the importance of considering human resource management issues in terms of their integration with wider business strategy. Driven by business and market considerations, this perspective treats trade unions as irrelevant and they are rarely if ever mentioned.

The second strand of work is captured in what might be termed the Harvard view of human resource management. This is essentially a generic approach which attempts to make the subject area comprehensible and interesting to Harvard MBA students and to general managers who have often been more attracted by the quantitative, financial, and strategic aspects of business (Beer *et al.* 1985). It is therefore an approach which tries to capture and re-present the field of what by tradition had been personnel management. Apart from providing a much more contemporary 'feel', the resulting analytic and descriptive material does not differ significantly from a number of personnel texts. Furthermore it explicitly acknowledges the role of trade unions in its conceptual framework by introducing the concept of 'stakeholder interests' as one of the key contingent variables helping to shape policy choices. However, once the more detailed material and the case studies are presented, trade unions are relegated to a very minor role. It was left to Kochan and his colleagues at MIT to present a more comprehensive framework which made explicit both the influences in the wider economic system and the potential role of trade unions.

The third strand, which perhaps links in more directly to Peters and Waterman (1982) as well as to the non-union case studies of Foulkes (1980) and some of the work of academics such as Lawler (1986, 1992) presents human resource management as an approach which is concerned with the full integration and full utilization of the workforce. This overlaps with the initial new industrial relations interest in the work of people like Maslow and McGregor. Indeed it is captured perhaps best in the writing of Walton (1985) and his contrast between the old control philosophy and the preferred new philosophy of high commitment. Both Lawler and Walton acknowledge that in high commitment organizations trade unions could have a role to play, but they tend to pass on quickly to consider non-union environments. Foulkes is explicitly writing about policies in large non-union companies. This perspective maps out the potentially distinctive features of human resource management which have been developed and presented elsewhere (Guest 1987). With its focus on an integrative, unitarist perspective, in which emphasis is placed on commitment to the organization, the role of trade unions is called into question. Indeed, one of the key research questions which emerges is whether it is possible to display commitment to both company and trade union (Guest and Dewe 1991).

This discussion of the emergence of human resource management and the new industrial relations in the United States is relevant partly because, at a key period in the 1980s, the United States was held up as the model to emulate in the UK. This was reflected in the warm relationship between Reagan and Thatcher at a political level and in the interest in monetarist free market economies at a policy level. Another source of interest was the legislative framework for industrial relations which in the United States reflected the dominance given to the operation of the market economy and made it more difficult for the unions to act as a significant economic constraint. Of course, as Beardwell (1991) has emphasized, there are dangers in taking the comparison too far. The context in the UK in the early 1980s was different in some important respects from the United States; in particular, the trade unions were more powerful and membership was much higher. However, there was a vacuum created by the apparent failure of the pluralist industrial relations strategy to deliver either good industrial relations or an efficient and productive industry. This resulted in a major policy debate about the need for new legislation and about the appropriate role for trade unions. As Beardwell acknowledges, much of the rhetoric of the debate was drawn from America.

What this meant was that the UK became susceptible to American ideas about human resource management and the new industrial relations. Beardwell (1992) has drawn a distinction between two approaches to the new industrial relations. He sees one as concerned with the reform of industrial relations, manifested in interest in job control, single union agreements, pendulum arbitration, and the like. The second approach is concerned with the new ideology of human resource management, with its focus on individualism and therefore its potential to replace the traditional pluralist system. The typical illustration of the reformist approach is the new Japanese manufacturing site, perhaps Toshiba (Trevor 1988) or Nissan (Wickens 1987) where management appears willing to accept a single union on their own terms. The American high technology firms such as IBM, Hewlett-Packard, Texas Instruments, and DEC (Buchanan and Boddy 1983) represent the stereotype of the second approach. However, as Garrahan and Stewart (1992) have argued in the case of Nissan and McLoughlin (1994) has shown in the case of high technology companies, the two approaches overlap, implying that the idea of the two perspectives existing Janus-like is too sharply drawn. Recognition of overlap has also been apparent in some of the debates about industrial relations and human resource management (Guest 1989; Storey 1992). What this implies is that managements' broad policy choices are not about a reformist industrial relations or human resource management but about options along two dimensions.

The first dimension is concerned with industrial relations. Following the Beardwell analysis, the type of industrial relations sought by management may range from the unreconstructed pluralism still found in some corners of the public sector, through a reformist type of new industrial relations complete with single union deal and pendulum arbitration to an absence of trade unions.

The second dimension is concerned with human resource management. Managers must decide how far they wish to embrace it. If they consider the issue strategically, they may opt to pursue a full-utilization model through policies designed to generate employee commitment, flexibility, and quality; and they may choose to do this for all or part of their staff. Alternatively, they may deliberately set out to pursue a strategy of cost-minimization, seeking high flexibility through short-term contracts and a policy of hire and fire. In such contexts, there is no pretence of seeking workforce commitment to the organization.

Considering the policy choices using these two dimensions takes us away from the conventional debates about the new versus the old or industrial relations and trade unions versus human resource management. Instead it opens up a variety of possible arrangements including trade unions operating alongside a set of human resource management initiatives. Alternatively, management may try to abandon any semblance of either traditional or new industrial relations and at the same time avoid any of the mutual commitments implied by human resource management. Any consideration of this wider set of choices forces us to look at the key contextual influences in the economy and the market place. It also requires a reconsideration of the ideological framework. The contrast between pluralism and unitarism may need to be replaced by notions of coexistence or complementarity. The possibility that some managers may choose to avoid both trade unions and human resource management opens up the question of the black hole of non-unionism, for too long neglected by researchers. At present we know too little about the policy choices that managers actually make, about what influences them and about their consequences. In our view the debate about human resouce management and the new industrial relations has probably gone on long enough and the best way to take the debate forward is to generate empirical data which can inform it.

The kind of research required must be both sufficiently wide-ranging to detect key trends and developments and sufficiently detailed to explore beneath the surface. Both surveys and case studies are required. We need to know more than whether unions survive; we need to know whether they play an active role or have become an empty shell. We need to know more than whether an organization has introduced single status or quality circles. To explore any comprehensive theory of human resource management we need to understand how these techniques combine to provide some sort of integrated approach.

Researchers have already embarked upon this task. The breadth is provided in the WIRS. WIRS3, carried out in 1990 (Millward *et al.* 1992; Millward 1994), can find little evidence of major advances in human resource management. Such advances as there have been are more likely to have occurred in unionized workplaces. Non-union workplaces apparently avoid human resource management practices, preferring, it seems, to treat the workforce harshly with consequent costs for both employer and employees. Such evidence further reinforces scepticism about the value of debates about trade unions or human resource management. Looking at the impact of human resource management, Fernie *et al.* (1994), in their analysis of WIRS3, have shown that those workplaces that adopt single status and employee involvement are more likely to report better performance. However we can only take the debate about human resource management and the new industrial relations forward a little with WIRS3 because the survey omitted large areas of human resource management policy and practice.

McLoughlin (1994) and Beardwell (1994), in their research on non-union establishments, have met the research criteria spelt out above by combining survey and case study material to highlight the diversity of practice in the non-union sector. They explore the question of whether a human resource management strategy reduces the propensity of workers to join a union. The conclusion appears to be that although this may contribute, a range of other factors, centring around the low perceived instrumental value of union membership and lack of encouragement from trade unions, are more important. Whatever the reasons, only 5 per cent of the establishments in their sample of high technology companies in South-East England recognize a trade union. Useful as it is, their research concentrates on issues of union joining and related management strategy rather than the detailed application and impact of human resource management.

In many respects their work is reinforced and complemented by the findings of the CLIRS2 (Marginson *et al.* 1993). For example, this survey reports diversity of practice about trade union recognition at new sites. Recognition is more likely where there is centralized pay bargaining and less likely in companies which, strategically, can be classified as financial controllers. Perhaps predictably, the decision about whether or not to recognize a trade union at a new establishment is usually taken centrally. This survey also finds that only a few companies practise what can be described as 'sophisticated' human resource management, reflected in eight indicators, but those that do are more likely to recognize a trade union.

These major surveys, together with a certain amount of detailed case study work, help to shed some light on the relationship between aspects of the new industrial relations and human resource management. However, they are unable to explore in sufficient detail the issue of the impact of trade unions on human resource management policy, practice, and performance. If we take the range of practices associated with human resource management, are there any which are more likely to be found in union or non-union workplaces? Are unions inhibitors or facilitators of human resource management initiatives and, keeping an eye on the new industrial relations, does it matter whether the presence of a union is based on traditional UK multi-unionism or a single union deal? The aim of the remainder of this chapter is to report research which helps to answer these questions.

In seeking to answer the question of whether human resource management is compatible with trade-unionism, we will operationalize the two dimensions described above. Along the dimension concerned with industrial relations policy and the union role we group establishments into four categories according to whether they recognize no union, recognize a single union in the context of a single union deal, recognize a single union but without any special deal, and whether they recognize multiple unions. On the human resource management dimension, we identify four categories acccording to whether they have an explicit human resource management strategy and the extent to which they make use of a range of human resource management practices. This provides us with a classification which we have initially applied to non-union establishments (Guest and Hoque 1994) but which can equally well be applied to any workplace.

Those with an explicit human resource strategy and a high use of human resource practices we label the Good. They adopt an approach close to the kind of 'high involvement' management espoused by Lawler (1986, 1992). At the other extreme, those with no human resource strategy and a low adoption of human resource practices we label the Bad. This could be construed as cautious pragmatism, but it is more likely to be poor, ill-thought through management. Those with an explicit strategy but one which results in a low take-up of human resource practices we label the Ugly. By implication, since they claim to have a strategy, they have thought through how they wish to manage their human resources and decided not to adopt a 'full utilization' approach. They fit the pattern outlined by Millward (1994) of bleak environments and limited rights. The Good and the Ugly have some parallels with the 'soft' and 'hard' versions of human resource management identified among others by Keenoy (1990) and Storey (1992). Finally, those with no human resource strategy but a high use of human resource practices we label the Lucky. They are lucky in that they have stumbled on a set of practices, perhaps through outside guidance, perhaps through emulation or perhaps by following fads. The potential value of a classification of this sort is that it explicitly takes into account the issue of strategic integration, emphasized by many writers on human resource management. Good human resource management should be based on a strategy and on extensive rather than narrowly focused application of human resource management practices. The research can explore the association between the two dimensions.

The second central research question is whether the trade unions act as a drag or a spur to performance. To explore this we will again use the same classification but add data on outcomes. Three types of outcome will be explored since they are the most central to the debates on the new industrial relations, the role of the unions, and the efficacy of human resource management. These outcomes are those predicted as first level outcomes by human resource management theory (Guest 1987) such as levels of commitment, staff quality, and flexibility. The second are employee relations outcomes such as industrial conflict, labour turnover, and absence. The third are performance outcomes including resilience in the face of recession and benchmark estimates of establishment quality and productivity.

2. The Research Setting and Method of Analysis

The data reported here are part of a larger study of human resource management in greenfield sites—new, often purpose-built factories and offices. The main study has three central aims; it examines what happens when greenfield sites turn brown; that is, as they age. The second part is concerned with the impact of ownership and in particular foreign ownership on the nature of human resource management. The third question is concerned with the impact of human resource management. An overriding question is the extent to which human resource management has become established as a preferred management option, on the assumption that this will be most clearly manifested in new establishments where managers have greater freedom to express their preferred choice. There are three parts to the study; the first is a reanalysis of part of WIRS3; the second is a survey of greenfield sites in the UK; and the third is a number of case studies in some of the surveyed establishments.

For our present purposes we will use data collected from the survey of greenfield sites. The survey was conducted in mid-1993, when a postal questionnaire was sent to just over 1,000 establishments in the UK employing more than fifty staff, including about 800 set up since 1980. We received responses from 393 establishments, subsequently reduced to 344 since some had less than fifty employees. Of the 344, 96 are purpose-built greenfield sites, new plants or offices being used for the first time; 152 are 'refurbished' sites, where there had been a major change of ownership and usually of activity, often following a shut-down period for the refurbishment; and 96 were set up before 1980.

For this analysis, we have restricted the sample to the greenfield and refurbished sites set up after 1980. This cut-off date was chosen as it marks the point at which Thatcherism began to have an impact at work, launching the debate about the new industrial relations. Establishments started since then provide what is arguably the best setting in which to explore the choices managers make about how to operate in the new industrial relations environments. At new establishments, unconstrained by history and tradition in the workplace, managers are most free to introduce the policies and practices of their choice. Equally, they provide the most exacting test of how far trade unions are able to respond to the challenges they face in the new industrial relations. If they can flourish in such settings, then we can be more confident about their ability to retain a viable long-term role. In operating with new establishments we recognize that there is a different argument that could be made about looking at processes of change in older establishments. However, we believe that the cutting edge of innovations and emerging patterns in human resource management and the new industrial relations is likely to be found in new establishments.

The sample therefore contains 248 post-1980 establishments of which 166 (66.9 per cent) are non-union and 82 (33.1 per cent) are unionized. These figures are in line with what we might expect from the analysis of WIRS3 (Disney, Gosling, and Machin 1993). Analysis by ownership reveals 104 UK-owned establishments, 45 American-owned, 52 Japanese-owned, 19 German-owned, and the remaining 24 owned by companies from the rest of the world which in practice means predominantly European Union and EFTA countries. Comparison with WIRS3 shows that the sample is broadly representative in size, based on number of employees and allowing for exclusion of those employing less than fifty staff. It is weighted towards manufacturing industry; indeed 84 per cent are manufacturing establishments, 10 per cent are in financial services, and 6 per cent are other services.

The questionnaire contained four sections. The first asked for background information on issues such as size, ownership, sector, age, and location. The second contained items about the presence of mission statements, human resource management strategy, and the degree of 'parental' influence. The third contained twenty-six items describing a range of contemporary human resource management practices and asked whether they are currently in existence at the establishment and whether they were used one year after start-up. The final section asked about a range of outcomes. These fall into three groups concerned with human resource management, employee relations, and establishment performance. The vast majority of questionnaires were completed either by the head of personnel at the establishment or by the most senior line manager with special responsibility for personnel issues, which in practice often meant the Managing Director, General Manager, or Plant Manager.

3. Results

Human Resource Management and Trade Unions

In this subsection we examine the impact of trade unions on human resource management strategy and human resource management practices. We do this by comparing the establishments falling into the four trade union categories. These are those with no union ($n = 166$), those with a single union deal ($n = 31$), those with a single union but no single union deal ($n = 18$), and those with multiple-unionism ($n = 33$). In the questionnaire we were unable to explore the content of the single union deals, so there are risks in assuming that they are similar in nature. However, the question was quite explicit in asking whether there was a single union agreement.

How helpful is a union presence?   One indirect way of exploring the impact of the unions was to gauge whether managers considered their presence to be helpful to the achievement of company goals. Sixty-six per cent of managers in establishments where unions were recognized considered the unions to be helpful. This ranged from 70 per cent in the case of single union deals to 55.6 per cent where there are single unions but no special deal. Multi-union establishments fell between the others with 62.5 per cent considering them helpful. The differences are not significant so we must be cautious, despite the apparent trend, in concluding that unions in the context of single union deals are seen as more helpful. This is a somewhat surprising result if we accept the popular assumption that single union deals are explicitly designed to foster cooperation. It suggests that single union deals, assuming they have been correctly identified, do not have the clear-cut advantages sometimes claimed for them by their enthusiastic advocates. On the other hand, with two-thirds of managers taking the view that the unions are helpful, it is possible that new establishments provide an opportunity for managers to develop the kind of cooperation they want irrespective of whether or not they have a single union deal.

Unions and human resource strategy   The questionnaire contained a section of items on aspects of policy and strategy. The responses in this section are important in setting a key part of the context for human resource management. It is hypothesized that those who take strategy more seriously will have better outcomes. However, as noted elsewhere (Guest and Hoque 1994) the content of the strategy will be as important as having a strategy. The comparison of the 166 non-union establishments with those where various union arrangements were recognized is presented in Table 2.1. In this table we present the descriptive statistics, together with a Chi2 test of differences between the categories. In the Appendix, we include Table 2.A1 which

Table 2.1. Human Resource Strategy

	Numbers saying yes[a]				
	Non-union	Single union deal	Single union	Multi-union	Chi2
Mission statement	80 (50.96)	22 (84.62)	14 (77.78)	22 (75.86)	0.000
If yes:					
Explicitly refers to human resource issues	47 (58.75)	19 (86.36)	11 (78.57)	16 (72.73)	0.060
Altered since first written	24 (39.34)	9 (45)	1 (9.09)	7 (36.84)	0.224
Human resource strategy supported by top site management	82 (50.31)	23 (76.67)	11 (76.11)	16 (53.33)	0.059
Strategy altered since first written	68 (42.5)	11 (36.67)	9 (50)	16 (53.33)	0.548

[a] The first no. in each of the columns is the frequency, the second (in brackets) is the percentage.

presents the multivariate statistical analysis. This controls for background variables and is a more rigorous test of differences between the categories.

The results in Table 2.1 show that all types of unionized establishment are more likely to have a mission statement than non-union establishments. However, Table 2.A1 shows that when we control for factors such as size and ownership, the difference is only significant for establishments with single union deals. Where there is a mission statement, it is more likely to include explicit reference to human resource issues in non-union establishments. Although the Chi2 result falls just short of significance, the multivariate test in Table 2.A1 is significant and reveals that once again the differences can be accounted for mainly by the establishments with a single union deal. The third key issue is the presence of a human resource strategy, formally endorsed and actively supported by the top management team at the establishment. Once again the unionized establishments are more likely to report the existence of such a strategy, although in both tables the results fall just short of significance. Table 2.A1 once again confirms that the differences can be accounted for mainly by the establishments with single union deals. One indication of an effective strategy is that it is reasonably consistent over time. Although the differences are not significant, the results in Table 2.1 indicate that where a mission statement or a human resource management strategy exists, the non-union establishments tend to be more likely to have altered both.

The results from this first set of data are reasonably clear-cut. Those new establishments where a union is recognized are more likely than non-union establishments to have a mission statement and to include in it specific reference to human resource issues, and more likely to have an explicit human resource strategy. These differences remain when we control for a range of background factors so they cannot be accounted for by variations in size, sector, or ownership. However, the presence of all these reflections of a strategy varies within the unionized establishments and is much the most likely to be found where there is a single union deal.

We cannot establish cause and effect. It is possible that those who think strategically opt for a single union deal. Alternatively, agreement to consider a single union deal forces establishments to confront related strategic human resource issues. It is probably most plausible to suggest that since we are dealing with new establishments, the development of human resource strategy and the planning of a single union deal go hand in hand. In this context, the role of the parent, as Marginson *et al.* (1993) have indicated, appears to be important in shaping attitudes towards trade union recognition and the form it takes. Whatever the reasons, the key finding is that it is the unionized rather than the non-union establishments that take the lead in developing human resource strategy.

Unions and human resource practices The data in Table 2.1 indicate that a union presence is associated with a greater likelihood of a human resource strategy and a mission statement. However, it is wise to be somewhat sceptical about both unless they are clearly reinforced by a set of relevant practices. This subsection therefore takes us a step further by examining the presence at the new sites of the sort of practices commonly associated with human resource management. The list is not exhaustive and it concentrates on human resource practices rather than some of those that might be associated with the more narrowly defined industrial relations aspects of the new industrial relations. This reflected the key focus of the study and also our knowledge that most of the establishments in the sample would be non-union and therefore issues like pendulum arbitration would be irrelevant. The list of items is shown in Table 2.2. Once again the multivariate analysis is shown in the Appendix in Table 2.A2.

Perhaps the most interesting result in Table 2.2 is the lack of consistent differences between union and non-union establishments. In both sets of new establishments, the use of a majority of the innovative human resource management practices is now the norm. Nevertheless significant differences emerge on seven of the items. Two of these concern status and harmonization. Here the differences are not so much between union and non-union as between non-union and single union deals on the one hand and other forms of union recognition on the other. However, in both cases it is the non-union establishments that are most likely to report these practices; and, as Table 2.A2 reveals, the differences between the non-union and single union deal establishments are significant. Therefore, although establishments with single union deals are more like the non-union establishments, they still fall some way short on single status. The pattern is somewhat similar for two other items, merit pay and appraisal. Non-union establishments are well ahead of all forms of unionized establishment in the use of merit pay. The differences are much less

Table 2.2. Human resource practices

	Non-union (%)	Single union deal (%)	Single union (%)	Multi-union (%)	Chi 2	Observations
Harmonized terms and conditions	69.88	63.33	50	36.67	0.003	244
Single status	55.35	40	29.41	23.33	0.003	236
Internal promotion the norm	83.73	83.33	73.22	83.33	0.676	244
No compulsory redundancy	37.58	33.33	16.67	20	0.112	243
Trainability as a major selection criteria	67.48	90	52.94	53.33	0.01	240
Use of psychological tests for all selection	17.47	16.67	16.67	26.67	0.67	244
Realistic job previews during recruitment	57.23	62.07	62.5	43.33	0.432	234
System to communicate values to new staff	68.07	80	83.33	70	0.361	244
Deliberate development of a learning organization	57.32	75.86	66.67	53.33	0.221	241
Minimum annual training requirements for all	10.84	13.33	5.56	23.33	0.212	244
Flexible job descs. not fixed to one task	72.39	86.21	72.22	80	0.39	240
Jobs designed to make full use of skills	51.55	43.33	41.18	46.67	0.733	238
Teamworking for majority of staff	73.78	79.31	72.22	63.33	0.559	241
Staff involved in setting performance targets	57.93	50	50	40	0.296	242
Staff responsible for their own quality	83.85	90	94.44	76.67	0.319	239
Majority involved in quality circles or quality improvement teams	43.03	40	61.11	53.33	0.35	243
Regular use of attitude surveys	23.03	30	16.67	20	0.708	243
Team briefing/Information cascades	62.05	76.67	55.56	66.67	0.39	244
Information on market position/company performance	78.18	90	66.67	73.33	0.234	243
Merit pay for all staff	64.85	37.93	38.89	30	0.000	242
Formal appraisal for all at least annually	72.89	68.97	61.11	43.33	0.014	243
Human resource policy integrated with business strategy	56.33	89.66	58.82	53.33	0.007	234
Human resource policies integrated with each other	55.06	82.14	47.06	50	0.033	231

marked on appraisal where it seems that the multi-union establishments are less likely to operate it.

The three remaining items are those where establishments with a single union deal stand out as most likely to have adopted a practice. One is the use of trainability as a major selection criterion; the others are concerned with integration of strategy. Establishments with single union deals are much more likely to claim that human resource policies are integrated with business strategy and that the various human resource policies are integrated with each other. This would fit with the earlier claims to be more likely to have a human resource strategy.

Taking the set of practices as a whole, it appears that they are most likely to be reported in establishments with a single union deal, closely followed by non-union establishments. However, the other unionized establishments are often little different, indicating that a union presence is no bar to most human resource practices. Despite this, the exceptions may be important. Unionized establishments are less likely to have progressed towards single status and less likely to be using appraisal-linked merit pay. These touch on traditional trade union territory and it would seem that in this territory they are still able to exert some influence on workplace practices.

Unions and types of human resource strategy   There is some evidence from the preceding analysis that unionized workplaces, and more particularly those with a single union deal, are more likely to have developed a coherent human resource strategy. However, not all establishments have a strategy and not all have introduced human resource management practices. To explore whether a union presence is compatible with the kind of high utilization human resource strategy sometimes associated with best human resource practice but also often seen as inimical to a trade union presence, we can reclassify establishments.

The basis for this classification was introduced earlier. Those establishments labelled Good have a human resource strategy, defined in the questionnaire as being formally endorsed and actively supported by the top management at the site; and also a high use of human resource practices, defined arbitrarily as more than half of those listed in Table 2.2. The Bad are the opposite in that they have no strategy and use less than half the practices listed. The Ugly have a strategy but use less than half the practices while the Lucky have no strategy but use more than half the practices. If strategic integration is at all important, we would expect the Good to report better outcomes than the Bad. If strategic integration around a distinctive set of human resource practices confers an advantage then we would also expect to see the Good report better outcomes than the Ugly and Lucky. By comparing across the groups we can also identify whether adoption of practices without a strategy—the approach of the Lucky—also has an impact on outcomes. In our total sample of 245 establishments, 107 (43.7 per cent) were classified as Good, 70 (28.6 per cent) as Bad, 28 (11.4 per cent) as Ugly, and 40 (16.3 per cent) as Lucky.

The key question for the debate about human resource management and the

Table 2.3. Unions and type of human resource strategy

	Good	Lucky	Bad	Ugly
Union (%)	50	6.1	29.27	14.63
Non-Union (%)	40.49	21.47	28.22	9.82
Chi2 sig.	0.157	0.002	0.864	0.263
Observations	107	40	70	28
Single union deal (%)	63.33	0	23.33	13.33
Single union no deal (%)	50	5.56	33.33	11.11
Multi-Union (%)	16.67	13.33	33.33	36.67
Chi2 sig.	0.099	0.014	0.815	0.717
Observations	107	40	70	28

Notes: The percentages given are based on a total sample of 245.
Single–Multi-Union Chi2 scores calculated in comparison with non-union category.

new industrial relations is whether the Good are compatible with trade-unionism. The results are shown in Table 2.3. The multivariate analysis can be found in the Appendix in Table 2.A3.

The results in Table 2.3 confirm that a union presence is compatible with a high utilization model of human resource management. Indeed, if we examine the distribution, a higher proportion of union than non-union establishments fall in the good category. This is due to the greater likelihood that they will have a human resource strategy. In contrast, more of the non-union establishments fall into the lucky category. They have adopted the practices but have not developed a strategy. The multivariate analysis confirms this pattern but reveals where the differences lie. It is the establishments with a single union deal that are significantly more likely to fall within the Good category while the non-union are significantly more likely to be Lucky. No group stands out as more likely to be Bad or Ugly, although, contrary to expectation, there is a slight tendency for them to be unionized rather than not.

Summarizing the results to date, we have shown that at new establishments, those set up in the 1980s or more recently, industrial relations, manifested in a trade union presence and human resource management are able to exist side by side. However, we can go further than this. It appears that, more particularly in the case of single union deals, it is less a matter of the systems coexisting as of being integrated through a coherent strategy. Indeed, unionized workplaces are more likely than their non-union counterparts to have a human resource strategy. There do appear to be some differences between the types of union presence. Without a single union deal, there is a slightly lower use of human resource practices and slightly less evidence of the sort of strategic pursuit of a high utilization policy categorized as the Good.

We have shown that with perhaps two exceptions, represented by single status and appraisal-related merit pay, the unions do not inhibit human resource management practice. The next key question is whether they have any impact on performance.

The Impact of Unions on Outcomes

If we wish to conduct a rigorous test of the impact of unions on performance and other outcomes, it is firstly necessary to see if there are links between human resource policy and practice and outcomes. If there are, then it will be necessary to hold this factor constant in order to ascertain the effect which unions have on performance *per se*, irrespective of the policies which are being used. The wider and controversial literature concerning the impact of unions on performance suggests that on balance they act as a drag. However, it is plausible to hypothesize that where a union presence is part of a planned human resource strategy in a new workplace, this is less likely to be the case.

The first step is to examine the impact of human resource policy and practice on outcomes. This is an important and interesting topic in its own light. For this purpose, we retain the integrative distinction between the Good, the Bad, the Ugly, and the Lucky. The results, for the three sets of outcomes— human resource outcomes, employee relations outcomes, and performance outcomes—are shown in Table 2.4. The multivariate results are shown in Table 2.A4 in the Appendix.

These results show that there are consistent differences between the policy types and it will therefore be necessary to hold policy effects constant when testing for union effects. While Table 2.4 has been included in order to demonstrate this necessity, it is also of great interest in itself. It shows the strength of the links between the use of strategically integrated human resource policies and performance. Specifically, the good establishments, those with a human resource strategy and a high uptake of human resource practices, consistently report better outcomes. At the other extreme, those with the poorer outcomes, revealed most clearly in Table 2.A4, are the Bad, those without a strategy or much use of human resource practices. The Ugly and the Lucky both report consistently poorer performance than the Good on all three types of outcome. This result will be of great encouragement to those who are attempting to implement a high utilization human resource strategy. This is the first UK study to date which demonstrates the benefits of such a strategy so clearly.

We can now hold the human resource policy variable constant while examining the impact of unions on outcomes. The resulting multivariate analysis is shown in Table 2.A5 in the Appendix. First, however, we can examine the descriptive results presented in Table 2.5.

The results in Table 2.5 reveal few significant differences between the various categories. There are some exceptions. Establishments with a single union deal claim to have weathered the recession more successfully than multi-union establishments. Industrial disputes are predictably less likely in non-union establishments. Finally there is a trend towards higher quality of staff in single union deal establishments compared with the multi-union.

Only when the controls are imposed do the differences become clearer. Table

Table 2.4. Human resource strategy and outcomes

	Good	Lucky	Bad	Ugly	Chi2	Observations
Human resource outcomes						
Commitment of lower grade staff	3.776 (0.731)	3.675 (0.764)	3.143 (0.785)	3.429 (0.742)	0.001	245
The quality of staff employed	4.056 (0.596)	3.9 (0.709)	3.559 (0.632)	3.929 (0.716)	0.000	243
Quality of work of lower grade staff	3.972 (0.621)	4.05 (0.714)	3.671 (0.607)	3.75 (0.752)	0.031	245
Quality of human resource policies and practices	3.701 (0.633)	3.154 (0.63)	2.706 (0.875)	3.333 (0.733)	0.000	241
The flexibility of staff	4.234 (0.681)	4.05 (0.677)	3.681 (0.795)	4.107 (0.875)	0.001	244
Ability to move between jobs as needed	4.085 (0.692)	3.8 (0.758)	3.557 (0.792)	4.036 (0.838)	0.002	244
Flexibility to adjust workforce size	3.424 (1.121)	3.25 (1.193)	3.206 (1.087)	3.185 (1.075)	0.651	241
Line manager enthusiasm for human resource policies	3.813 (0.646)	3.436 (0.718)	2.806 (0.875)	3.071 (0.766)	0.000	241
Employee relations outcomes						
Industrial dispute 'yes' (%)	16.82	10	18.57	25	0.43	245
Labour turnover in 1992 (%)	7.18 (7.826)	9.375 (10.166)	12 (13.263)	11.423 (13.03)	0.224	219
Absenteeism in 1992 (%)	4.229 (3.026)	5.879 (6.684)	4.681 (3.044)	6 (5.721)	0.259	186
Performance outcomes						
Quality targets attained (%)	91.554 (13.177)	88.565 (25.443)	88.618 (10.592)	88.429 (20.887)	0.068	145
How well was the recession weathered	4.047 (0.773)	3.925 (0.656)	3.716 (0.735)	3.929 (0.858)	0.033	241
Productivity benchmarked against UK	4.174 (0.829)	3.917 (0.776)	3.441 (0.705)	3.783 (0.795)	0.002	167
Quality benchmarked against the UK	4.437 (0.773)	4.192 (0.694)	3.714 (0.926)	4.043 (0.706)	0.000	171
Prod'y benchmarked against World	3.64 (1.029)	3.348 (0.982)	3.172 (0.848)	3.526 (0.964)	0.485	154
Quality benchmarked against World	3.988 (0.97)	3.8 (0.912)	3.429 (1.034)	3.7 (0.979)	0.133	158

Notes: Means given (minimum 1, maximum 5) with standard deviation in brackets.

Table 2.5. Unions and outcomes

	Non-Union	Single Union Deal	Single Union	Multi Union	Chi2	Observations
Human resource outcomes						
Commitment of lower grade staff	3.56 (0.79)	3.6 (0.814)	3.667 (0.686)	3.233 (0.817)	0.7	244
The quality of staff employed	3.884 (0.659)	3.967 (0.615)	3.834 (0.857)	3.733 (0.64)	0.071	242
Quality of work of lower grade staff	3.928 (0.693)	3.9 (0.662)	3.778 (0.428)	3.633 (0.556)	0.106	244
Quality of human resource policies and practices	3.259 (0.831)	3.552 (0.736)	3.111 (0.963)	3.241 (0.872)	0.449	238
The flexibility of staff	4.018 (0.777)	4.267 (0.691)	4.056 (0.802)	3.9 (0.803)	0.802	243
Ability to move between jobs as needed	3.898 (0.776)	4.033 (0.765)	3.833 (0.707)	3.724 (0.922)	0.676	243
Flexibility to adjust workforce size	3.252 (1.146)	3.667 (0.884)	3.556 (1.097)	3.103 (1.175)	0.612	240
Line manager enthusiasm for human resource policies	3.435 (0.82)	3.5 (0.777)	3.222 (1.003)	3.003 (0.928)	0.255	239
Employee relations outcomes						
Industrial dispute 'yes' (%)	5.42	33.33	22.22	60	0.000	244
Labour turnover in 1992 (%)	9.619 (10.178)	12 (14.397)	6.706 (12.02)	6.261 (6.864)	0.754	216
Absenteeism in 1992 (%)	4.815 (4.986)	4.552 (3.101)	5.231 (3.468)	4.826 (1.969)	0.592	184
Performance outcomes						
Quality targets attained (%)	89.13 (18.151)	93.571 (6.896)	90 (6.305)	89.133 (13.856)	0.84	145
How well was the recession weathered	3.963 (0.767)	4.214 (0.686)	3.889 (0.676)	3.433 (0.679)	0.021	240
Productivity benchmarked against UK	3.964 (0.838)	4.211 (0.787)	3.818 (0.874)	3.591 (0.796)	0.547	238
Quality benchmarked against the UK	4.202 (0.854)	4.318 (0.716)	4.273 (0.786)	4 (0.894)	0.23	237
Prod'y benchmarked against World	3.569 (1.02)	3.579 (0.838)	2.9 (0.994)	3.333 (0.966)	0.146	234
Quality benchmarked against World	3.838 (1.02)	3.762 (0.7)	3.7 (1.337)	3.85 (0.988)	0.314	233

Notes: Means given (minimum 1, maximum 5) with standard deviations in brackets.

2.A5 in the Appendix shows that the unionized establishments, taken as a whole, report poorer outcomes on almost all variables. On a number they are significant. However, as expected, there are variations according to the type of union arrangement. The rest of Table 2.A5 indicates that the poorer outcomes are most likely to be found at the multi-union establishments. In particular, they appear to have poorer human resource outcomes. In contrast, the only significant factor among the single union establishments is the greater likelihood of industrial conflict compared with the non-union establishments. Indeed, on issues associated with flexibility they appear to be at an advantage. What these results indicate is that the presence of a union still acts as a modest but sometimes significant drag on performance. The effects are greater for multi-unionism and least for single union deals. Despite the earlier evidence of a willingness on the part of union establishments to embrace human resource practices, it seems that the unions still exert some influence on workplace outcomes. Finally, it is worth noting that the human resource strategy types appear to exert more influence than the unions. Performance is poorer in the Bad establishments than in the multi-union establishments.

4. Conclusions and Discussion

The first key question we set out to explore through the study of greenfield sites is whether human resource management and trade-unionism can coexist. The answer from this study is an unequivocal yes. Most human resource management practices are just as likely to exist at unionized establishments as at those without unions. There are some variations on this general pattern.

The first important variation is the finding that the presence of a trade union is associated with a greater use of a human resource management strategy and a mission statement, which, in addition, is more likely to refer explicitly to human resource issues. This needs to be qualified by the analysis of types of trade union presence. A strategy and mission statement is particularly likely to exist where there is a single union deal. We cannot tell from this cross-sectional data whether the union presence encourages managers to think strategically or whether those who think strategically opt for a single union deal. Although we suspect that the causal direction varies from context to context, since the choice of whether to recognize a union is an increasingly open one, we suspect that management thinks strategically about both human resource management and the new industrial relations and decides to opt for a single union deal. Multiple unionism, by contrast, may come into operation in those establishments where a parent company already has a central collective agreement with a number of unions. It follows that the majority of such cases are likely to be British-owned. Examination of the national ownership patterns confirms that this is indeed the case. The UK- and USA-owned establishments where any union is recognized are the least likely to report a single union deal.

The pattern across the range of human resource management practices also reveals some specific differences and helps to sharpen the distinction between the new industrial relations, reflected in single union deals, and the traditional industrial relations reflected in multi-unionism. Any type of trade union presence is associated with less use of single status and use of performance appraisal and merit pay for all staff. Single union deals on the other hand are associated with a set of practices broadly similar to non-union establishments but with the added advantage of having a more coherent human resource strategy. These results are strongly supported by Millward's (1994) analysis of the new industrial relations based on WIRS3. He finds that establishments with single union deals are consistently more likely to have a range of innovative practices, implying once again that they think strategically about single union deals and human resource management issues together.

The second major question we have explored is whether a union presence facilitates or constrains aspects of performance. The general conclusion is that unions inhibit performance and multi-unionism inhibits it more. However, this conclusion requires some qualification since single union deals have far less impact on performance, compared with non-union establishments.

The similarity between non-union establishments and those with a single union deal brings us back to the question of whether this type of unionism is an empty shell. It does not appear to constrain management. Indeed, it is associated with what managers believe to be greater commitment to the organization among lower level staff and with greater flexibility than even non-union establishments. In contrast, multi-unionism is associated with poorer outcomes on all variables except labour turnover and absenteeism; and on five of the outcomes, the differences with non-union establishments are significant. Thus multi-unionism is associated with poorer performance. This confirms the economic research on the impact of unions.

Before reaching the general conclusion that multi-unionism is bad for performance, we should recall the data on human resource management types. The Bad establishments are more clearly associated with poor outcomes than the multi-union establishments, implying that decisions about human resource strategy are more important for outcomes than decisions about multi-unionism—assuming that managers take decisions about these issues and that in practice the two can be disentangled. In one sense, this marginalizes the union issue. On the other hand, unions may always have been marginal to performance in the great majority of organizations although industrial relations specialists, with their distinctive focus on unions, have been understandably reluctant to acknowledge this.

To summarize, the new trade-unionism, reflected most strongly in single union deals, is compatible with human resource management. There is more of a question mark against multi-unionism. This raises the question of why any company will recognize a trade union at a new establishment. A single union deal has very little impact compared with non-union establishments suggesting that they turn unions into empty shells. Multi-unionism has a somewhat negative impact. In our sample of post-1980 establishments, approximately a third recognized one or more trade unions. However, this fell to 20 per cent in the 'pure' greenfield sites compared with 42 per cent in the refurbished sites. The great majority of managers have already decided that there is no value in recognizing a trade union. So why do others do so?

The evidence from our case studies supports the more extensive data from the CLIRS2 (Marginson *et al.* 1993). This indicates that unions will be recognized in those companies which have a centralized system of collective bargaining which they wish to retain. Secondly, as our comparison of green-field and refurbished sites suggests, unions may be recognized at those work-places which are taken over, even if shut down for a while and refurbished, and where a union was already recognized. It is possible that in some cases there may be scope for the operation of individual values. Some managers, including perhaps personnel managers in particular, may value the presence of a trade union as a counterweight to arbitrary management treatment. Since we have found little evidence of any trade union official presence in our case studies, it appears that the personnel manager may act as promoter and recruiter for the union. However, this is likely to become less common. The evidence from this study suggests that as we learn more about the impact of the new industrial relations, in the absence of any change towards a government that more actively encourages them, the outlook for trade unions is bleak.

REFERENCES

Beardwell, I. (1992), 'The New Industrial Relations? A Review of the Debate', *Human Resource Management Journal*, 2/2: 1–7.

——— (1994), 'Managerial Issues in the Non-Union Firm', Paper prepared for the LSE CEP Workshop on Non-Unionism, Apr.

Beer, M., Spector, B., Lawrence, P., Quinn Mills, D., and Walton, R. (1985), *Human Resource Management: A General Manager's Perspective* (New York: Free Press).

Buchanan, D. A., and Boddy, D. (1983), *Organizations in the Computer Age: Techno-logical Imperatives and Strategic Choice* (Aldershot: Gower).

Fernie, S., Metcalf, D., and Woodland, S. (1994), 'What Has Human Resource Manage-ment Achieved in the Workplace?', *Employment Policy Institute Economic Report*, 8/3.

Foulkes, F. (1980), *Personnel Policies in Large Non-Union Companies* (Englewood Cliffs, NJ: Free Press).

Garrahan, P., and Stewart, P. (1992), *The Nissan Enigma: Flexibility At Work in the Local Economy* (London: Mansell).

Guest, D. (1987), 'Human Resource Management and Industrial Relations', *Journal of Management Studies*, 24/5: 503–21.

——— (1989), 'Human Resource Management: Its Implications for Industrial Relations and Trade Unions', in J. Storey (ed.), *New Perspectives on Human Resource Management* (London: Routledge).

——— (1990), 'Human Resource Management and the American Dream', *Journal of Management Studies*, 27/4: 377–97.

——— and Dewe, P. (1991), 'Company or Trade Union: Which Wins Workers' Allegiance? A Study of Commitment in the UK Electronics Industry', *British Journal of Industrial Relations*, 29/1: 75–96.

——— and Hoque, K. (1994), 'The Good, the Bad and the Ugly: Employment Relations in Non-Union Greenfield sites', *Human Resource Management Journal*, 5/1: 1–14.

Keenoy, T. (1990), 'HRM: A Case of the Wolf in Sheep's Clothing?', *Personnel Review*, 19/2: 3–9.

Kochan, T., Katz, H., and McKersie, R. (1986), *The Transformation of American Industrial Relations* (New York: Basic Books).

Lawler, E. (1986), *High Involvement Management* (San Francisco: Jossey-Bass).

——— (1992), *The Ultimate Advantage* (San Francisco: Jossey-Bass).

McLoughlin, I. (1994), *Managing Without Unions: Human Resource Management in Non-Union Firms in Britain* (Brunel: Department of Management Studies WP no. 6).

Marginson, P., Armstrong, P., Edwards, P., Purcell, J., and Hubbard, N. (1993), *The Control of Industrial Relations in Large Companies: Initial Analysis of the Second Company-Level Industrial Relations Survey* (Warwick Papers in Industrial Relations, No. 45, Univ. of Warwick IRRU).

Miles, R., and Snow, C. (1984), 'Designing Strategic Human Resource Systems', *Organizational Dynamics* (Summer), 36–52.

Millward, N. (1994), *The New Industrial Relations?* (London: PSI).

———, Stevens, M., Smart, D., and Hawes, W. (1992), *Workplace Industrial Relations in Transition* (Aldershot: Dartmouth).

Newsweek (1981), 'The New Industrial Relations', *Newsweek* (May).

Peters, T., and Waterman, R. (1982), *In Search of Excellence* (New York: Harper and Row).

Schuler, R. (1989), 'Strategic Human Resource Management and Industrial Relations', *Human Relations*, 42/2: 157–84.

Storey, J. (1992), *Developments in the Management of Human Resources* (Oxford: Blackwell).

Tichy, N., Fombrun, C., and Devanna, M. (1984), 'Strategic Human Resource Management', *Sloane Management Review*, 23/2 (Winter), 47–61.

Trevor, M. (1988), *Toshiba's New British Company* (London: PSI).

Walton, R. (1985), 'From Control to Commitment in the Workplace', *Harvard Business Review*, 63 (Mar.–Apr.), 76–84.

Wickens, P. (1987), *The Road to Nissan* (Basingstoke: Macmillan).

APPENDIX

Table 2.A1. Multivariate analysis of human resource strategy

	Union = 1	R2	Observations	Single union deal	Single union no deal	Multi-Union	R2	Observations
Formal mission statement	0.819 (0.411)**	0.151	220	1.59 (0.734)**	0.874 (0.669)	0.587 (0.579)	0.165	216
If yes:								
does it refer to human resource issues?	1.157 (0.551)**	0.551	133	2.003 (0.797)**	1.306 (0.892)	0.46 (0.693)	0.213	131
has it been altered?	−0.625 (0.556)	0.084	106	0.145 (0.655)	−1.844 (1.192)	−0.703 (0.733)	0.092	113
Is there a human resource strategy supported by top management at the site?	0.703 (0.385)*	0.111	230	1.513 (0.603)**	0.458 (0.62)	0.12 (0.51)	0.132	226
Has there been any significant change made to human resource management?	−0.404 (0.381)	0.097	227	−0.632 (0.536)	−0.325 (0.598)	−0.007 (0.506)	0.097	223

Notes: Logit regression analysis used. Coefficients given (standard errors in brackets).
** significant at 5%; * significant at 10%.
R^2 is pseudo.
Regressions control for size, region, type of establishment, ownership, whether or not part of a larger organization, greenfield sites.

Table 2.A2. Multivariate analysis of human resource practices

Policy/practice (independent variables)	Single union deal	Single union no deal	Multi-Union	R2	Observations
Harmonized terms and conditions	-0.128 (0.582)	-0.346 (0.613)	-0.903 (0.542)*	0.165	229
Single status	-1.155 (0.512)**	-1.127 (0.512)*	-1.935 (0.573)***	0.168	222
Internal promotion the norm	-0.303 (0.696)	-1.238 (0.694)*	-0.285 (0.661)	0.121	229
No compulsory redundancy	-0.051 (0.532)	-0.751 (0.755)	-0.64 (0.59)	0.145	228
Trainability as a major selection criterion	1.319 (0.711)*	-1.032 (0.623)*	-1.024 (0.518)***	0.124	226
Use of psychological tests for all selection	-1.136 (0.785)	-0.3 (0.925)	0.579 (0.653)	0.191	231
Realistic job previews during recruitment	-0.068 (0.53)	-0.14 (0.631)	-0.748 (0.517)	0.087	221
System to communicate values to new staff	0.207 (0.595)	0.716 (0.730)	-0.363 (0.535)	0.091	229
Deliberate development of a learning organization	0.925 (0.574)	0.286 (0.605)	-0.174 (0.503)	0.119	226
Minimum annual training requirements for all	0.878 (0.777)	pfp	1.931 (0.774)**	0.141	212
Flexible job descriptions not fixed to one task	0.519 (0.712)	-0.114 (0.696)	0.565 (0.683)	0.172	226
Jobs designed to make full use of skills	-0.261 (0.474)	-0.408 (0.592)	-0.312 (0.498)	0.083	224
Teamworking for majority of staff	-0.141 (0.575)	-0.324 (0.643)	-0.799 (0.53)	0.103	226
Staff involved in setting performance targets	-0.494 (0.518)	-0.522 (0.594)	-0.972 (0.525)*	0.099	227
Staff responsible for their own quality	0.359 (0.716)	1.273 (1.11)	-0.674 (0.595)	0.084	224
Majority involved in quality circles or quality improvement teams	-0.37 (0.533)	1.074 (0.625)*	0.454 (0.522)	0.126	228
Regular use of attitude surveys	0.561 (0.529)	-0.84 (0.851)	-0.04 (0.621)	0.097	230
Team briefing/Information cascades	0.529 (0.56)	-0.515 (0.592)	-0.259 (0.515)	0.075	229
Information on market position/company performance	1.032 (0.825)	-0.646 (0.647)	-0.444 (0.581)	0.131	228
Merit pay for all staff	-1.039 (0.554)*	-0.908 (0.665)	-1.104 (0.552)**	0.183	227
Formal appraisal for all at least annually	-0.487 (0.632)	-0.835 (0.676)	-1.549 (0.582)***	0.212	228
Human resource policy integrated with business strategy	1.808 (0.714)**	0.009 (0.605)	-0.297 (0.514)	0.169	220
Human resource policies integrated with each other	1.186 (0.652)*	-0.23 (0.612)	-0.184 (0.559)	0.184	217

Notes: Coefficients given (standard errors in brackets).
Default category is non-union establishments.
*** significant at 1%; ** significant at 5%; * significant at 10%.
R2 is pseudo.
Regressions control for size, region, type of establishment, ownership, greenfield site, whether or not part of a larger organization. pfp = predicts failure perfectly.

Table 2.A3. Multivariate analysis of unions and type of human resource strategy

	Union = 1	R2	Observations	Single union deal	Single union no deal	Multi-Union	R2	Observations
Good	0.563 (0.384)	0.115	230	1.125 (0.534)**	0.611 (0.61)	0.09 (0.523)	0.126	226
Lucky	−1.851 (0.582)***	0.131	230	pfp	−1.696 (1.129)	−0.802 (0.687)	0.114	198
Bad	0.24 (0.406)	0.126	230	−0.056 (0.59)	0.422 (0.632)	0.464 (0.535)	0.134	226
Ugly	0.357 (0.529)	0.083	232	0.162 (0.669)	0.058 (0.867)	0.523 (0.659)	0.033	228

Notes: Logit regression analysis used. Coefficients given (standard errors in brackets).
*** significant at 1%; ** significant at 5%.
R2 is pseudo.
Regression control for size, region, type of establishment, ownership, whether or not part of a larger organization, greenfield sites.
pfp = predicts failure perfectly.

Table 2.A4 Multivariate analysis of human resource strategy and outcomes

	Lucky	Bad	Ugly	R2	Observations
Human resource/employee relations outcomes					
Commitment of lower grade staff	0.013 (0.224)	−0.79 (0.198)***	−0.493 (0.253)*	0.102	230
The quality of staff employed	−0.411 (0.235)*	−0.967 (0.212)***	−0.399 (0.263)	0.125	228
Quality of work of lower grade staff	0.098 (0.236)	−0.452 (0.205)**	−0.511 (0.265)*	0.133	230
Quality of human resource policies and practices	−1.176 (0.245)***	−1.429 (0.221)***	−0.821 (0.27)***	0.221	227
The flexibility of staff	−0.249 (0.229)	−0.849 (0.201)***	−0.094 (0.259)	0.108	230
Ability to move between jobs as needed	−0.542 (0.227)**	−0.79 (0.2)***	−0.094 (0.256)	0.09	229
Flexibility to adjust workforce size	−0.069 (0.214)	−0.281 (0.187)	−0.041 (0.243)	0.053	227
Line manager enthusiasm for human resource policies	−0.855 (0.236)***	−1.711 (0.223)***	−1.428 (0.27)***	0.199	227
Employee relations outcomes					
Industrial dispute 'YES'[a]	−0.058 (0.702)	−0.006 (0.505)	−0.07 (0.627)	0.282	234
Labour turnover in 1992 (%) [b]	1.173 (2.247)	3.103 (1.841)*	4.931 (2.395)**	−0.022	206
Absenteeism in 1992[b]	1.963 (0.991)**	0.601 (0.891)	2.128 (1.149)*	0.021	176
Performance Outcomes					
Quality targets attained (%)[b]	−2.842 (4.33)	0.498 (3.961)	−9.3 (5.509)*	0.015	138
How well was the recession weathered	−0.389 (0.227)*	−0.451 (0.204)**	−0.074 (0.26)	0.075	227
Productivity benchmarked against UK	−0.83 (0.293)***	−1.204 (0.286)***	−0.679 (0.289)**	0.115	159
Quality benchmarked against the UK	−0.475 (0.289)	−1.094 (0.273)***	−0.682 (0.287)**	0.122	163
Productivity benchmarked against World	−0.654 (0.287)**	−0.439 (0.281)	−0.133 (0.281)	0.094	146
Quality benchmarked against World	−0.262 (0.283)	−0.611 (0.288)**	−0.272 (0.292)	0.087	150

Notes: Ordered Probit regression analysis used, except for [a] logit, and [b] OLS. Coefficients given (standard errors in brackets).
Default category is Good.
*** significant at 1%; ** significant at 5%; * significant at 10%.
R2 is pseudo for logit and ordered probit, and adjusted for OLS.
Regressions control for size, region, type of establishment, ownership, whether or not part of a larger organization, greenfield sites and union recognition.

Table 2.A5. Multivariate analysis of unions and outcomes

	Union = 1	R2	Obs	Single union deal	Single union no deal	Multi-Union	R2	Obs
Human resource/employee relations Outcomes								
Commitment of lower grade staff	-0.082 (0.229)	0.104	226	-0.158 (0.276)	0.424 (0.316)	-0.485 (0.267)*	0.109	226
The quality of staff employed	-0.165 (0.207)	0.125	228	-0.142 (0.286)	0.072 (0.325)	-0.364 (0.28)	0.124	224
Quality of work of lower grade staff	-0.388 (0.209)*	0.133	230	-0.308 (0.289)	0.06 (0.332)	-0.716 (0.282)**	0.141	226
Quality of human resource policies and practices	-0.165 (0.206)	0.221	227	-0.078 (0.286)	-0.371 (0.324)	-0.183 (0.278)	0.215	223
The flexibility of staff	-0.056 (0.203)	0.108	230	0.118 (0.284)	0.146 (0.321)	-0.349 (0.272)	0.111	226
Ability to move between jobs as needed	-0.363 (0.201)*	0.09	229	-0.145 (0.277)	-0.366 (0.315)	-0.559 (0.272)**	0.093	225
Flexibility to adjust workforce size	0.21 (0.191)	0.053	227	0.442 (0.267)*	0.242 (0.302)	-0.083 (0.256)	0.057	223
Line manager enthusiasm for human resource policies	-0.435 (0.204)**	0.199	227	-0.407 (0.284)	-0.531 (0.32)*	-0.635 (0.272)**	0.203	223
Employee Relations Outcomes								
Industrial dispute 'yes'[a]	1.991 (0.478)***	0.282	234	1.805 (0.617)***	0.769 (0.732)	2.967 (0.732)***	0.325	230
Labour turnover in 1992 (%)[b]	-1.363 (1.895)	-0.022	206	2.663 (2.544)	-3.23 (2.947)	-4.425 (2.681)	-0.006	202
Absenteeism in 1992 [b]	0.12 (0.9)	0.024	176	0.318 (1.186)	0.03 (1.462)	-0.189 (1.236)	0.009	172
Performance Outcomes								
Quality targets attained (%)[b]	2.59 (4.022)	0.015	138	4.262 (5.104)	-1.509 (6.983)	2.821 (5.695)	-0.001	137
How well was the recession weathered	-0.553 (0.207)***	0.075	227	-0.046 (0.289)	-0.377 (0.309)	-1.104 (0.286)***	0.091	223
Productivity benchmarked against UK	-0.303 (0.246)	0.115	159	0.051 (0.344)	-0.56 (0.43)	-0.531 (0.323)*	0.119	156
Quality benchmarked against the UK	-0.127 (0.243)	0.122	163	-0.147 (0.334)	0.097 (0.446)	-0.254 (0.322)	0.12	160
Productivity benchmarked against World	-0.512 (0.256)**	0.094	146	-0.452 (0.333)	-1.29 (0.447)***	-0.329 (0.328)	0.106	144
Quality benchmarked against World	-0.174 (0.256)	0.087	150	-0.497 (0.335)	-0.1 (0.455)	0.07 (0.334)	0.095	148

Notes: Ordered Probit regression analysis used, except for [a] logit and [b] OLS. Coefficients given (standard errors in brackets).
*** significant at 1%; ** significant at 5%; * significant at 10%.
R2 is pseudo for logit and ordered probit, and adjusted for OLS.
Regressions control for size, region, type of establishment, ownership, whether or not part of a larger organization, greenfield sites and human resource policy.

3

THE STATE AND NEW INDUSTRIAL RELATIONS

Ian Clark

1. Introduction

The practices and process of 'new industrial relations' and human resource management have become the primary agenda of industrial relations research and teaching whether prescriptive or critical (see Storey 1992, 1995; and Edwards 1995); notwithstanding this primacy new industrial relations and human resource management are of no use in themselves; they are propagated as mechanisms to rejuvenate the British economy, its manufacturing sector in particular, and connect with current dynamics in capitalist production. Without an evaluation of the problematic nature of the wider dynamics of capitalist production new industrial relations and human resource management are both abstract and decontextual.

In the period since 1945 the dynamics of capitalist production have been generalized under two broad headings. The post-war period is generalized as 'Fordism', centred on the mass production of standardized commodities, institutionalized collective bargaining, and Welfare State capitalism (see Jessop 1991; Hyman 1994; and Nolan 1994). The contemporary period is generalized as 'Post-Fordism' premissed on the demise of mass consumer markets, the rise of niche markets, and the erosion of social democracy in the institutional base of the State. In particular, it has rejected collective bargaining and trade union recognition as 'good' industrial relations (see Jessop 1991, 1994; and Purcell 1993).

If we accept that Fordism and Post-Fordism generalize periods in capitalist production it is equally necessary to question the degree to which national pathways in capitalist production measure up to the generalization. We contend that national pathways predominate over generalized descriptions in the development of capitalist production. In consequence we must evaluate the relationship between capital, labour, and the State within national pathways in order to illustrate how historical formation within particular nation states weakens the viability of generalized description.

We suggest that the British State has been subject to a formative influence of libertarian *laissez faire* which emphasizes freedom and liberty from centralized and institutionalized measures enacted by the State. In the post-war period plural industrial relations and voluntary regulation epitomize this influence. Equally during the post-war period the British State was subject to the contextual influence of social democracy and plural public policy manifest in 'good' industrial relations as collective bargaining and trade union recognition. The contemporary erosion of social democracy and 'good' industrial relations has separated the State from an active interest in capitalist accumulation; in fact the disengagement of pluralism in industrial relations has wound up the contextual influence of social democracy and returned the formative influence of libertarian *laissez faire* as contemporary contextual influence in the State, its accumulation strategy, and public policy on industrial relations. However, the disengagement of pluralism, an accumulation stategy based on flexibility, and redefined 'good' industrial relations are all caught in the permanent yet unfolding contradiction of libertarian *laissez faire*; that is, a continuity in historical formation within a particular nation state and the predominance of this over generalized pathways in capitalist production. We contend that new industrial relations is in the British case isolated and disengaged from contemporary material dynamics other than promoting what can be termed 'extra flexibility'. This isolation illustrates the weakness of prescriptive generalization in capitalist production because Post-Fordism and Fordism are based on a presumed role for the State, which we suggest never developed in the British State.

This chapter seeks to illustrate the isolation of new industrial relations as informed by human resource management from market and production strategies which are portrayed as the (future) basis of capitalist production in the UK. The chapter develops a wide-ranging polemic and is eclectic in its discussion with references to the State and its current strategy of disengagement from active involvement in capitalist accumulation.

Since 1945 'good' industrial relations have been a central feature of public policy. For much of the post-war period 'good' industrial relations was constituted in terms of plural State institutions presiding over an economy where collective bargaining and trade union recognition were functional elements within an accumulation strategy centred on Fordism. By 1979 'good' industrial relations had become 'bad' industrial relations; almost overnight the Thatcher Government rejected the pluralism in the post-war settlement between capital and labour (see Gamble 1990: 149–57). More significantly the Thatcher Government came to power when the period of capitalist development generalized as Fordism was exhausted. The contemporary State has initiated a libertarian, that is individual accumulation, strategy, disengaged pluralism in industrial relations, and sought to roll back much of its previous social democratic orthodoxy in areas such as employment policy, the Welfare State, nationalized industry, and industrial relations (see Gamble 1988: 96–135). Good industrial relations has been reconstituted and now emphasizes the managerial prerogative and less industrial action as the basis of good (see Purcell 1991).

This chapter contends that the contemporary State's method of operation, disengagement from social democracy, actively frustrates its efforts to generate a positive flexible Post-Fordism in the UK. The chapter asserts that flexibility is a means to an end in the movement between stages of capitalist development whereas in the UK it has become an end in itself. In consequence, in the UK, flexibility is not a bridge between Fordism and Post-Fordism but a method of making the entrails of Fordism more flexible, thereby contributing to the development of a neo-Fordist low wage, low productivity, yet flexible, economy. Hence our contention that sovereign national pathways to capitalist development predominate over generalized periodizations. In order to develop this overall argument the discussion which follows is divided into four sections.

In Section 2 formative and contextual influences on the British State are briefly introduced in order to specify the limited nature of the British State. Section 3 evaluates the process of contemporary State disengagement from the post-war social democratic orthodoxy; the strategy of Conservative governments and their attempts to reconstitute good industrial relations is located in the process of disengagement. Section 4 evaluates new industrial relations, new market and production strategies, and suggests that institutional disengagement by the State isolates new (improved) industrial relations from new market and production strategies. In consequence typology–normative description of market and production strategies are removed from their actual constitution in the UK's national pathway. Section 5 builds on the arguments of the previous sections to illustrate the limited nature of new industrial relations in the generation of flexibility and sustainable improvement in productivity. This section is followed by a general summary (Section 6) and conclusions (Section 7).

2. Formative and Contextual Influences on the State

As a precursor to a more detailed evaluation of new industrial relations we briefly discuss formative and contextual influences on the British State. The aim of this section is to illustrate how a renaissance of formative influences on the State in terms of its public policy actually frustrates overall economic performance. The formative influence on the development of the British State is libertarian *laissez faire*. As an economic and political doctrine it eschews a centralized state and highlights voluntary regulation in all spheres through contract and status (see Fox 1985: 6). Notwithstanding its formative influence, *laissez faire* was discredited as the industrial revolution progressed during the nineteenth century. From the 1870s a contextual influence emerged on the State; social democracy and collectivism developed in response to industrialization and collective experience in the employment relationship. For example, between 1871 and 1906 trade unions were legalized so that their activities were given immunity from prosecution in specific instances. Additionally between 1832 and 1928 the franchise was extended to all adults over the age of 21. Lastly, between 1908 and 1911 the Liberal Government introduced the beginning of what later become a fully fledged Welfare State. In addition to these examples of collectivism and social democracy both concepts reached their height in the formulation of plural industrial relations as public policy in the post-war period. For a general survey on the emergence of collectivism in the UK, see Greenleaf (1983).

For much of the period since 1945 industrial relations were worked out plurally between employers and employees free from substantive legislative interference by the State (see Flanders 1951: 115; 1954: 307, 332; and 1970: 94–103; Clegg 1979, and McCarthy 1992). In substance pluralism in industrial relations was extra-contractual and socio-political in its constitution. By extra-contractual we mean it operated beyond the influence of individual contract, in consequence its method centres on the negotiation of collective agreements on the individual enforcement of contract. Pluralism was socio-political in its constitution because in public policy it was geared towards collective bargaining, trade union recognition, and State absenteeism with minimal negative use of the law; Kahn-Freund (1954, 1959) referred to this as 'collective laissez faire'.

The formative influence of libertarian *laissez faire* on the British State facilitated the development of voluntary industrial relations, projecting freedom from the State in the institutional base of industrial relations. Voluntary method in industrial relations illustrates the political foundation of *laissez faire* which prescribes a preference for voluntary regulation over State regulation. In the post-war period this equated to autonomous collective bargaining between employers and employees.

The central point in the making is the contradictory effect the formative influence of libertarian *laissez faire* has had. In many respects voluntary industrial relations replicated the formative influence of libertarian *laissez faire* by limiting active and positive State regulation of industrial relations, in particular the negative use of the law. By this we mean that voluntarism, that is collective *laissez faire*, encouraged a form of decentralized production politics where capital, labour (and the State) sought to keep the State out of their internal affairs and relations. Perkin (1969) argues that a pattern of pre-industrial class-formation, emphasizing maximum material freedom from the State was reproduced in industrial society. Barrington-Moore (1966: 413) refers to this as a peaceful bourgeois revolution expressing a continuity of interests in and between capital and free labour *vis-à-vis* the centralized State apparatus in the form of Monarchy or Parliament. I. Clark (forthcoming) illustrates this argument in relation to the development of State policy on productivity in the post-war period (see also Tomlinson and Tiratsoo 1993).

Notwithstanding the above, institutional freedom only extends to the method of industrial relations. Within a capitalist economy the State is always present in the institution of industrial relations; the State apparatus defends and maintains private property, capitalist reproduction, and the contractually determined employment relationship, that is the naturalized framework of capitalist production (see Hyman 1975: 22–5; and 1989: 84–9, and S. Clarke 1991: 82–6). A contradiction in industrial relations is its complete separation from the dynamics of capitalist production. Rule-making in capitalist production is beyond economics but central to industrial relations, this defines the fictitious nature of voluntary industrial relations; their method may be voluntary but their institution results from the framework of capitalist production.

Since 1979 the State has not been rolled back *per se*, it is the contextual influence of social democracy and collectivism which has been curtailed. As a result the formative influence of libertarian *laissez faire* has been repopularized in order to halt socio-political advances made by labour during the post-war period.

In essence the Thatcher–Major Governments have sought to restructure capital by eroding social democracy and reconstituting public policy as individual and liberal. A major element in this policy has been the removal of 'market rigidities' such as trade unions, elements of the public sector, and within employment inflexible collective agreements constituted beyond contract. A by-product of reconstituting public policy has been an effort to generate new industrial relations informed, initially by macho management and latterly by new management techniques amalgamated in 'human resource management'. In both cases individual contractual reward and regulation are highlighted. We now proceed to a more detailed discussion of new industrial relations.

3. The Generation of New Industrial Relations?

The previous section argued that since 1979 the formative influence of libertarian *laissez faire* has been paramount in the State's efforts to restructure the UK's industrial capitalism. In addition it was argued that voluntary industrial relations, constituted collectively or individually, replicate the libertarian bias in the British State which emphasizes freedom from centralized State action and regulation. The absence of centralized State action and regulation has been projected as vital to the generation of new industrial relations; this in turn has led to a rejection of pluralism and social democracy in the institutional base of the State. Both of these were primary contextual influences on the post-war State and public policy on industrial relations. This section examines the State as a functional entity which seeks to structure class conflict and provide co-ordination for the market by facilitating capitalist accumulation.

The period of capitalist development which followed the Second World War is generalized as Fordism; within this, economic co-ordination and class struggle necessitated the promotion of plural industrial relations and a Welfare State. Such innovations accommodated the balance of class forces which were determined by full employment and a diffusion of social democracy in the State. Since 1979 the contemporary State has disengaged this orthodoxy. It has been able to do this with such ease precisely because pluralism and social democracy were constituted beyond the formative influences on the State. One area where the pressure of disengagement has been most prominent is the generalization of new industrial relations.

What is New Industrial Relations?

In terms of our argument we suggest that new industrial relations represents three ideological images propagated by the contemporary State: first, the promotion of the managerial prerogative, employee compliance, and a low strike level; secondly, a rejection of collective bargaining and trade union recognition as public policy and their replacement with managerially determined regulation and individualism in the employment relationship; thirdly, a prescription for management labour use strategies centred on flexibility and extra-contractual commitment through human resource management. Each image evokes the formative influences of libertarian *laissez faire* informed by contract and status and rejects contextual influences centred on pluralism, collective bargaining, and trade unions.

Thatcherism emphasized the conservative nature of the British State and repopularized individualism and freedom from the State (see Hutton 1995: 89–95). Thatcherism sought to reduce financial and institutional dependence on the State and encourage self-reliance, both economically and socially. In so doing it attacked the contextual basis of the post-war State (see Gamble 1990).

By promoting contractual individualism Thatcherism launched a supply side attack on 'obstacles' to productive efficiency such as public debt, State-spending on the products of social democracy, and the social democratic acceptance of privileged trade unions. As Gamble (1993) makes clear, Thatcherism unwound the coil of social democracy in the UK's State apparatus (a socio-political retreat designed to promote economic advance). A rapid change in public policy on industrial relations in the use of the law and the promotion of individualism became the leading edge of State disengagement from the post-war plural orthodoxy (see Crouch 1990: 239–242; Purcell 1991, 1993; and McCarthy 1992: 39–42).

The rhetoric of new industrial relations attacks the acceptance of conflict in industrial relations; the failure of pluralist industrial relations as public policy. The substance of new industrial relations represents an effort to contextualize formative influences on the State. In consequence the State has sought to circumscribe or terminate key rights and immunities acquired by trade unions since the late nineteenth century (see Zeitlin 1986: 2; and McCarthy 1992). Pioneers of social democracy such as the Webbs (1897: 823, 828) saw the expansion of State activity and institutional recognition on behalf of labour as an imperative; that is, a functional response to the needs of industrial capitalism. The political erosion of social democracy since 1979 is also propagated on the basis of current imperatives in capitalist development; in crude terms, the orthodox pluralism of 'old' industrial relations was based on the contextual influences of collectivism, union recognition and the absence of law: 'new' industrial relations is based in the formative influence of libertarian *laissez faire*, State individualism, and freedom from extra contractual institutional regulation. Collectivism sat easily with the functional requirements of Fordism, whereas market individualism is propagated as essential for a successful movement to a Post-Fordist stage in capitalist development (see Boyer 1988; and Jessop 1991, 1994).

In order to avoid the charge of functional determinism there are two caveats which illustrate the problematic of function. First, old and new industrial relations are constituted through public policy; in both cases the extent to which the reality measures up to constitution is questionable (for a brief discussion of the limits in the post-war settlement see Eldridge *et al.* (1991: 20–1); for the limits of the contemporary settlement see Hutton (1995: 105–10)). The second caveat concerns the generation of new industrial relations and its role in the movement from Fordism to Post-Fordism. As Zeitlin (1986: 50) points out, States are not rational actors operating as historical subjects in defined periods but complex and contradictory associations. Hence there can be no guarantee that action by the State can be coherent or strategic. If this were the case order in industrial relations would be the norm.

The interesting question is how public policy becomes dysfunctional; the role and motivation of the State is a key factor as are its formative limitations. In the post-war period contextual influences on the State, pluralism, and social democracy became almost exclusive. For example, the Donovan prescription for industrial relations reform had no linkage to economic performance other than the social democratic assertion that formalized procedures at company level would arrest the use of restrictive practices, unofficial industrial action, and informal sectionalism (see Crossley 1968; Reid 1968; Turner 1969; Goldthorpe 1974; Nolan and Walsh 1995; and I. Clark, forthcoming). Since 1979 public policy has sought to sweep away social democracy and pluralism in industrial relations precisely because it inhibited economic performance via its method of extra-contractual (collective) rigidity. In both periods public policy became dysfunctional; first, it failed to address the issue of management (see Edwards 1995: 7–10). In the 1960s management practice was largely ignored by the Donovan proposals. Flanders (1970: 70) argued that procedural reform would improve management; however, as Hyman (1973: 110–12), S. Clarke (1988: 293), and Hutton (1995: 84) point out management did not necessarily improve its own practice in terms of cost and production control or work study. In the contemporary period management is assumed to be improved by measures which promote the managerial prerogative. However, British management practice was not necessarily connected to the broader material dynamics of Fordism or Post-Fordism (see Carew 1991: 65; Tomlinson 1991; and I. Clark, forthcoming).

A second reason for State policy becoming dysfunctional centres on the form of the State; in the post-war period contextual influences were determined extra-contractually whereas in the contemporary period extra-contractual influences have been curtailed. The contradiction for the State is its limited form. In the era of pluralism the State could not structure an integration of formative and contextual influences, whereas today the State has rejected the latter and seeks to operate through the former. Hence human agency within the institutional base of the State has gone from social democracy without a consideration of economic performance to a singular consideration of capitalist accumulation without a consideration of social democracy or comparative economic performance.

Use of law and the rejection of anything approaching good industrial relations in public policy are the dysfunctional consequences of State policy: the absence of the latter and pivotal role of the former have enabled the State to go back to its formative influences of contract, status, and the market. All three now drive human agency within the State's institutional apparatus. For example, in the pluralist era 'status rights' were determined extra-contractually through the acceptance of collective bargaining, trade unions, and the minimal use of the law. In the contemporary era 'status' is not attached to anything collective, but instead, the individual contract of employment, which the prescription behind human resource management encourages individual employees to go beyond in order to progress up a single status hierarchy (see Storey 1992: 30–41; and Storey and Sisson 1993: 15–19).

By disengaging from an institutional interest in good industrial relations the State has no industrial relations or overall industrial strategy which can lever the UK economy into Post-Fordism other than the purported benefits of market-oriented flexibility and statistically engineered improvement in productivity (see Nolan 1989a, and 1989b; and Hutton 1995: 188). As Zeitlin (1986: 12) points out, functional explanations become tautological if any development can (retrospectively) be advantageous or compatible with functional requirements in capitalism.

The critical issue is the disconnection of cause and positive effect. Changes in the use of law and the generation of new industrial relations as enterprise-based public policy are largely negative in their effect because in the UK they fail to connect with production and market strategies essential in a movement to positive Post-Fordism. In the main, new industrial relations operates in Fordist product and market strategies which in the majority of areas encourage low productivity and low wages (see Elger 1990; and Hutton 1995: 8). Business operates in a climate of perennial uncertainty and instability which in the absence of an overall industrial strategy encourages short-term responses to marketing, production, and management in general. As enterprise responses such moves are expressions of rational self-interest; however, the absence of an overall industrial strategy, other than the pursuit of flexibility, provides no positive dynamic for employers to follow.

The Basis of Industrial Relations Change

The first Thatcher administration visualized trade unions as operationally uncontrollable and restrictive. Trade unions were held to be uncontrollable in the sense that industrial action was often unofficial, secondary, and involved the use of mass picketing. In addition highly particular restrictive practices were generalized to be operative throughout the economy. Such practices created inflexibility and rigidity in the supply side of the economy blunting its efficiency. Inefficiency manifested itself in a failure to use new technology in a competitive manner (for definitive examples of this line of argument see Muellbauer (1986) and Crafts (1988, 1991)).

Supply side measures attacked obstacles to productive efficiency such as trade unions. Early legislation (1980–4) was designed with two purposes in mind: first, to challenge established patterns of behaviour and conduct in industrial disputes, and secondly, to improve the managerial prerogative. The latter effect is a function of the former; measures such as secondary picketing and unofficial industrial action were often traditional responses to managerial unreasonableness and unilateralism. In the new legal environment of the trade union as legal personality, fines and possible sequestration make such action less likely. Hence in operational terms the likelihood of trade union financial loss facilitated a potential improvement in the managerial prerogative (see Purcell 1991: 41).

The Employment Acts of 1980 and 1982 were not primarily directed at the internal activity of unions or their (restrictive) practices but at their conduct within industrial disputes. The 1980 Act outlawed secondary industrial action and secondary picketing whereas the 1982 Act made the continuation of these now illegal activities more pressing by narrowing the definition of a trade dispute and restoring the legal personality of trade unions. As Brown and Wadhwani (1990: 61) comment, these changes substantially weakened the position of unions which traditionally relied on secondary action.

Thus, the first attack on the working of established industrial relations was to weaken its mode of operation in times of dispute. The second attack can most effectively be seen within the wider attack on, and rejection of, elements within the supply side of the post-war settlement.

The attack on the post-war settlement and the supply side in particular was the Thatcher Government's response to the failure of economic and social regulation in the orthodoxy of the social democratic State; that is, the capacity of the State to manage this orthodoxy. The presence of near full employment was visualized as reducing pressures on employers to be efficient thereby resulting in uncompetitive productivity levels especially in manufacturing. In addition the restrictive nature of trade unions stifled enterprise and the effective operation of market forces (see Crafts 1991). Initially the strategy of attack was to shake out the manufacturing sector by severe deflation, an indirect effect of which was to promote the managerial prerogative on the basis of 'macho management' which later appeared more reasoned in 'new industrial relations' centred on the idea of human resource management. By implication the Government argued that the manufacturing sector would re-emerge leaner, fitter, more flexible, and free of the rigidity imposed by previously acceptable restrictive practices. Crouch (1990: 339) sees this as a 'rejection of compromise': what we have termed the social democratic orthodoxy in the post-war settlement. Crouch argues that the State has rejected the need for good industrial relations and failed to institute anything in its place.

Whilst Crouch is generally correct it must be pointed out that human agency which is driving the contemporary State does not want to institute anything in the place of good industrial relations; precisely because the basis of the comtemporary State's effort to generate new industrial relations is institutional disengagement from the employment relationship; an effect of which is a loss of political citizenship for trade unions.

Efforts to politically reconstitute good industrial relations are a response to the incapacity of the social democratic orthodoxy in the post-war State. It is best visualized as an effort to modify the working of market forces to counter the tendency for the rate of profit to fall. For sustainable success such a policy must be grounded in a solid industrial policy.

Lane (1989: 256) has argued that since 1979 the State has disengaged itself from industry and the circuit of capital precisely because of its overt free market ideology which denies the need for an active industrial policy. This is exactly the case because current accumulation strategies and industrial policy express the contradiction of the formative influence on the State; that is, the libertarian bias of freedom from State regulation. Jessop *et al.* (1988: 135) has highlighted this as a central flaw in the libertarian accumulation strategy of the contemporary State. Dynamic efficiency within any accumulation strategy requires the active, that is collective, cooperation of both parties in the employment relationship. The political reconstitution of good industrial relations expressly avoids this via its rejection of pluralism (see also Streeck 1992: 64–72). This point can be amplified through a brief discussion of these changes at the level of the firm.

The Basis of New Industrial Relations at the Level of the Firm

The rejection of the post-war settlement and higher levels of unemployment, together with the empty libertarian accumulation strategy, has placed economic uncertainty at the centre of corporate strategy. As Hyman (1991: 262) argues the primary effect of this uncertainty is budgetary pressure supplemented by management empowerment–prerogative to introduce new initiatives in industrial relations centred on labour control under the label human resource management. Hyman's point is reinforced by Streeck (1987: 283) who highlights the attack on 'status rights' within the contract of employment which new industrial relations promotes via its location in the wider reassertion of market principles. The message of human resource management replaces the notion of social stability and extra-contractual status (in collective bargaining) with the promotion of cooperative 'extra' flexibility based on individual status and extra-contractual obligation, what Storey (1992: 35) terms going beyond contract.

The template of so-called 'soft' human resource management focuses on the individual to legitimize more authoritarian employment practices which undermine the institutional framework of 'old' industrial relations. However, the devices of contractual regulation, extra-contractual obligation, and individual status are insufficient to raise productivity and counter the tendency for the rate of profit to fall. An active industrial strategy is essential to focus the material objectives behind greater flexibility and improved productivity; in the absence of this the pursuit of flexibility has become an end in itself not a means of capitalist regeneration.

The contemporary libertarian accumulation strategy centres on the deregulation of markets, especially the labour-market, privatization, the stimulation of small businesses, and the enterprise culture. It is based on a highly particular stereotypical image of private sector capitalism which the individualist and contractually bound State generalized as the norm.

In summary it can be concluded that elements of new industrial relations have been introduced but there are two caveats; first, if we evaluate new industrial relations in terms of the historical development of the British State and its formative influences, the disengagement of pluralism in industrial relations further separates the State from active involvement in capitalist production; that is, new industrial relations cannot by itself connect with contemporary material dynamics. Secondly and relatedly, in the absence of an active industrial strategy new industrial relations largely operate in a vacuum; that is, the atomized firm and individual accumulation strategies. In the following section we can address the question of why we need new industrial relations by examining product, employment, and labour-market changes in more detail.

4. The Need for New Industrial Relations?

The previous section made clear that the generation of new industrial relations is of no use in itself. The management and regulation of employment; that is, its industrial relations is a requirement of industrial capitalism and its wider production dynamics. In consequence it is necessary to examine wider economic and social restructuring which are alleged to be the crucial impetus for the dissemination of new industrial relations.

The central components of economic and social restructuring are twofold: first, new forms of production and associated market strategies, and second, social restructuring. The former is generalized in terms of flexible specialization and a movement to 'Post-Fordism' whereas the latter is generalized as 'flexibility' in civil society and its prevailing attitude to work.

This section briefly details both flexible specialization and flexibility and then evaluates each in terms of the UK's contemporary accumulation strategy and the historical development of the State. It propagates an argument which suggests that, in the UK at least, flexibility does not measure up to either dominant model; as a result, we contend that in the UK flexibility is constituted in the entrails of Fordism. In consequence the substance of new industrial relations cannot connect with market and production strategies on which it is premissed. Hence in large measure it is rhetorically based to justify a deterioration in the quality of the employment relationship. However, because of its individual constitution new industrial relations does benefit some workers who are empowered to go beyond contract; that is, become more flexible.

Conventional Flexibility: Flexible Specialization and the Flexible Firm

As a theory of production flexible specialization concentrates on changes in the production process which result from the application of new technology and computerized production equipment. The demand side dynamic of flexible specialization is the saturation and collapse of mass Fordist markets together with the promulgation of more determined consumer sovereignty. The supply side dynamic of flexible specialization represents a market strategy based on the pursuit of niche markets. The economics of flexible specialization are simple: improvements in the technological base of production enable niche markets to be pursued because the fixed costs of set-up times can be drastically reduced, thereby enabling small batch customized products to be profitably produced at standardized prices. The primary advocates of this strategy, Piore and Sabel (1984), see flexible specialization facilitating the re-emergence of craft products and in consequence multi-skilled craft workers; for a critical review of evidence for the UK see Nolan and Walsh (1995: 76–9).

In the absence of stable accumulation and production strategies based in Fordism, alternatives such as flexible specialization are propagated as the harbingers of economic and social stability in a movement to Post-Fordism. We can now turn to flexibility as a labour utilization strategy at the level of the firm.

Flexibility as a management-use strategy for labour was first repopularized in a typology presented by Atkinson (1984). This typology centred on management segmenting its labour force into a core, with structured internal labour-markets and a periphery of plug-in-unplug jobs. Hutton (1995: 105–10) refers to these groups as privileged: the 40 per cent of the labour-market whose market power has increased since 1979 and the marginalized and insecure whose market position has deteriorated since 1979, as a result of flexibility and new industrial relations. Segmentation leads to the possibility of functional flexibility in the core and numerical flexibility in the peripheral groups. Hyman (1991: 275–9) argues that flexibility has become the theme of the 1980s wherein industrial relations is integrated into business strategy in order for management to cope with economic uncertainty. If we accept that flexibility is the main theme in contemporary business strategies we must add that it represents one result of the State's disengaged accumulation strategy. This positions the management of macroeconomic uncertainty at the level of the individual firm.

It is important to make clear that in the UK flexibility is a management strategy (flexible firm) and more. Flexibility also refers to labour-market outcomes which result from deregulation, the enhanced managerial prerogative, human resource management, and the disengagement of the social democratic State. We term this 'extra flexibility' in order to distinguish it from flexibility inherent to the flexible firm and flexible specialization.

Jessop *et al.* (1988) generalize flexible specialization and flexibility into a post-recession settlement which forms the basis of a movement to Post-Fordism in the UK; that is, it is a functional response to the needs of British capitalism. The effect of this movement, the success of which is highly uncertain (see below), impacts on industrial relations in three ways. First, industrial relations have become less collective and more differentiable. Core workers who presumably are the focus of new industrial relations are themselves integrated into the organization for whom they work by their location in secure internal labour-markets. The mechanics of human resource management are prescribed to be the basis of this integration (see Bassett (1986: 171–9) for a hopeful account of these developments). Secondly, collective industrial relations are of declining significance; as a response to heightened uncertainty in market conditions, the wage relation itself is made more flexible for both the core and the periphery. WIRS3 (1992) data (pp. 218–34, tables 7.1–7.7) concludes that the majority of workers do not have their pay determined as a result of collective bargaining. For manual and non-manual workers in 1990 the figures were 45 per cent and 24 per cent respectively whereas in private services the figures for manual and non-manual workers were 32 per cent and 27 per cent. Only in the public sector did the majority of manual and non-manual workers have their last pay increase determined by collective bargaining (78 per cent and 84 per cent respectively). Where pay was not determined through collective bargaining the most significant determinant was management at establishment level. A third effect of the post-recession settlement on industrial relations is the disappearance of many full-time jobs, some of which are reconstituted via subcontracting, or the use of non-standard labour in the form of agency workers and part-timers.

For Boyer (1988) these types of labour-market and industrial relations flexibility are essential because capitalism has moved beyond Fordism. In consequence methods of industrial relations regulation and the quasi-right to full-time employment are unsuitable in Post-Fordism or neo-Fordism stages of capitalist development. We can now evaluate flexible specialization and the generalized flexibility thesis within the UK's current accumulation strategy and the stance of the State.

Economic and Social Restructuring: the State's Accumulation Strategy

The libertarian accumulation strategy espoused by the State during the 1980s and 1990s is centred on extra-flexibility popular (individualist) capitalism and the enterprise culture. It assumes social and economic stability will result from the stance of the State; that is, its disengagement from the economy and further separation from civil society.

Within the libertarian accumulation strategy flexible specialization and flexibility are more or less left as free-standing strategies with which the mechanics of new industrial relations can connect. In short the chimeric content of the contemporary accumulation strategy has generated an enterprise strategy based around numerical flexibility between core and peripheral workers. The potential benefits of flexible specialization have been relegated to a concentration on changes in current production and labour processes which in themselves create functional flexibility. Hence both flexibility as a labour-use strategy and attempts at flexible specialization place the emphasis on labour input in isolation from the wider context of such movements (see Lane 1989; Elger 1990; and Knell 1993). Lane argues that flexibility in the UK has been brought about by an overall reduction in terms and conditions of employment, with functional flexibility pushing more labour into the periphery. In consequence the potential benefits of new industrial relations and human resource management are irrelevant to large sections of the employed labour force because they are not in its locus. Elger argues that flexibility in British manufacturing is based in job intensification and job enlargement not multi-skilling. Knell concludes that foreign-owned multinational firms who invest in British regions do not necessarily bring flexible specialization to such regions but adapt production to local flexibility as generalized by the accumulation strategy of the host State; that is, in the UK low productivity, low value production by marginalized and insecure labour. As a result flexibility becomes functional and rhetorical.

Flexibility is functional in the sense that its actual dissemination as distinct from prescribed type is seen by the State as a response to the imperative and pressures of capitalist accumulation in the movement to Post-Fordism. Such passive facilitation is rhetorical in that as a response it solves problems in a deterministic manner. In short the passive response of the State, evident in the absence of industrial strategy, coordinates production dynamics and resolves industrial relations conflict in civil society precisely because it meets the changing requirements of British capitalism as defined by the *laissez faire* State. That is, an accumulation strategy based on flexibility and low wages is likely to reproduce a Hong Kong style economy with the worst traits of the deregulated US labour-market (see Hutton 1995: 110), wherein regions seek to attract foreign-owned non-European multinationals. Besides providing employment this is likely to reduce indigenous profitability in similar sectors by exposure to greater international competition (premissed on flexibility and low wages) creating pressure for further financial engineering to remain competitive via flexibility and reductions in labour numbers and standards. This is likely to reduce the level of capital stock per employee, reducing the need for investment in human capital. Sadly, this course of action has led to an evaluation of economic performance solely in terms of the productivity of human labour in the absence of attention to longer term capital renewal, precisely because generalizing low wages (by European Union standards) but high (in comparison to the recent past) productivity is the basis of the contemporary accumulation strategy. The absence of the potential for class conflict or even a collective employee voice mechanism has resulted in extra flexibility being conflated and generalized as a direct result of flexibility as presented by Atkinson.

Storey (1992: 36) describes the presence of human resource management under four headings: beliefs and assumptions, the pre-eminence of line managers, strategic aspects, and key levers. All four are premissed on a 'can do' outlook which eschews and goes beyond contract, a movement which empowers employees and management to become more committed to their organization. We term this an individual status-obligation fulcrum.

The fulcrum and its mechanisms listed under the four headings may well define an organization as one where human resource management philosophy prevails; however, the whole approach is premissed on the absence of employee interests, a benefit of which is greater flexibility. Clark (1993: 80) argues that flexibility is only useful as a means, therefore it must be allied to existing procedures, not seen as an end which was absent in 'old' industrial relations.

The disengagement of the State at the level of the economy combines with the institutional prescription of individualism and individual values which permeate civil society; this combination is dysfunctional. It promotes the managerial prerogative together with entrepreneurialism without stimulating an active context for individualism to operate in. Storey and Sisson (1993: 50) argue that much of the individualist prescription in the human resource management literature is decontextualized from the real world; in the case of the UK we can add to this that much of it is decontextualized from the way the State operates (see also Sisson 1994). For example, the voluntarist principle on apprenticeship training was virtually destroyed in the early 1980s as a result of the shake-out in manufacturing industry. Voluntary destruction illustrates a contradiction in new industrial relations as informed by human resource management; its prescription empowers commitment and multi- or re-skilling, but the absence of formally administered and regulated training systems promotes a logic of improving flexibility in current production systems and methods of work organization. The resultant trend of such inertia is the development of a low productivity, low value-added, low pay manufacturing sector.

Hence in respect of decontextualized position there is a double contradiction; new industrial relations and human resource management are decontextualized from the voluntary basis of much of the UK's industrial relations framework; equally and relatedly, management in the UK is unlikely to consider the benefits of human resource management and might prefer not to use it because of its resource demands. (See also Keep (1994) for a critical survey of current training provision for the youth labour-market).

The fact that this point is rarely made clearly indicates the organization-specific pathway to new industrial relations and human resource management. The pathway rejects a collective employee voice mechanism as irrelevant because it is based only in input analysis. This is likely to be the case because of an absence of focused industrial strategy on economic and social restructuring, the basis of the State's industrial strategy: placing extra flexibility centre stage in the status-obligation fulcrum of new industrial relations and human resource management at the level of the firm; that is, flexibility based largely in the productivity of human labour.

Core workers are assumed to collaborate with management in the socio-economic restructuring of the labour process through the mechanics of new industrial relations and human resource management. Individualism, trust, empowerment, quality circles, briefings, and improved communication encourage and empower workers to enter the restructuring process themselves.

Here we can see how flexible specialization, the flexible firm plus extra flexibility have been fused together to create an enterprise strategy derived from direct and indirect pressure on labour independent of market production pressures. This point illustrates the argument presented above that flexibility in the UK is itself an atomized concept and an end rather than a means. Recent empirical evidence (Hunter *et al.* 1993) seems to confirm that the main thrust of flexibility as a labour-use strategy is not functional and numerical flexibility as prescribed in the Atkinson typology but an exercise driven by cost and financial pressures. In many cases this resulted in the continued use of non-standard labour in the form of part-timers, agency or other temporary workers, and subcontracting. Another significant conclusion of the study suggested that many employers were now moving away from the use of non-standard labour and returning to a reliance on standard full-time labour because of the competitive and organizational benefits it brings.

In the UK the focus of economic and social restructuring through flexible specialization and flexibility has been politically mediated through the active disengagement of the State. As Jessop (1991: 142) argues, it has resulted in a form of flexibility too flexible for the generation of Post-Fordism by the flexible specialization route. Nolan and O'Donnell (1991*a*) assert that this results from a neglect of positive interventionary industrial policy which is essential to conduct and focus individual enterprise strategies. This is the case because individualism permeates the current institutional framework of the State and informs human agency within the apparatus of the State. Both are crucial to the generation of extra flexibility and the avoidance of a centrally determined industrial policy. Libertarian *laissez faire*, that is freedom from the State, the basis of the current accumulation strategy, is a political leitmotiv, nothing more. It is a theme without substance which is replicated in much of new industrial relations and human resource management. Both are rhetorically based in the managerial prerogative and flexibility as an end in management labour-use strategies.

Human agency which drives the State has determined to separate the State, civil society, the locus of new industrial relations, and human resource management; in consequence the collective State apparatus cannot focus the accumulation strategy it has determined. The State has, however, succeeded in attaining increased extra flexibility within the employment relationship. As Sisson (1993: 201–11) shows, at the level of the firm, much of this rooting is at the 'soft' end of human resource management. The short-term benefits of new industrial relations and soft human resource management are likely to be constituted in improved productivity figures and tighter wages costs; however, it is as yet unclear what the economic benefits of this extra flexibility are (other than it being visualized as an end in itself). We can follow Boyer (1988) in suggesting that flexibility within economic and social restructuring can be either positive or negative. In the UK's case it appears to be negative in the sense that flexibility represents movement within current structures and does not represent a transition to something new. The form of the State and the absence of positive interventionary industrial and employment strategies are central to this process.

In the light of this argument we can now proceed to discuss the limited potential of new industrial relations in the generation of increased flexibility and improved productivity in the wider context of the UK's neo-Fordism.

5. New Industrial Relations and Economic and Social Restructuring

The previous section located the prescription behind new industrial relations within economic and social restructuring and the emergence of new market strategies such as flexible specialization and the pursuit of increased labour flexibility. In this section we seek to consolidate the argument developed in the previous section which centred on the relative failure of new market strategies and flexibility as pathways to a new stage in capitalist production. The argument will suggest that in the absence of an overall industrial strategy and the pursuit of extra flexibility as an end, the capacity of new industrial relations to generate a movement to positive flexibility and sustainable improvements in productivity is limited. This limitation is mainly a product of State disengagement (see Crouch 1990: 350; 1994: 265; and Streeck 1987: 283). In the UK we can term this development neo-Fordism rather than Post-Fordism. Such a distinction is justifiable on two grounds; first, as the previous section argued, flexibility does not connect with new market and production strategies. As a result extra flexibility is largely constituted in existing systems of production and work organization. Secondly, the productive benefits of extra flexibility have in the main been the result of downward demarcation flexibility; that is, core to periphery. This type of movement requires greater (self- or peer) supervision and is based on labour intensification not multi- or re-skilling in a genuine sense.

As a basis for accumulation neo-Fordism is premissed on deskilling, but unlike the Fordist era, without a collective treatment of employees. Individualism within neo-Fordism does not recognize labour as a producer or consumer; the earning potential and propensity of labour which are the basis of income streams for firms and the economy in general are ignored. We now move to a more detailed critique of extra flexibility in the UK, indicating why new market strategies are, in the context of State disengagement, likely to be less than successful.

Flexible specialization as a market and production strategy cannot be fully deployed in the UK for two reasons. First, as Hyman (1988: 52) points out, the methodology of flexible specialization is steeped in production changes in manufacturing. In the UK only four million members of the employed population are now employed in the manufacturing sector. Economic restructuring pursued through severe deflation in the early 1980s has not led to the development of a leaner and fitter manufacturing sector but the emergence of a small unit manufacturing sector. Secondly, flexible specialization requires a highly skilled functionally flexible workforce. The absolute decline in the size and scale of the manufacturing sector reduces the need for this. Additionally in the UK the destruction of craft status through downward adjustments in terms and conditions of employment and labour intensification is the basis of extra flexibility.

In order to strengthen this argument we can draw on data from CLIRS2 and WIRS3. CLIRS2 evaluates the existence and effect of labour utilization policies which purport to emphasize task flexibility. The survey found that task flexibility is readily pursued at local level with 30 per cent of the sample having such a policy, although only 7 per cent of firms made task flexibility mandatory. Overall CLIRS2 concluded that the coverage and presence of task flexibility appeared little connected to the existence of policy on flexibility, suggesting that firms tend not to have a considered view on flexibility, with only a loose connection between task flexibility and other elements in flexibility. Indeed, task flexibility appears more integral to communication and participation rather than changes in production systems (see CLIRS2: pages 34–8, 47–9, 64–5, and table 5.10 for more detail).

WIRS3 data appears to confirm the lack of movement in production systems. Changes in working practices designed to increase flexibility centred on what we have termed extra flexibility. The use of part-timers, non-standard labour, and subcontracting all scored relatively highly. However, there is virtually no mention of multi-skilling or changes in production systems other than working practices in current production systems, see WIRS3 (1992: 329–43).

The State's industrial strategy really boils down to one of encouraging employers to pursue extra flexibility at all costs. This stance of disengagement and the denial of the need for any positive self-help via an interventionary policy revolves around the rejection of the legitimacy in good industrial relations. As Crouch (1990: 342) argues, this essentially encourages employers to follow any industrial relations policy they like.

In the context of non-focused industrial strategy employers have geared the pursuit of functional flexibility to improved technical-organizational efficiency as described above. As Gough (1992: 32) argues, there is no guarantee that such a strategy will lead to a general economic revival. Thus, in large measure we can conclude that productivity improvements in manufacturing are largely derived from reductions in the employment to output ratio; that is, they are based in extra flexibility not positive flexibility. In the British context new industrial relations and human resource management are themselves largely based in this movement. Employers respond to increased competitive pressure on production costs in markets by examining the deployment and utilization of human resources as distinct from the deployment of capital resources or the value base of human resources in training and development (see Evans *et al.* 1992).

Crouch (1990: 351) denies a significant presence of new industrial relations based around either active worker participation with or without the presence of unions. Alternatively Crouch posits the emergence of simple 'spot' contracting without unions. Sisson (1993: 206–10) consolidates this assertion by suggesting the emergence of 'dualism' in industrial relations. Central to this is the emergence of human resource management and new industrial relations in organizations where collective bargaining is present combined with the emergence of employment areas largely unprotected by an employee voice mechanism.

These arguments lead us to the conclusion that new industrial relations can take two forms in the UK: first, a congruence between labour-use strategies and corporate strategy in the overall context of restored managerial prerogative; second, the emergence of individualism at the workplace. Here non-collective worker involvement and participation operate within labour use strategies focused on individualism in the form of spot contracting and unilateral deployment. (See O'Doherty (1993) for a single-sector, but multi-employer, study of this phenomenon.)

Both forms of new industrial relations are enterprise responses to uncertain economic conditions, conditioned by the wider rejection of the institutional orthodoxy in the post-war State and the contemporary State's disengagement–separation stance. In combination these factors have encouraged short-term policies to improve flexibility and productivity, a policy furthered by the exclusion of collective employee voice mechanisms in the determination of State industrial policy and industrial relations strategies. In summary the generation of popular capitalism and the enterprise culture has enabled the contemporary libertarian State to privatize industrial strategy. In consequence new industrial relations and human resource management operate in isolation from an end because as with flexibility they are seen as an end.

Flexibility in new industrial relations and human resource management has become a negatively based tactical strategy for economic survival. Eldridge *et al.* (1991: 42) argue that during the early 1980s this centred on generating one 'big stop' in the UK's post-war stop–go cycle. Recovery from the stop legitimized what has turned out to be extra flexibility in current production strategies (see MacInnes (1987: 113–24) for a discussion of workplace flexibility between 1979–1986). This represents technical-organizational efficiency determined through diverse economic and social changes, which do not equate to the rhetorical prescription of flexibility as popularized by Atkinson or a movement to flexible specialization. Instead it represents improved extra flexibility within the declining and disparate elements of the UK's post-war Fordism.

Market and production strategies such as flexible specialization and flexibility are premissed on a presumed role for the State; that is, government policies will themselves be conducive to stable reproduction. The accumulation strategy initiated during the 1980s lacks the presence of such a presumption. In consequence there has been weak sponsorship of market-led industrial recovery. As Leys (1985) points out, by 1980 corporatist-cum-pluralist influence in the CBI was folding under the perceived need to legislate on trade unions and industrial relations. Perhaps unbeknown to CBI supporters the political aim of Thatcherism was to destroy the post-war accumulation regime by attacking its social and economic basis; the routine of Fordism. In larger measure this required the destruction of the State's social democratic orthodoxy and the elevation of naked market forces: what we have termed the process of State disengagement.

The combined effect of CBI manœuvring, trade union reform, and State disengagement has been the collapse of large-scale manufacturing industry. Leys argues the whole process of manufacturing collapse and re-emergence as neo-Fordism illustrates an undiminished ideological and political weakness in British manufacturing industry. We can add that this weakness has facilitated the main thrust of the State's accumulation strategy; the generation of extra flexibility at all costs premissed on the assumption that this will itself create jobs and industrial recovery. Thus, it is an expression of ends not means.

The strategy of disengagement and further institutional separation propagated by the State reverses the presumption role and actually assumes an effective organization of employers in general. As Streeck (1987: 283) points out, such organization is only likely in the presence of favourable economic and institutional conditions. In the absence of this and the political stance of the contemporary State, new developments in industrial relations start and finish at the level of the individual firm as individual strategies. The effect of this in the UK has not been wholly unsuccessful but has encouraged firms in the manufacturing sector to improve productivity through extra flexibility in current high-volume low-margin markets.

The well-rehearsed Metcalf–Nolan productivity debate is instructive in this respect. Metcalf (1989 and 1990) has argued the case for successful and sustainable improvements in the economy and manufacturing productivity in particular during the 1980s. In contrast Nolan (1989*a*, 1989*b*, and 1993) and Nolan and Marginson (1990) argue that such improvements are the result of windfall benefits through the shock effects of Thatcherite policy and disparate measures, here termed extra flexibility.

The central point is that Metcalf describes the benefits of extra flexibility and labour fall-out whereas Nolan in particular argues the unsustainable nature of technical-organizational improvements in productivity. In consequence we can argue that Metcalf sees the benefits of current industrial policy whereas Nolan centres his critique of such in its longer term negative implications which derive from the lack of an interventionary industrial strategy as a conductor for disparate firm-specific measures. Visualized in this manner the debate can be seen as an outcome of extra flexibility and the absence of a determined State strategy for industrial recovery.

The contemporary State is not confronting the need for capital accumulation head on but has sought to facilitate it through its more interventionary mode of regulation in the employment relationship by the generation of new industrial relations. As Gough (1992: 42) argues, changes here have been constructed by a crisis of accumulation instead of being constituted in a movement to a new stage in capitalist production such as post-Fordism. Such a movement requires the generalization of changes in the labour process to actively encourage a movement to flexible specialization via positive flexibility. In this respect we must concur with Nolan and O'Donnell (1991*b*: 168) who suggest that a low-productivity low-wage manufacturing sector is what the State actually wants. This in itself is presumed to further extra flexibility within high-volume low-margin manufacturing. In consequence the UK becomes an attractive location for inward investment. In the short term such a policy has not been without success; in the longer term, however, it is likely to inhibit the upgrading of the domestic skill base in the UK's manufacturing sector (for individual case studies see Crowther and Garrahan (1988) and Knell (1993)).

Hence the basis of growth within the State's accumulation strategy is determined on a flexible low wage economy, where productivity improvement results from job enlargement in the work process, which in turn predetermines low labour costs (see Hutton 1995: 75). As Coates (1994: 164, 246) argues, such a policy makes the UK attractive for overseas investment by multinational corporations, but only to the extent of the development of a 'screwdriver economy'.

The circuit of capital is conditioned by the determinant role of industrial capital in the overall accumulation process. The failure of the State to address this through an interventionary accumulation and industrial strategy accentuates specific tendencies in the current accumulation strategy which deny and eschew the need for such a positive role. In consequence new industrial relations cannot connect with market and production strategies on which it is premissed. As Crouch (1990: 342) argues, new industrial relations is whatever employers say it is in a particular organization. Streeck (1992: 65) argues that new industrial relations has become one input element in corporate strategy which in the current situation has been individual and isolated.

The rejection of pluralism and the social democratic post-war State represent a determination to end traditional forms of workplace authority and control. In its place new industrial relations and human resource management have been given the contradictory tasks of reasserting the managerial prerogative, gaining active workplace cooperation, and exploiting extra flexibility. The status–obligation fulcrum inherent to new industrial relations and human resource management in particular is unlikely to build a lasting economic recovery precisely because of its atomized and uncertain nature.

6. Summary

Industrial relations whether old or new cannot be evaluated comprehensively in isolation from the material dynamics of capitalist production, which move in stages of capitalist development. In the post-war period the dynamic centred on Fordism and associated State apparatus and mechanisms; during this period the apparatus and mechanisms of the British State was dominated by contextual influences of pluralism and social democracy which expressed a configuration of class forces materially supported by the dynamic of economic stability, manifest in full employment and a generalized Welfare State (see Hyman 1995*a*: 20–2; 1995*b*: 47).

Since the mid-1970s material conditions have become uncertain and unstable; as a response the State has sought to dislodge contextual influences no longer amenable to capitalist reproduction. A central component of this process has been the reconfiguration of capitalist regulation in new industrial relations.

Economic restructuring in the British economy via a libertarian accumulation strategy has so far been largely negative. In civil society it represents a thinly disguised shift in the balance of power between capital and labour. This has been promoted on the basis of more unitary industrial relations as an individual-oriented class compromise.

Between 1979 and 1982 Thatcherite economic policies were pro-cyclical in that they accelerated the destruction of Fordism in an effort to vitalize a movement to Post-Fordism. The contradiction for the overtly libertarian State was the depth of pro-cyclical economic restructuring. The disengagement of the State which allowed market forces to valorize capital was not without initial success: labour productivity improved dramatically during the early 1980s; however, it was not accompanied by a comparable increase in the productivity of units of capital (see Hodgson 1984). This leads us to the general conclusion that disengaged industrial policy and the promotion of extra flexibility has done little to counter the destruction of Fordism. Indeed the pro-cyclical nature of Thatcherite economic policy together with the disengagement of plural industrial relations have led to the destruction of Fordist modes of production and made future market and production strategies largely irrelevant to the UK. Hence our assertion that capitalist production is primarily determined by the relationship between capital, labour, and the State in national pathways. The permanent yet unfolding effect of formative influences on a particular capitalist state has the potential to hinder and inhibit economic and political prerequisites in the generalization of models of capitalist development and production.

Recession during the 1980s was not vitalizing but debilitating. The central flaw in the Thatcher-cum-Major programme is the ideological determination to destroy the contextual orthodoxy of the post-war State. The wholesale replacement of social democracy with libertarian individualism renders new industrial relations and flexibility isolated from new market and production strategies. It is an industrial strategy without a reindustrialization programme, other than firm-specific policies which themselves express the movement to an individualist enterprise culture.

The erosion of pluralism in public policy on the employment relationship together with the denial of active State intervention in industrial policy has resulted in labour, collectively and individually, being relegated to an input issue within firm-specific corporate strategy. Extra flexibility is the basis of such individual strategies.

'Flexibility' in the absence of stable economic and institutional conditions actually sustains extra flexibility as an end. The discourse and rhetoric of the 1980s as propagated by the Thatcher Governments did effect an ideological break with the orthodoxy of the post-war social democratic State; however, the rigorous institutional separation of economics, politics, and ideology in the British State overestimates the application of ideologically motivated economic policy and law as generators of industrial renewal and economic stability.

Peeling back collectivism in the social democratic State exposed the weakness of the market as an initiator of the libertarian accumulation strategy and generalized Post-Fordism. The rhetoric and discourse of the 1980s have side-tracked this by highlighting two issues: first, the inability of the State to manage the economy and its industrial relations, often expressed in the sound bite 'there is no alternative'; secondly, the presence of unstable economic and institutional conditions world-wide. Both are then used to justify disengagement from the economy and pursuit of extra flexibility to generate industrial recovery in globalized capital beyond the European Union.

New industrial relations and human resource management are visualized as the atomized mechanics by which this recovery can be generated. Industrial strategy has focused on the facilitation of naked market forces which in the current accumulation crisis centre on change and flexibility as an end within existing patterns of production.

A contradiction evident for the State is located in the slippage between economy and civil society where the State mediates its activity. The libertarian bias in the State, its peripheral intervention, and its form make representation of capital's general interest problematic. The very disengagement and separation of the State from the economy and civil society is a contradictory measure of its success and its failure. The material conditions of production are still beyond the responsibility of the State whereas the regulation of wage labour is even more voluntarily determined within new industrial relations and human resource management. This heightens the formative influence of contract precisely because it is something to go beyond; that is, the status–obligation fulcrum of human resource management.

Conclusions

From the eclectic nature of the argument developed in this chapter four overall conclusions can be made.

First, a recurrent element in all three images of new industrial relations and human resource management in the UK is extra flexibility; the discourse and rhetoric of the State since the 1980s has turned this into a virtue, which was largely absent during the plurally defined post-war social democratic orthodoxy. Alleged institutional rigidities created by pluralism have been generalized into the major supply side problem in the UK. Hence, the pursuit of flexibility as an end. An effect of this is the rejection of collectively defined employee interests constituted in good industrial relations and its associated voice mechanisms. In turn this has relegated industrial relations to the status of an input problem in management labour use strategies. Within the British pathway, capitalist restructuring in the contemporary period is uniquely particularized in the hegemony of formative influences on the State, not a movement to a new phase in capitalist production.

Secondly, the State has further separated itself from the regulation of the employment relationship, the economy and civil society. The vehicle for this separation has been chimeric industrial policy and labour-market strategies which both centre on freeing up market forces. This devolution of industrial strategy to the level of the firm consolidates the need for extra flexibility and State disengagement through the libertarian accumulation strategy.

Thirdly, extra flexibility cannot generate sustained improvements in productivity unless they are derived from technical-organizational changes. Additionally extra flexibility is not suited to a movement to Post-Fordism constituted in the flexible specialization route. In the absence of an active industrial strategy increases in flexibility and productivity via improvements in the input and productivity of labour have become more important than what labour is producing, who owns it, and the distribution of productivity improvements. Hence we have to conclude that extra flexibility constitutes neo-Fordism; that is, flexibility in existing production structures and what can be inwardly attracted as a result of this. For the national pathway this concentrates production in high-volume low-margin sectors where low wages and increased productivity result from extra flexibility. For civil society it has led to a breakdown or marginalization of plurally mediated institutions such as local government, the Welfare State, free-standing higher education, and the voice mechanisms of (old) industrial relations.

Lastly, the rooting of new industrial relations and human resource management in extra flexibility and the rhetorical rise of individualism is a success which expresses the contradiction in the UK's libertarian State. At the level of civil society the status–obligation fulcrum of new industrial relations and human resource management has generated what the State wants: a decline in the perceived rigidity of collective industrial relations. However, this success in the longer term is likely to be reined in because the State, although it has shaken off its post-war orthodoxy, cannot shake off its own form and methods of intervention which have continued to be empty and institutionally peripheral. In the likely event of continued uncertainty and instability in economic conditions extra flexibility in the UK's national pathway is likely to sustain the current accumulation strategy and weaken the industrial, manufacturing, and service base of the economy, inhibiting the emergence of 'Post-Fordism'.

The State itself is inflexible and rigid in the conception of its form and function; without change here the UK is likely to become a Morris Minor economy: one which goes on forever but which becomes increasingly detached from generalized developments in capitalist production, to the extent that maintenance of its engine, once the basis of its success, itself becomes an individual niche market.

REFERENCES

Atkinson, M. (1984), 'Manpower Strategies for Flexible Organisations', *Personnel Management*, (Aug.), 28–31.

Barrington-Moore, Jun. (1966), *The Social Origins of Dictatorship and Democracy, Lord and Peasant in the Making of the Modern World* (Harmondsworth: Penguin).

Bassett, P. (1986), *Strike Free* (London: Macmillan).

Boyer, M. (1988) (ed.), *The Search for Labour Market Flexibility* (Oxford: Clarendon Press).

Brown, W., and Wadhwani, S. (1990), 'The Economic Effects of Industrial Relations Legislation since 1979', *National Institute Economic Review*, 131 (Feb.), 57–70.

Carew, A. (1991), 'The Anglo-American Productivity Council (1948–1952): The Ideological Roots of the Post-War Debate on Productivity in Britain', *Journal of Contemporary History* 26/1: 49–71.

Clark, I. (forthcoming),'The State, Regulation and Industrial Relations', Ph.D. thesis, University of Leeds.

Clark, J. (1993), 'Procedures and Consistency versus Flexibility and Commitment in Employee Relations: A Comment on Storey', *Human Resource Management Journal*, 41: 79–81.

Clarke, S. (1988), *Keynesianism, Monetarism and the Crisis of the State* (Aldershot: Elgar).

———(1991), *Marx, Marginalism and Modern Sociology* (2nd edn., London: Macmillan).

Clegg, H. (1979), *The Changing System of Industrial Relations*, (Oxford: Blackwell).

Coates, D. (1994), *The Question of UK Decline: The Economy, State and Society*, (Hemel Hempstead: Harvester Wheatsheaf).

Crafts, N. (1988), 'The Assessment: British Economic Growth over the Long Run', *Oxford Review of Economic Policy*, 4/1: 1–21.

———(1991), 'Reversing Relative Economic Decline? The 1980s in Historical Perspective', *Oxford Review of Economic Policy*, 7/3: 81–98.

Crossley, R. (1968), 'The Donovan Report: A Case in the Poverty of Historicism', *British Journal of Industrial Relations*, 6/3: 296–302.

Crouch, C. (1979), *The State and Economy in Contemporary Capitalism* (London: Croom Helm).

———(1990), 'United Kingdom: The Rejection of Compromise', in G. Baglioni and C. Crouch (eds.), *European Industrial Relations: The Challenge of Flexibility* (London: Sage).

———(1994), *Industrial Relations and European State Traditions* (Oxford: Clarendon Press).

Crowther, S., and Garrahan, P. (1988), 'Invitation to Sunderland: Corporate Power and the Local Economy', *Industrial Relations Journal*, 19/1: 51–60.

Edwards, P. (1995), 'The Employment Relationship', in P. Edwards (ed.), *Industrial Relations Theory and Practice* (Oxford: Blackwell).

Eldridge, J., Cressey, P., MacInnes, J. (1991), *Industrial Sociology and Economic Crisis* (Hemel Hempstead: Harvester Wheatsheaf).

Elger, A. (1990), 'Technical Innovation and Work Re-Organisation in British Manufacturing in the 1980s: Continuity, Intensificatiion or Transformation', *Work, Employment and Society* (May), 67–102.

Evans, S., Ewing, K., Nolan, P. (1992), 'Industrial Relations and the British Economy in the 1990's: Mrs Thatcher's Legacy', *Journal of Management Studies*, 29/5: 571–89.

Flanders, A. (1951), 'Industrial Relations', in G. Worswick and P. Ady (eds.), *The British Economy 1945–1950* (Oxford: Oxford University Press).

—— (1954), 'Collective Bargaining', in A. Flanders and H. Clegg (eds.), *The System of Industrial Relations in Great Britain* (Oxford: Blackwell).

—— (1970), *Management and Unions* (London: Faber).

Fox, A. (1985), *History and Heritage* (London: Allen & Unwin).

Gamble, A. (1988), *The Free Economy and the Strong State: The Politics of Thatcherism* (London: Macmillan).

—— (1990), *Britain in Decline: Economic Policy, Political Strategy and the British State* (3rd edn., London: Macmillan).

—— (1993), 'The Entrails of Thatcherism', *New Left Review* 198 (Mar./Apr.), 117–28.

Goldthorpe, J. (1974), 'Industrial Relations in Great Britain: A Critique of Reformism', *Politics and Society*, (repr. in T. Clarke and L. Clements (1977) (eds.), *Trade Unions Under Capitalism* (Glasgow: Fontana/Collins).

Gough, J. (1992), 'Where's the Value in Post Fordism', in N. Gilbert, R. Burrows, and A. Pollert (eds.), *Fordism and Flexibility: Divisions and Change* (London: Macmillan).

Greenleaf, W. (1983), *The British Political Tradition*, i. *The Rise of Collectivism* (London: Methuen).

Hodgson, G. (1984), 'Thatcherism: The Miracle that Never Happened', in E. Nell (ed.), *Free Market Conservatism: A Critique of Theory and Practice* (London: Allen & Unwin).

Hunter, L., McGregor, A., MacInnes, J., and Sproull, A. (1993), 'The Flexible Firm: Strategy and Segmentation', *British Journal of Industrial Relations*, 31/3: 383–409.

Hutton, W. (1995), *The State We're In* (London: Jonathan Cape).

Hyman, R. (1973), 'Industrial Conflict and the Political Economy', in R. Miliband and J. Saville (eds.), *The Socialist Register* (London: Perkin Press), 101–54.

—— (1988), 'Flexible Specialization: Miracle or Myth?', in R. Hyman and W. Streeck, *New Technology and Industrial Relations* (Oxford: Blackwell).

—— (1975), *Introduction to Marxist Industrial Relations* (London: Macmillan).

—— (1988), 'Flexible Specialisation: Miracle or Myth?', in R. Hyman and W. Streeck, *New Technology and Industrial Relations* (Oxford: Blackwell).

—— (1989), *The Political Economy of Industrial Relations* (London: Macmillan).

—— (1991), 'Plus Ca Change? The Theory of Production and the Production of Theory', in A. Pollert (ed.), *Farewell to Flexibility* (Oxford: Blackwell).

—— (1994), 'Theory and Industrial Relations', *British Journal of Industrial Relations*, 32/2: 165–81.

—— (1995*a*), 'Industrial Relations in Europe: Theory and Practice', *European Journal of Industrial Relations*, 1/1: 17–46.

—— (1995*b*), 'The Historical Evolution of British Industrial Relations', in P. Edwards (ed.), *Industrial Relations Theory and Practice* (Oxford: Blackwell).

Jessop, B. (1982), *The Capitalist State* (Oxford: Blackwell).

—— (1990), *State Theory: Putting the Capitalist State in its Place* (Oxford: Blackwell).

—— (1991), 'Thatcherism and Flexibility', in B. Jessop, H. Kastendiek, K. Nielsen, and O. Pedersen, *The Politics of Flexibility* (Aldershot: Edward Elgar).

—— (1994), 'Post-Fordism and the State', in A. Amin (ed.), *Post-Fordism: A Reader* (Oxford: Blackwell).

—— Bonnett, K., Bromley, S., and Ling, T. (1988), *Thatcherism* (Oxford: Polity/Blackwell).

Kahn-Freund, O. (1954), 'The Legal Framework', in A. Flanders and H. Clegg (eds.), *The System of Industrial Relations in Great Britain*.

——— (1959), 'Labour Law', in M. Ginsberg (ed.), *Law and Public Opinion in England in the 20th Century* (London: Macmillan).

Keep, E. (1994), 'Vocational Education and Training for the Young', in K. Sisson (ed.), *Personnel Management: A Comprehensive Guide to Theory and Practice in Britain* (2nd edn., Oxford: Blackwell).

Knell, J. (1993), 'Transnational Corporations and the Dynamics of Human Capital Formation: Evidence from West Yorkshire', *Human Resource Management Journal*, 3/4: 48–59.

Lane, C. (1989), *Management and Labour in Europe* (Aldershot: Edward Arnold).

Leys, C. (1985), 'Thatcherism and British Manufacturing Hegemony', *New Left Review* (May/June), 151: 5–25.

McCarthy, W. (1992), 'The Rise and Fall of Collective Laissez Faire', in W. McCarthy (ed.), *Legal Intervention in Industrial Relations* (Oxford: Blackwell).

MacInnes, J. (1987), *Thatcherism at Work* (Milton Keynes: Open University Press).

Marginson, P., Armstrong, P., Edwards, P. K., and Purcell, J. (1993), *Control of Industrial Relations in Large Companies: An Initial Analysis of the Second Company Level Industrial Relations Survey* (Warwick Papers in Industrial Relations, 45; Warwick).

Metcalf, D. (1989), 'Water Notes Dry up: The Impact of the Donovan Reform Proposals and Thatcherism at Work on Labour Productivity in British Manufacturing Industry', *British Journal of Industrial Relations*, 27/1: 1–33.

——— (1990), 'Union Presence and Labour Productivity in British Manufacturing Industry: A Reply to Nolan and Marginson', *British Journal of Industrial Relations*, 28/2: 249–67.

Millward, N., Stevens, M., Smart, D., and Hawes, W. (1992), *Workplace Industrial Relations in Transition* (Aldershot: Dartmouth).

Muellbauer, J. (1986), 'The Assessment: Productivity and Competitiveness in British Manufacturing', *Oxford Review of Economic Policy*, 2/3: 1–25.

Nolan, P. (1989a), 'Walking on Water: Performance and Industrial Relations under Thatcher', *Industrial Relations Journal* 20/2: 81–93.

——— (1989b), 'The Productivity Miracle', in F. Green (ed.), *The Restructuring of the UK Economy* (Hemel Hempstead: Harvester Wheatsheaf).

——— (1993), 'The Past Strikes Back', Public Lecture, *University of Leeds Review*, 36: 199–210.

——— (1994), 'Fordism and Post-Fordism', in P. Arestis and M. Sawyer (eds.), *The Elgar Companion to Radical Political Economy* (Aldershot: Elgar).

——— and Marginson, P. (1990), 'Skating on Thin Ice? David Metcalf on Trade Unions and Labour Productivity', *British Journal of Industrial Relations*, 28/2: 227–49.

——— and O'Donnell, K. (1991a), 'Restructuring and the Politics of Industrial Renewal: The Limits of Flexible Specialisation', in A. Pollert (ed.), *Farewell to Flexibility* (Oxford: Blackwell).

——— ——— (1991b), 'Flexible Specialization and UK Manufacturing Weakness', *Political Quarterly*, 62/1: 106–24.

——— and Walsh, J. (1995), 'The Structure of the Economy and Labour Market', in P. Edwards (ed.), *Industrial Relations Theory and Practice* (Oxford: Blackwell).

O'Doherty, D. (1993), *Banking on Part-time Labour* (Leicester Business School Occasional Papers, 8; Leicester).

Perkin, H. (1969), *The Origins of Modern English Society 1780–1880* (London: Routledge).

Piore, M. and Sabel, C. (1984), *The Second Industrial Divide: Possibilities for Prosperity* (New York: Basic Books).

Purcell, J. (1991), 'The Rediscovery of the Management Prerogative: The Management of Labour Relations in the 1980s', *Oxford Review of Economic Policy*, 7/1: 33–43.

—— (1993), 'The End of Institutional Industrial Relations', *Political Quarterly*, 64/1: 6–23.

Reid, G. (1968), 'An Economic Comment on the Donovan Report', *British Journal of Industrial Relations*, 6/3: 303–15.

Sisson, K. (1993), 'In Search of HRM', *British Journal of Industrial Relations*, 31/2: 201–11.

—— (1994), 'Paradigms, Practice and Prospects', in K. Sisson (ed.), *Personnel Management in Britain* (2nd edn., Oxford: Blackwell).

Storey, J. (1992), *New Developments in the Management of Human Resources* (Oxford: Blackwell).

—— (1995) (ed.), *HRM: A Critical Text* (London: Routledge).

—— and Sisson, K. (1993), *Managing Human Resources and Industrial Relations* (Milton Keynes: Open University Press).

Streeck, W. (1987), 'The Uncertainties of Management in the Management of Uncertainty: Employers, Labour relations and Industrial Adjustment in the 1980s', *Work, Employment and Society*, 1/3: 281–308.

—— (1992), *Social Institutions and Economic Performance* (London: Sage).

Tomlinson, J. (1991), 'The Failure of the Anglo-American Productivity Council', *Business History*, 33/1: 82–92.

—— and Tiratsoo, N. (1993), *Industrial Efficiency and State Intervention in Labour 1939–1951* (London: Routledge).

Turner, H. (1969), 'The Donovan Report', *Economic Journal*, 79: 1–10.

Webb, S. and B. (1897), *Industrial Democracy* (London: Longmans).

Zeitlin, J. (1986), 'Shop Floor Bargaining and the State: A Contradictory Relationship', in S. Toliday and J. Zeitlin, *Shop Floor Bargaining and the State: Historical and Comparative Perspectives* (Cambridge: Cambridge University Press).

4

TRADE UNION LAW SINCE 1979

Stephen Dunn and David Metcalf

1. Introduction

Allan Flanders once suggested that 'the tradition of voluntarism cannot be legislated *against*' (1974: 365). By voluntarism he meant the collective bargaining system that had developed over the century in the UK with scant help or hindrance from the law (Kahn-Freund's 'collective *laissez faire*' (1959)). His judgement was made when the Industrial Relations Act, an ambitious labour code introduced at a stroke, was nearing the end of its short, blighted life. The Act's failure reinforced a then conventional academic wisdom that legislation was unhelpful in reforming Britain's troubled system. As Flanders himself stated 'it is clear that the law is a very inadequate, dangerous and dubious means for trying to modify any established modes of conduct of trade unions' (1974: 365).

Twenty years on, this proposition looks falsified. After eight major acts since 1979, unions' conduct is so altered that the union debate has gone cold. For example, only 27 per cent of people considered the unions too powerful in 1992 compared to 80 per cent in 1979 (MORI: quoted in Taylor in 1993: 369). Celebrating 'improvements which would have been inconceivable' in the 1960s and 1970s, the Conservative Government claims that 'without doubt, . . . trade union law played an essential part in transforming Britain's industrial relations' (Employment Department 1991: 1, 6). Improvements mentioned include all-time low strike levels; declining restrictive practices; safeguards for union democracy; protection of businesses, jobs, individuals, and community from flying pickets and closed shops; and a fair power balance between employers and unions. Although the Conservatives do not attribute all the 'improvement' to legal intervention, their emphasis is understandable. While other aspects of Thatcherism have tarnished in the 1990s, its union curbs have retained widespread support (Taylor 1993: 370). More deeply, the market liberal philosophy

We thank Ray Richardson, Lord Wedderburn, and Simon Milner for their detailed comments on earlier drafts. The chapter is part of the Centre for Economic Performance's industrial relations programme. The CEP is an ESCR-funded research centre based at the LSE.

underpinning Thatcherism assumes that unions stifle economic growth. If the law reduces their power, so the argument goes, then axiomatically the economy will blossom. Reason enough for celebration and never mind the empirical complexities.

We are interested in the empirical complexities. We try to isolate the impact of the law from other factors that might be equally or more important in altering union behaviour and employee performance. The one previous attempt concluded that 'the economic effects of the legislation have been limited and, to some extent, perverse . . . It is implausible that employers were stimulated to manage their labour better as a result of the altered legal circumstances of trade unions. Far more likely is that they were given more freedom to do so by high unemployment and more incentive to do so by product market crisis' (Brown and Wadhwani 1990: 2, 31). This appears partially to retrieve Flanders's proposition. Put strongly, the implication is that legislation has been peripheral. It began to leech on a trade union body already draining of strength in adverse market conditions and, as unions became increasingly enfeebled, it had the opportunity to take hold—irritating, parasitic, but not the main source of union discomfort.

Given that reduction of union power was central to Thatcherite ambitions anyway, why it is important to determine how far law abetted this task? Is it not sufficient that the legislation is compatible with a broader attempt to liberate market forces, alongside monetarism, the end of exchange controls, privatization, market testing in the public sector, withdrawal of State subsides to industry, and a preference for allowing unemployment, rather than inflation, to rise? Apart from academic curiosity, three reasons for investigation are offered. First, Thatcherite sympathizers make big claims about the law's importance and advocate further legal restrictions on unions to complete the project (Hanson and Mather 1988; Hayek 1984; Minford 1983; Tur 1982). Second, critics have been quick to flay the Conservatives for treading on internationally accepted union rights (Ewing 1989; Hendy 1989; Wedderburn 1991). Third, European Union employment policy clashes with Conservative ideology, as in Britain's opt-out from the Maastricht Treaty's Social Chapter. All three suggest that UK law is far from settled. It would be useful to know, therefore, whether measurable benefits have accrued from the legislation that make further statutory intervention, continued stigmatization, and voluntary exile from European policy-making worth while.

The task is difficult. It involves finding whether economic outcomes have changed, whether these changes have stemmed from altered union behaviour, and whether the alteration in union behaviour is due to the legislation. Making links is not always possible. It is much easier to trace the law's impact on unions than on the economy. Where links are elusive, we explore plausible alternatives. Our method is to review different types of research, including analysis of cases, surveys of institutions and processes, and econometric tests. We examine their usefulness and limitations in developing an overall assessment. As a yardstick against which to measure the law's effect, we begin by describing Conservative ideology and the intent behind the most important statutes.

2. Ideology

Whether the Conservative's legal programme was driven by ideological rigour has been widely discussed (see Fosh *et al.* 1994). Probably, as Marsh asserts, the Thatcher Government came to power in 1979 without a coherent industrial relations policy, save an ambition to bring the unions to heel (1992: 54–64). More clearly, as Auerbach suggests, increasingly bold legislative probing took it in directions unmarked on any ideological map (1990: 230–6). Nevertheless, the programme is lifted above pragmatism and, to its supporters, redeemed from mere union-bashing by its association with the philosophy of Hayek (see Hanson and Mather 1988; Hayek 1960: ch. 18; and 1984; and, hostilely, Wedderburn 1991: ch. 8). His contribution was to clothe neo-classical economics in a propagandist coat that, in the aftermath of the 1978–9 Winter of Discontent, made traditional public policy towards unions, particularly its weak legal restraints on their behaviour, look threadbare. In a famous quote, he was adamant that 'there can be no salvation for Britain until the special privileges granted to the trade unions three-quarters of a century ago are revoked' (Hayek 1984: 58). The word 'salvation' seemed apt. The slant he gave to conventional free market economics demonized unions and fitted the political mood of the country. For him, the issue at stake was saving us from union coercion and liberating us to pursue economic success.

Put briefly, the Hayekian analysis is as follows. A competitive market is beyond grand human design. Left to itself, it distributes rewards according to individual energy, talent, skill, risk, and luck. Its manipulation, whether by the State or by private monopolies and cartels (notably unions in pursuit of fairness, equality, security, or a share of rents), invariably tends towards coercion. Individuals become subjugated to a collective will. Moreover, in restricting enterprise, such manipulation enervates those entrepreneurs who thrive on risk. And, in interfering with complex processes, it causes a misallocation of resources. The result is a poorer economy and a less free society than would exist if the market were left to itself.

Accordingly, Hayek accused British unions of being 'the biggest obstacle to raising the living standards of the working class. . . . The chief cause of the unnecessarily big differences between the best- and worst-paid workers . . . the prime source of unemployment . . . [and] the main reason for the decline of the British economy in general' (1984: 52), adding that 'the problem of inflation . . . and the problem of excessive [union] power . . . have become inseparable' (for comment on the extravagance of such claims, see Richardson 1995). As an accessory to these economic atrocities, the State stood in the dock too. By 'irresponsibly' (Hayek 1984: 64) granting unions 'a licence to coerce' via the immunities written into the 1906 Trade Disputes Act and the 1974 TULRA, it had handed unions power on a plate. The immunities deprived the judiciary of common law remedies to which unions would otherwise have been immensely vulnerable. In industrial disputes, they permitted unions to behave in ways that would have been found criminal or tortious if the law had not been hobbled. They allowed unions to conspire to induce breaches of employment and commercial contracts and to act in restraint of trade. For Hayek, this was a gross dereliction of the State's duty to maintain a rule of law that minimized coercion, fostered free contract and free trade, and indulged no favourites.

Hayek's solution to the union problem was a complete repeal of the immunities, effectively outlawing the strike and other bargaining tactics. However, he mused on whether the government would have the courage to do it. So far, the Conservatives have not. This means we cannot truly test Hayek's proposition about the salvation of Britain. Nevertheless, looking at his earlier, and more detailed, agenda for trade union reform (1960: ch. 18), we can see that the Conservatives have progressed significantly towards the Hayekian ideal. As he advocated, they have banned mass picketing, closed shops, preferential hiring of union members, and secondary action. Moreover, even while failing to implement his final solution, which seems a bridge too far for any democratic government, they have tackled union power by other, more subtly penetrative means, unimagined by Hayek. It seems reasonable therefore to expect that, if the Hayekian analysis is right, and, provided the law has altered union behaviour in ways that Hayek and the Government wanted, quite dramatic economic benefits would have accrued.

3. Intent

Divisions and caution meant the Conservatives proceeded incrementally. Targets were selected tactically, lines of least resistance followed, opportunities grasped, and holes plugged. Now, looking back, it is possible to trace the Conservatives' advance and see what compromises between free market individualism and traditional collectivism were made along the way. The sheer volume of legislation requires some basic classification. Our summary is organized under three headings: Responsibility, Voice, and Exit (for a chronological, non-technical description of successive acts, see McIlroy 1991).

Responsibility

Before 1979 the voluntarist system was underpinned by what Kahn-Freund called abstentionist law. The immunities gave unions the freedom to organize, bargain, and strike, and (oversimplifying) employers and unions were left to develop their own procedures and agreements. In one sense, therefore, more intrusive legislation curtails the responsibility of the two sides to resolve their differences voluntarily. But, in other senses, the law brings new responsibilities. Most obvious are the new penalties on unions and their members. Less direct are the opportunities offered to employers and workers, with legal protection against unions, to grasp the nettle and be responsible for their own relationship in a competitive market.

On penalties, the fundamental change was to make unions, as organizations, legally responsible for the actions of their officials and lay organizers. Since 1982, and for the first time since 1906 except during the 1971 Act, union funds have been at risk upon a breach of the immunities. Previously only named officials had been liable. Now the union itself is recognized as a corporate entity and can be brought to court not only by employers and others whose contractual relationships are affected, but by anybody whose life they disrupt (with the help of a Commissioner for Protection Against Unlawful Industrial Action: 1993 Act). The union faces unlimited fines and sequestration for contempt if injunctions are flouted, and damages if cases are pursued. The intent is to make union bureaucrats reluctant to step beyond the immunities and risk financial catastrophe for the union. And, to inhibit them from trying to protect funds by washing their hands of unlawful acts by local activists, all strikes are regarded as official for legal purposes unless repudiated in the strongest written terms by the union (1982 and 1990 Acts).

To discourage such repudiated, unofficial action, legislation has recently put strikers' jobs in greater jeopardy. Official strikers are still protected by 1970s' law that requires employers to dismiss all or none of them. Under the 1990 Act, however, unofficial strikers can be selectively dismissed. Shop stewards and ringleaders face a greater prospect of 'victimization' and are therefore under pressure to heed their union's repudiation. A different kind of penalty is aimed at strikers in general. Domestic responsibilities are emphasized in the deduction of part of their families' social security payment during a strike (originally under the 1979 Finance Act). The deduction is notionally equivalent to strike pay, but applies whether it is received or not. This is a nod towards the dubious 'State subsidy theory' of strikes which suggests that industrial action is likely to be more frequent and longer when workers can dull the financial pain by doses of welfare.

On new opportunities under legal protection, the main thrust of the law is to insulate individual firms, even workplaces, from outside union influences. In 1980 secondary picketing was outlawed. The 1982 Act prevented industrial action by outsiders to force a closed shop or union recognition on a firm or establishment. The scope of the immunities was reduced further by tightening the definition of a trade dispute to cover only industrial action between employees and their own employer and by outlawing, finally in 1990, all secondary strikes and boycotts. Certain State-sponsored routes, legacies of the 1974 Labour Government, by which trade-unionism and its effects could penetrate the firm, were also shut off. Union recognition machinery was abolished in 1980, as was Schedule 11, which allowed employees to pursue comparability claims at the Central Arbitration Committee and, in practice, threatened to develop into a kind of national arbitration system by which the results of collective agreements might ripple back and forth over firms, trades, and industries. Older machinery eventually went as well. The Fair Wages Resolution of the House of Commons, which spread union standards among government contractors, was rescinded in 1982. More importantly, 1993 saw the abolition of the wages councils whose dual role in 'sweated' trades had been to establish statutory minimum terms and conditions and to encourage independent negotiating machinery.

So far, all this begins to add up to a market liberal second preference. If the first preference is to legislate collective bargaining out of existence, diminishing unions to harmless Friendly Societies and workers' advice bureaux, then, should that prove too difficult, the fall-back position is to cordon off union enclaves and prevent them contaminating the existing non-union sector and new-born enterprises. It is also to isolate union enclaves from each other (Wedderburn calls it 'salami slicing' (1991: 222)), giving individual compa-nies a better chance either to tailor agreements to their own business needs or to opt out of unionism altogether. Significantly, although they flirted with the idea in the early 1990s, the Conservatives have not made collective agreements legally binding. Thus, one of the pillars of voluntarism still stands. But, of course, voluntary agreements make derecognition just a little bit easier. So too does the late addition to the 1993 Act which allows employers to treat union members differently to non-members, permitting, for example, more favour-able terms to be offered as an incentive for employees to opt out of collective bargaining and, instead, sign bespoke contracts.

The implication of the law described here is that, if legislation stops the spread of collectivism among market rivals, individual unionized companies and their employees have to face up to the costs of trade-unionism in an increasingly non-union world. The law is agnostic on whether they continue with it or not. That remains their responsibility. However, the ideology says: on your own head be it.

Voice

Following Crouch (1982), 'voice' is used here as a shorthand for union democracy and involves legislation on ballots together with members' rights to challenge maladministration. Tensions exist between such legislation and market liberal ideology. For instance, it is not an item on Hayek's reform agenda. On strike votes, Hanson and Mather put the Hayekian position succinctly: 'a ballot . . . cannot validate or legitimise the industrial action itself. . . . Yet the introduction of the democratic process of the ballot undoubt-edly lends a spurious legitimacy to such action. . . . Insofar as pre-strike ballots perpetuate the strike threat, a clumsy and outdated concept, they are wholly unwelcome' (1988: 76–7). So, the voice legislation might also be seen as a second-best preference. But tensions remain. First, the responsibility aspect of the law appears to be attempting to limit the horizons of union members to the company, while such voice aspects as leadership and political fund votes focus members' gaze on the union as a national institution. Second, the responsibility aspect encourages caution among union bureaucrats and stimulates them to control rank and file militancy, whereas voice introduces a wild card into the hierarchical deck. Ballots might produce militant leaders and reckless strikes. So, if the legislation's intent is to chime with Conservative ideology, a particular model of union government is required.

The most obvious would assume a silent majority in unions whose interests are somehow smothered. Such a model is conventional enough, although opinions vary about whether this majority is potentially more militant or more moderate than the controlling group. The old left-wing 'iron law of oligarchy' (Michels 1915), for instance, presumed that moderate union bureaucrats betrayed the class interest of the membership but remained unassailable because of their expertise, manipulative skills, and psychological dominance. A right-wing model would start as a mirror image of this, with militant 'union barons' leading members where they would prefer not to go. But it is more complicated than that. Research has indicated that unions' internal political systems, involving officials, lay activists, and ordinary members in cliques and alliances, cannot be plausibly reduced to Michels's iron law (see Hemingway 1978; Undy and Martin 1984). For the left, the crucial check on oligarchy is 'participative democracy' at workplace and branch meetings and upwards to conferences of mandated delegates. For the right, this is exactly the problem. Participation requires a level of dedication beyond most ordinary, commonsensical members. They leave it to the committed minority or, if they do become involved, they are quickly discouraged by the labyrinthine procedures and machinations of the active cliques (for a sanitized version of this, see Department of Employment 1983).

Such a model suggests that mandatory ballots would give the moderate majority a greater voice in key decisions, while avoiding the chore of active participation. Indeed, if legal responsibilities make the nation leadership more cautious at the same time as its authority is strengthened by popular support, then the active minority, the stewards and other lay volunteers who have traditionally given British trade-unionism some radical energy, are likely to find themselves sandwiched and sandbagged (on the Conservative Party's debate, see Auerbach 1990: ch. 6).

Preceded by State financial support for voluntary secret ballots in 1980, the principle of legally enforceable voting was established in the 1984 Act. Of the three issues subject to such regulation, election of national executives (and general secretaries from 1988), ratification of political funds, and industrial action decisions, the latter only could be conducted by workplace, as opposed to postal, ballot. That dispensation was removed in 1993. The preference for postal ballots fits the model. They distance the membership from group pressures at work and substitute domestic considerations, as well as making administration more complicated and more expensive (State funding was withdrawn in 1993 also) for the union. In fact, a shift in emphasis can be detected from 1988. Ballot rules became increasingly complex, backed by a lengthy code of practice. Following the 1993 changes, for instance, it has been estimated that the time needed for a union to jump through all the legal hoops lengthened from two to eight weeks (Labour Research Department 1993: 16). Moreover, since 1988 individual members, not just employers and other aggrieved parties, have been empowered to challenge legal breaches with the help, if necessary, of the CROTUM. Her brief also includes supporting members' new rights to scrutinize union accounts and the application of rule books. In short, having strengthened the majority voice in 1984, the Government began to support minority dissidents, even single voices, in the late 1980s.

Exit

Here we are on less ambiguous ground. Hayekian ideology puts a high premium on freedom of choice. That is why it appears sceptical about majority rule, and why it expresses particular abhorrence at the closed shop. Under the heading 'exit', we include legislation affecting the closed shop, check-off, and union disciplinary powers. The main intent here is to make it easier for workers to get out or stay out of unions, and, if they choose to stay in, to avoid some of the consequences of collective decisions.

Under voluntarism, the closed shop spread with only sporadic interference from the law. Not only did the immunities allow disputes to force people into union membership, but, without unfair dismissal protection until 1971, workers could be sacked for any reason, including non-unionism (see Dunn and Gennard 1984; Hanson *et al.* 1982; McCarthy 1964). Temporarily outlawed in 1971, although not suppressed, the closed shop would have regained its previous voluntarist legal status in 1974 except that the incoming Labour Government continued the 1971 Act's unfair dismissal principle. Condoning the closed shop, therefore, meant allowing fair dismissal of non-unionists.

So unswervingly hostile were the Conservatives to the closed shop that its abolition might have been expected straightaway. Gross coercive power was attributed to the practice, and dire economic effects—over and above the standard union monopoly impact (Burton 1978; Hanson *et al.* 1982; Hayek 1960: 275). Yet, characteristically, the Conservatives advanced cautiously, taking a full ten Thatcher years to outlaw it completely.

The advance was two-pronged (see Dunn 1985). One followed the line of the immunities. The 1982 Act outlawed secondary industrial action to force a closed shop on an open firm or workplace. In 1988 this was extended to any industrial action to promote or defend the practice. The other prong followed the line of individual rights. Beginning in 1980, the grounds for claiming unfair treatment in a closed shop were systematically extended until in 1988 it became automatically unfair to harass or dismiss any non-member in any circumstances, thus restoring the symmetry between the right to belong and not to belong to a union enshrined originally in the 1971 Act. The legal pincer finally closed two years later when preferential hiring of union members (or non-members) became unlawful.

Outlawing the closed shop reflected an adjustment of Conservative policy away from voice and towards exit legislation. The 1988 Act can be seen as pivotal. Until then, the legal status of the closed shop had depended on ratification by a substantial ballot majority (1980 and 1982 Acts). Now that no longer applied. The will of the majority no longer prevailed. But, more subtly, the increasing preference for exit forked along two paths. One encouraged simple defection from unions, as illustrated by the 1993 Act's regulation of check-off facilities. This gave members a right to confirm periodically the deduction of union dues from their pay packets—a regular reminder that union membership is voluntary. The other path veered towards voice legislation when it too shifted in 1988 towards giving members rights of investigation and complaint. In offering protection to members disciplined by their union for refusing to obey a strike call, for instance, the 1988 Act lowered the cost both of exit from collective decisions and of expressing a minority voice. Each is about escaping majority rule, but the latter suggests that the Conservatives saw scope for unions to be gnawed at from within by even a few dissenters (see Auerbach 1990: ch. 8).

Before turning to the law's impact, it is worth repeating that the Government has not gone the whole Hayekian hog. The immunities still exist and strikes within companies or workplaces can still be lawful. Moreover, legislation has gone in directions that Hayekians disapprove of, notably on balloting. Yet, the Conservatives have offset this by increasingly detailed regulation of union affairs, setting legal traps for unions that require a degree of alertness and expense to avoid. The Government's ingenuity is not in doubt. But has it worked?

4. Impact

Legal Cases and Their Ramifications

Analysing how the courts interpret statutes cannot reveal whether legislation is being widely observed or disregarded. Nor can the volume of litigation clarify matters. If it is low, for example, do we infer that unions are being law-abiding? Or do we infer that employers are turning a blind eye to union transgressions? Nevertheless, legal cases provide a valuable jumping-off point. Given the difficulty of attributing behavioural change to legislation, they corroborate survey and econometric results. We concentrate on three related areas: civil disobedience, injunctions, and the demonstration effect of important cases.

Civil disobedience brought the 1971 Act into disrepute. Especially damaging were the difficulties that the National Industrial Relations Court had in making judgements stick (Weekes *et al.* 1975). The 1980s and early 1990s saw no disobedience on a similar scale. True, union funds have been sequestrated and bitter disputes waged unlawfully. But ultimately the will of the courts prevailed. Although this far from demonstrates that the new law has been generally observed, it does suggest that the conditions exist for such observance. When cases turn into a shambles, then it is less likely that unions elsewhere will be cowed into lawfulness or employers feel confident that the law is a reliable ally. When, on the other hand, the judicial process seems inexorable, both sides are likely to accept that they operate within fresh legally defined norms.

The interlocutory injunction contributes to this sense of inexorability. A quick method of stopping possible unlawful action in its tracks, injunctions lay defiant unions open to unlimited fines or seizure of assets for contempt. Of course, these existed in 1971. But since a Law Lords' ruling in 1975, they have become easier to obtain. No longer need the plaintiff offer a prima-facie case, only evidence of a serious question to be tried (see Wedderburn 1991: ch. 7). Ron Todd, when General Secretary of the TGWU, put it bluntly. 'Employers', he said, 'can wake up a judge at the dead of night, give him a drop of brandy, show him a headline from *The Sun* and get him to sign an injunction' (quoted in Turnbull *et al.* 1992: 219). Such cynicism is illuminated by research. Between 1980 and 1989 over 90 per cent of injunction against unions were granted (Evans 1985, 1987; Marsh 1992: 86).

Evan's work suggests that injunctions had an effect from the outset. 'Contrary to the assertions of the abstentionist argument', he concluded from studying thirty-eight strikes in 1982, 'even managements with character-istically accommodative orientations to unions could be brought to use legal sanctions' (1985: 128). On the union side, 'the effect of the injunction threat was generally as intended by managements, to shift control over the strike away from shop stewards towards union leaders' (1985: 137). Note that this was before the 1982 Act made unions, as corporate bodies, responsible for unlawful action by their officials and stewards. It might be expected that after the Act unions would have been even keener to get a grip on the conduct of disputes. However, the initial union reaction to the new legal hazards was defiant. Between 1982 and 1984, 69 per cent of injunctions were resisted, compared to 11 per cent between 1980 and 1982 (Marsh 1992: 86–7). It was as if unions were testing their power against the judiciary, encouraged perhaps by the militant tone of the TUC's 1982 Wembley Special Conference. That the defiance rate fell to 23 per cent in the second half of the 1980s suggests that unions learned some hard lessons from their encounters with the courts, as expressed in the 'new realism' that emerged from the 1984 Congress.

The four hard lessons most frequently cited punctuate the 1980s, as though reminding unions of the new era. These were at the Stockport Messenger

(1983–4), at News International (1986–7), at P&O and Sealink Ferries (1988), and in the docks (1989) (on some or all of these, see Dunn 1985; Gennard 1984; McIlroy 1991: 69–72, 108–16, 143–51; Turnbull *et al.* 1992). The feature common to all was the pre-entry closed shop which, in each case, operated on a multi-employer basis. These labour supply or labour pool arrangements dictated that employers recruit only approved union members. Over time, they had given the unions bargaining leverage to impose considerable costs, in terms of wages and job controls, upon management. To preserve them, the unions had to stop firms escaping their territory. A prime weapon was secondary action, particularly 'blacking' and picketing, against the offending company. The Messenger Group was one such company. It set up a non-union shop in an increasingly competitive sector (local newspapers), using new technology and non-craft labour. Until the 1980 and 1982 Acts, the chances of the company succeeding would have been slim. Even though computer technology was already undermining old skills, the NGA had slowed its introduction and kept its members' craft status remarkably intact by virtue of its ability to control the labour supply. Fought in the heartlands of strong trade-unionism, the dispute was thus the sternest of tests for the new law. Wielding its traditional weapons, the NGA was met with a volley of injunctions, followed by fines and sequestration. By the time it abandoned the dispute, its funds had been drained by fines, costs, and damages. As a similar penalty was likely each time the NGA tried to overwhelm a non-union firm in the traditional style, the old weapons appeared to have little future.

The Messenger dispute was a clear instance of the law working as intended against entrenched union monopoly power. Not only did it demonstrate to unions what legal responsibility entailed, it also showed how well the new legislation could protect individual firms from union harassment, if they chose the non-union path. The encouragement it gave to employers in the printing industry is revealed by the fact that, between 1984 and 1987, 36 per cent of all injunctions involved printing disputes. Indeed, provincial newspaper proprietors increasingly adopted union exclusion policies (see Gall 1993; Smith and Morton 1990, 1993). And the lesson could be repeated. At News International, the issue was the firm's flight from restrictive Fleet Street to a new plant at Wapping where a non-print union, the EETPU, was to be recognized. At P&O and Sealink Ferries, it was restructuring in preparation for competition from the Channel Tunnel and an attempt by the union to defend its industry-wide solidarity. On the docks, it was the decentralization of bargaining and derecognition in the aftermath of the Government's abolition of the Dock Labour Scheme upon which the TGWU's labour pool shop was built. In the first two cases, the unions began at the head of a crusade, much as the NGA had done in 1983, wilted in the face of injunctions, then backed off, despite rank and file anger. Significantly, the TGWU was more circumspect from the outset in handling the dockworkers' dispute. Its leaders refused to be bounced into unlawful action and, according to Turnbull *et al.* (1992), delayed until the cause was lost.

Room exists, of course, to challenge the importance of these cases as a deterrent to unions and an encouragement to managers. But even Elgar and Simpson, whose interviews with management and union representatives tended to make them sceptical about the law's importance, nevertheless reported a feeling that the new legislation 'contributed to a climate where there was a general awareness of a continuing shift in the balance of bargaining power' (1993*a*: 106). Another sceptic, McCarthy, admits that 'the government could claim that its laws were being observed: the myth that British unions are in some way above or beyond the law is no longer credible' (1992: 70). Certainly, as the 1990s arrived, unions were far less likely to approach legal problems like a bull at a gate. We have not seen the kind of trials of strength in this decade that lent drama to industrial relations in the 1980s. Rather, unions began to learn the art of the possible. They became more adapt at exploring the boundaries of lawfulness (Metcalf and Dunn 1989). The most successful instance was the 1990 national engineering dispute over shorter working hours (Richardson and Rubin 1993). To avoid the legal repercussions of trying to organize multi-employer action, the AEU and its allies conducted a series of discrete single-employer strikes in key firms which opened the way to a host of agreements on the issue. More pyrrhic were the successes unions had in using unofficial hit and run tactics to make legal interference difficult (McIlroy 1991: 166–7) and in manipulating ballot constituencies (Wilkinson 1987). Both brought a tightening of the law. Indeed, the 1988 and 1990 Acts seemed to be the beginning of a cat and mouse game in which unions started to wriggle from the law's clutches, only to be grabbed by a fresh set of statutory claws. In short, the art of the possible became an increasingly futile pastime.

Surveys of Industrial Relations Institutions and Processes

From the Intent section, we would expect that, if the law were to have an impact, it would reduce union membership, erode the coverage of both the closed shop and collective bargaining, and curb strikes. Where bargaining survives, we would hypothesize that it would have become increasingly decentralized. We would also expect greater use of ballots within unions and anticipate votes for moderation. Surveys abound to test these propositions. Isolating cause and effect, however, is always difficult. Even though the evidence often shows that changes are in the direction hoped for by the Conservatives, how far they can be attributed to the law, rather than to structural, economic, sociological, or managerial variables, is a vexed question.

Union membership In reversal of the 1970s trend, unions since 1979 have suffered their longest sustained membership fall ever. Beginning the period at 13.3 m., numbers declined to 8.9 m. in 1992 (Certification Officer 1993). Other surveys suggest an even lower figure. Calculations of the proportion of workers who are members also vary (see Kelly and Bailey 1989). A conservative estimate would be that union density has evaporated from 55 per cent to near 40 per cent, although some credible sources put it way down in the 30 per cent range.

We are not short of theories to explain this drop. Favourite would be 'business cycle' theory, which presents wages and unemployment as particularly important variables, followed by composition theory, which prefers workforce characteristics and industrial structure. This makes Freeman and Pelletier's calculations all the more startling. Controlling for the variables fundamental to the other two theories, and using an index to chart, Act by Act up to 1986, the favourableness of legislation to unions, they concluded that 'the vast bulk of the observed 1980s decline in union density in the UK is due to the changed legal environment for industrial relations' (1990: 156). No room is left for reconciliation with an increasingly refined business cycle theory by which Disney (1990) explains (though slightly overpredicts after 1983) annual union density to 1987, and with a persistent composition theory by which Booth (1989) explains over 40 per cent of the density decline to 1987. Somebody must be wrong (for a review, see Waddington 1992).

One criticism of Freeman and Pelletier is that they do not establish cause and effect, merely statistical association. Nor do they consider the possibility that, in an intense period of confusing economic, industrial, and political upheaval, trade union decline caused an increasingly confident government to enact legislation. Also, the index assumes that the law's impact is instant, whereas evidence, explored below, suggests strongly that its effects elsewhere were lagged. Indeed, not until the second half of the 1980s, after Freeman and Pelletier's cut-off date, did it begin to alter the institutional shape and possibly the economic outcomes of the industrial relations system. Without a plausible story to convince us why the legislation should have had such an exceptional immediate effect on union membership, we are left with Metcalf's (1991) 'safe' conclusion that none of the major theories can be discarded in favour of one dominant explanation.

The closed shop   The closed shop population has also plummeted since 1979. The latest figures indicate 0.3 to 0.5 m. people covered by such arrangements in 1990 (Millward *et al.* 1992: 96–101) compared to over 5.2 m. ten years previously (Dunn and Gennard 1984). Attributing this to the law is tempting. So, too, is linking it to the drop in union membership. If we follow Olson (1965: ch. 3), for example, the rationality of 'free riding' is so strong that widespread defections would have been expected, once members were given the opportunity to exit.

According to the first two Workplace Industrial Relations Surveys (WIRS1 and 2), the initial fall in the closed shop population (about 1.5 m. by 1984) was due to the disappearance or contraction of closed shop establishments in the recession, rather than to people 'exiting' under the protection of the new legislation (Millward and Stevens 1986: 301; also Labour Research Department

1985). Although bad news for Freeman and Pelletier, this finding seems consistent with the legal changes. Until 1988 the practice could survive in law, despite a limited extension of the right not to belong, compulsory ballots, which were rare but usually in favour (McIlroy 1991: 127), and restrictions on industrial action to spread the closed shop principle. Subsequently, the picture alters. WIRS3 showed that in 1990 only 4 per cent of establishments (in contrast to 20 per cent in 1984) had closed shops covering manuals and only 1 per cent (9 per cent in 1984) covering white collars (Millward *et al.* 1992: 97). Here, Millward and his colleagues prefer legislation to compositional factors as an explanation. Again, this seems reasonable, although they do not elaborate greatly. The best evidence comes from the public sector. The virtual elimination of closed shop agreements in the nationalized industries, where they had become universal in the 1970s, and in the public services, reflects the pressure on managers to be law-abiding. In the private sector, managers did not generally impose the new legal regime so assiduously. Instead, the closed shop has been dying a slow death. Commonly, managers have grown unwilling to sack non-unionists and unions reluctant to force the issue. Where closed shops have survived the longest, in general printing, say, or among small groups of skilled workers, or where traditional solidarity still persists, managers may still tacitly support them (Dunn and Wright 1993). Frequently, though, managerial endorsement has been downgraded from making union membership a condition of employment to a strong encouragement to join. How many such instances can be classified as informal closed shops, masked from the law, is difficult to estimate. If the basic criterion for a closed shop is that people get sacked for non-unionism, the answer is probably that not many 'encouragement' clauses qualify.

While a robust case can be made that the law is killing off the closed shop, alternative explanations are worth considering. For instance, mass unemployment and the collapse of union confidence in the mid-1980s gave firms an opportunity to escape it. Market liberal theory would suggest that the costs of the closed shop are such that any rational employer would leap at the chance. Indeed, well before the 1980 Act, pre-entry shops, the most restrictive, were under threat from de-skilling technology and employer 'runaway' (Dunn and Gennard 1984: ch. 3). Would this escape have happened to the extent it eventually did without legislative help? Our best guess is that the erosion of pre-entry shops would have continued, but more slowly. The ban on secondary action seems to have been decisive in speeding things up, even before the 1990 Act outlawed the preferential hiring of union members upon which pre-entry shops depend.

In the case of the more common post-entry shop, the weaker variety in so far as it performs no entry control function, the process of decline has been different. The word 'escape' seems inappropriate here. While the 1980s' rise of human resource management, with its stress on individualism and commitment (see e.g. Guest 1987), has made companies less tolerant of the collectivism embodied in the closed shop (Dunn and Wright 1993), they did not have the same incentive to destroy post-entry arrangements as they did the costlier pre-entry type. The waning of union power certainly gave managers the opportunity to sidestep union channels when dealing with the workforce. Yet, where unions were well entrenched, human resource management techniques often developed alongside existing union practices and procedures (see Dunn 1993; Millward *et al.* 1992: ch. 10). Indeed, procedural agreements survived surprisingly well (Dunn and Wright 1994). The exception was the closed shop which was by far the most likely arrangement to have been deleted. As, unlike other union security clauses, it was by then legally indefensible, our conclusion is that the motive behind its removal tended to be a (sometimes tardy) desire to conform with the law, not primarily some concerted effort to escape collectivism while market conditions remained unfavourable to unions.

What effect has the closed shop's decline had on union membership? The evidence is patchy and our estimate rough. If we assume that the closed shop population fell by 5 m. (probably too high an estimate) in the eighties, perhaps 2 m. (probably too low) were lost through plant closures, rather than any legal impact. If we then assume that the law helped in the elimination of the rest, we need to know what proportion of members leave unions when compulsion is removed. Using a NIESR survey, Gregg and Yates (1991) reported an average 9 per cent drop in membership where closed shop agreements were withdrawn between 1985 and 1990. Similarily, Millward *et al.* found that, where a comprehensive closed shop survived among manuals, union membership stood at 98 per cent, while it was down to 88 per cent when management only strongly endorsed such membership, a typical replacement for a deleted closed shop clause. Looking at WIRS panel data, they also found that, in those establishments that had operated the practice in 1984, density had fallen only to 93 per cent by 1990 (1992: 100–1). Perhaps we can therefore select, somewhat heroically, a 10 per cent drop as typical up to 1990, which would mean that some 0.3 m. quit their unions as a result of being given the right not to belong. As Millward and his colleagues conclude, 'the decline of the closed shop had only a limited part to play in the overall drop in union membership' (1992: 101). Nevertheless, once the haemorrhage starts, there is no reason why it should stop at any particular level. Indeed, recent research has suggested that during the 1990–3 recession, nearly three-quarters of the accelerating decline in union membership in large private sector companies was in firms where unions remained otherwise secure (Geroski *et al.* 1993)—and this before the 1993 Acts check-off rules came into play.

The coverage and structure of collective bargaining   If the intent of the Conservatives' policy is to discourage collective bargaining, then, as with the closed shop, they can claim a gradual success. The proportion of establishments that recognized unions rose slightly between 1980 and 1984, prompting many observers (e.g. Kelly 1990; MacInnes 1987) to emphasize the durability of bargaining machinery. By contrast, the 1990 WIRS3 evidence showed a 'stark, substantial and incontrovertible' fall (Millward *et al.* 1992: 352) from

66 per cent to 53 per cent in six years (1992: 71). And, because collective agreements encompassed fewer employees within workplaces, the drop in numbers covered was even greater, from 71 per cent to 54 per cent (1992: 94). Bringing in those very small establishments excluded by WIRS, the estimate is that collective bargaining now extends to less than half of both workplaces and employees. Inevitably this has assumed major symbolic importance. Millward *et al.* have called for a 'substantial revision to the traditional characterisation of the British "system"' (1992: 351), while Purcell has called it 'the end of institutionalised industrial relations' (1993: 6). But what had the law to do with it?

The preferred explanation, confirmed by WIRS data, for this remarkable decline is that unions have failed to penetrate a sufficient quantity of young workplaces to replace those bargaining units lost through closure (Millward *et al.* 1992: 73; Millward 1994: ch. 2). Thus, in private manufacturing (a traditional union stronghold), workplaces born after 1979 are 30 per cent less likely to recognize unions than those set up before then (Disney *et al.* 1994: 12). Why? Disney *et al.*'s econometric analysis finds little room for either composition or business cycle effects. Rather it pinpoints the interaction between industrial product markets, labour-market regulation (proxied by union density), management attitudes, and legislation (for which their 'pre–post 1979' variable is the proxy—no Freeman and Pelletier-style index). The often-floated idea that what is being captured here is not a legal impact but merely the fact that post-1979 plants are too new for unions to have organized as extensively as the older places is countered by evidence that the relationship between age and recognition is not smooth (Disney *et al.* 1994: 10). Millward supports this with evidence that in 1980 unions were recognized in 45 per cent of young establishments, whereas in 1990 the proportion was 24 per cent (1994: 28). So, there seems to be a 1980s' effect. Yet, despite Disney *et al.* pulling in the law as the handiest suspect, the case is purely circumstantial. They do not offer any concrete evidence that it has prevented recognition. Can we help?

A relevant legal change was the abolition in 1980 of Labour's statutory recognition machinery. Millward mentions this as a possible factor (1994: 29). Yet the now defunct machinery was generally regarded as pretty feeble, even by trade unions. Their opposition to its removal was lukewarm (Beaumont 1987: ch. 3). Had the machinery survived, it might have made a marginal difference. But it would scarcely have repaired the damage to bargaining coverage that actually occurred from 1984. A second obvious change was the outlawing of secondary action, specifically action to impose bargaining on a workplace where unions were not recognized (1982 Act). There is little systematic evidence on how frequent such tactics were in the 1970s. However, Millward *et al.* (1992: 72) note an exceptionally steep decline in recognition in the printing and publishing sector where, as previously described, secondary action was once a standard method of bringing non-union companies into the fold. Here the legislation does seem to have had an impact in preventing recognition.

Apart from this latter, and frequently cited, example, it is almost impossible to isolate the law's contribution from a range of factors often lumped together under the label 'industrial relations climate' or 'the Thatcher effect'. If required to tell a plausible story about the lack of recognition in new workplaces, we would emphasize, first, that the law does not prevent workers taking industrial action to force their management to concede collective bargaining rights. To that extent, the legal position is not a major obstacle in most cases. It seems less relevant than the slow build-up of management confidence to resist unionization together with a growing wariness among a committed minority of trade-unionists about sticking their necks out. Seeking recognition may be seen as increasingly deviant, especially as unionization shrinks. Fear of the consequences of that deviancy in a continuingly slack labour-market is a powerful deterrent to even the most resolute union activist. It is significant, for example, that, in the 27 per cent of young workplaces where recognition was achieved, the commonest method was via managerial sponsorship in multi-plant companies where unions were already accepted elsewhere (Millward 1994: 24). The union behaviour involved was, in managerial terms, conformist.

Such managerial sponsorship was important to unions even in the more combative 1970s (Brown 1981). That management has not been weaned off unions more extensively since 1979 provides grounds for disappointment among market liberals. Indeed, managers in unionized environments seem to have continued to display conformity themselves, as indicated by Disney *et al.*'s finding that new recognitions are positively related to the degree of unionization in the industry concerned. Stealing a possible competitive edge by avoiding the costs of collective bargaining seems to have been tempered by a willingness to follow industrial relations norms. The limited extent of dere-cognition is relevant here too. WIRS3 found that only 3 per cent of unionized establishments in 1984 had dispensed with collective bargaining by 1990 (Millward *et al.* 1992: 74; confirming earlier work by Claydon 1989). Admittedly, the panel sample of private sector workplaces contradicts this by revealing that a fifth that had had unions in 1984 had none six years later. The anomaly is explained by Millward and his colleagues in terms of bargaining withering away in areas of declining union density. This, they thought, was likely to have been under-reported in the retrospective questionnaire put to the main sample because no act of formal derecognition had taken place. For us, the important thing is that worker apathy towards or disillusionment with unions seems to have been the cause, rather than any managerial offensive, backed by the law. Sometimes it has also been the product of long-term institutional change in the bargaining system. Ever since the 1950s, there has been a trend towards decentralized bargaining arrangements (Brown 1981; Royal Commission on Trade Unions and Employers' Associations 1968). During the 1980s the move accelerated to the extent that by 1990 membership of employers' associations in the private sector had fallen from 25 per cent to 13 per cent of establishments (Millward *et al.* 1992: 45). while multi-employer bargaining as the basis for pay increases had fallen from 27 per cent to 16 per cent (1992: 221). In engineering, where the industry-wide agreement collapsed in 1989 after many years of declining influence, derecognition was particularly marked (1992: 72). The implication here is that small firms that had traditionally followed the industry rate and recognized unions informally via national institutions, merely dropped out of a somewhat tattered union net and began setting pay unilaterally. All this fits the ideology behind the new laws, evidence of firms wanting to take responsibility for their own industrial relations, rather than be tied in with common deals involving their business rivals. But, as Purcell (1991) suggests, such decentralization or dropping out is an adjunct to broader managerial changes. The existence of the legislation seems coincidental. To sum up, managers appear so far to have confined their derecognition activities largely to the weak, the apathetic, the peripheral, the inappropriate, and, exceptionally, the defeated. Only in the latter instance has the law played much direct part.

Ballots, militancy, and strikes Perhaps the most convincing evidence of the law's influence comes from research into unions' balloting arrangements. Unions have strenuously tried, if reluctantly, to conform with the 1984 Act and subsequent regulation of their democratic processes (Martin *et al.* 1991; Smith *et al.* 1993; Steele 1990). Whether the result has been less militant trade-unionism, however, as the voice of an assumed moderate majority has shaped union policies and actions, is far less clear-cut.

We do know that all the political fund votes were in favour of their continuation and that some new funds were created as a result of ballots (Steele *et al.* 1986), which was probably not what the Conservatives intended. More broadly, the Imperial College–ESRC survey of leadership elections found that the legislation left 'an indelible if uneven mark upon the structures of union government, which in turn has affected political outcomes in a number of unions' (Smith *et al.* 1993: 380). Yet it also discovered that these outcomes did not necessarily accord with Conservative hopes. Although some militant leaders had been overturned in elections, so had moderates. There was also evidence that the legal insistence on postal ballots had reduced participation, suggesting that the voice of the membership was still often disinclined to speak, even in private. (Judging by the CROTUM's workload, the litigious union member remains a rare breed too.) Moreover, the removal of electoral colleges, like delegate conferences, from the democratic process sometimes hampered opposition factions and, as a result, may have increased the oligarchical position of incumbent leaders (Smith *et al.* 1993: 379). This last point is the most intriguing when trying to judge the law's success from a Conservative standpoint. We discussed at length in the Voice subsection, above, whether the Government really wanted greater democracy in unions or just internal processes that produced greater moderation. We suggested that, if the priority were moderation, the hope must be, not to remove oligarchical barons necessarily, but to muffle the active minority which has tended to be more militant than either the professional leadership or the rank and file. Smith *et al.* hint that such muffling may have happened, although they deny that the legislation has initiated 'a reorientation of union policy in a "moderate" direction' (1993: 380). Of course, such a conclusion depends on how moderation and militancy are defined. A time-travelling union activist from the 1970s might find most of today's union leaders, even those labelled as left-wing, breathtakingly moderate in their acceptance of legal changes, managerial reforms, and the free market. It would be far-fetched to say that such moderation was caused by the balloting laws. Yet, leaders who are shielded to some extent from the sniping of more militant cliques by a popular vote are likely to be more consistent in pushing moderate agendas.

Pre-strike ballots have to be judged against a background of declining union militancy too. Thus, when ACAS (1990) reported that, of 1,023 statutory ballots up to 1989, 908 were in favour of industrial action, the Hayekians' scepticism about the wisdom of the 1984 Act superficially appeared justified. Nor does this proportion appear to have changed much in the 1990s. In 1992, for example, eight large unions held 209 ballots of which 199 were pro-strike (Labour Research Department 1993: 15). However, nobody suggests that the legislation has unblocked a spring of rank and file militancy. The most plausible explanation is that unions pick and choose, avoiding ballots they think will be lost. According to the Imperial–ESRC survey, 'union officials were usually confident in their ability to predict the outcome of ballots' (Martin *et al.* 1991: 202). Indeed, they appear to have become increasingly expert, the proportion of 'yes' votes rising from 78 per cent in 1985–6, to 94 per cent in 1989, to 95 per cent in 1992. This is also indicative of the way in which the law has made it imperative for full-time officials to control the strike weapon in order to avoid legal penalties. Its unsheathing has become much more bureaucratic (1991: 205). But has it reduced the number of strikes? On one level, it can be surmised that those strikes once railroaded through without a vote or by a show of hands no longer occur, not least because, in the ballot era, strikes tend not to take place where majorities are slender (Elgar and Simpson 1993*b*: 5). On top of that, most pro-strike ballots do not result in action. The Labour Research Department, for example, discovered that in 1992 only 48 per cent produced strikes (1993: 15).

From the Conservative standpoint, however, this may be unwelcome because the predominant reason why decisive strike votes fail to produce action is that management settles the dispute (Brown and Wadhwani 1990: 62; Elgar and Simpson 1993*b*: 13). In other words, secret ballots seem to have made the strike threat, so despised by market liberals, more potent by sending a clear signal of solidarity to management. Strikes may be fewer, but wage settlements, say, be more inflationary. Indeed, later Conservative attempts to weaken union solidarity in order to offset unwanted consequences of the 1984 Act may have worsened the problem. The argument goes as follows. Between the introduction of ballots in 1984 and the 1988 Act, bargaining became more efficient because asymmetries of information were reduced. The vote was an accurate barometer of support in so far as the union could use its disciplinary powers to stiffen the backbone of waverers or tactical voters. Therefore, those unwilling to strike had a strong incentive to vote 'no', rather than a fake 'yes' to put the wind up their employer. In turn, the employer could regard a positive vote as a reliable indicator of intent and opt to make concessions. Since 1988, however, strike breakers have been protected from union discipline. This has lessened the cost of voting 'yes' because the voter cannot be held to the democratic decision. The result is a restoration of the asymmetry of information. Strikes or erroneous concessions by employers become more likely.

Union organizers involved in the Imperial–ESRC survey were reluctant to admit that they exploited this uncertainty (Martin *et al.* 1991: 203). Nevertheless, ballots have clearly increased the room for manoeuvre and bluff in negotiations. They have also, according to union officials, helped galvanize support for industrial action and increase worker commitment to it (Martin *et al.* 1991: 206; Elgar and Simpson 1993*b*: 14). On the other hand, if the ballot threat has become a potent one, employers too have an enhanced legal deterrent. Of 846 union negotiators questioned by Elgar and Simpson, 28 per cent of those who had seriously considered industrial action had also received some kind of legal threat from management, half relating to ballots (1993*b*: 5). Rather more common (reported by 35 per cent), however, was the older, pre-Thatcherite, threat to dismiss the strikers. The traditionally weak legal position of British strikers becomes particularly acute in periods of job scarcity (1993*b*: 6, 14). And the sacking option has been pushed to the fore by the compulsory wording on ballot slips that reminds voters of the breach of employment contract involved in striking.

Although balloting is the most intrusive aspect of the new strike legislation, the best research concludes that its impact has been 'ambivalent' (Martin *et al.* 1991: 206). The effect of more specific legal restrictions targeted on secondary action, however, seem wholly unambivalent. WIRS found experience of secondary blacking in 4 per cent of establishments in 1980 and just 1 per cent in 1990 (Millward *et al.* 1992: 309), while 'secondary picketing almost disappeared' (1992: 309). Sympathy strikes were also far fewer (1992: 289). But then, whichever way you look at strikes since 1979, they are far fewer. Take any kind of industrial action. Workplaces that had experienced it in the previous year halved to 12 per cent between 1984 and 1990 (1992: 279). Take national aggregates. Strike incidence, duration, and mass have fallen even more dramatically than union membership. For instance, 211 stoppages were reported in 1993, the lowest since records began in 1891 (Employment Department 1994). This compares with an annual average of 2,601 in the 1970s and continues the downward trend of the 1980s when the annual average was 1,129 (Kessler and Bayliss 1992: 210). Similarly, 1992 saw a record low of 528,000 days lost through strikes (annual average in the 1970s: 12.8 m.). Reason enough for Conservative triumphalism, even if the ballot policy were to have misfired. However, four qualifiers must be added. First, the virtual elimination of the coal mining industry, traditionally a big contributor to the figures, partly accounts for the meagreness of strike activity in the 1990s (Metcalf and Milner 1993: 257). Second, when days lost per union member, rather than per employee, are considered, the fall looks less marked (1993: 239), suggesting that overall the drop is partly a function of the growth of non-unionism. Third, international comparisons show a widespread decline in industrial action, which indicates that the effect of parochial changes in the law can be exaggerated (Agence Europe 1994; Kessler and Bayliss 1992: 214). Britain, for instance, stood seventh in a twenty-country league table of strike-proneness at both the beginning and end of the 1980s. Fourth, looking back over the longer pattern, it is the militant 1970s that look anomalous, while the increasingly pacific 1980s and 1990s seem 'a return to the underlying trend of strike activity apparent since 1930' (Milner and Metcalf 1993: 238) when voluntarism ruled.

Theories to explain the pattern of strikes are plentiful. Forecasts of the strikes' withering away in industrial societies, as they 'modernize' economically, socially, and politically, have existed since the 1950s (e.g. Ross and Hartman 1960). By contrast, long-wave theory would see the phenomenon cyclically in terms of the post-war boom collapsing into a prolonged economic downturn of union exhaustion and retrenchment (Cronin 1979). Others emphasize how global changes in the capitalist system have undermined the collective regulation of markets, rendering unions weak and vulnerable (Lash and Urry 1987). All these could accommodate both the lack of industrial action and the introduction of restrictive strike law as an outward sign of greater forces, but they are too broad to pinpoint the precise link between the two.

More modestly, economists have tried to predict strike patterns using equations roughly akin to those mentioned above in relation to union density and bargaining coverage. Takla (1988), for instance, adapted the familiar Ashenfelter and Johnson (1969)–Pencaval (1970) model to incorporate a legislation dummy. Using UK data 1970–85 and having controlled for macroeconomic variables, she found that strike activity was lower after 1979 than previously on all three measures (frequency, workers involved, and days lost). The reduction was statistically significant only in the case of the number of stoppages, which dropped by a quarter. Similarly, McConnell and Takla (1990) used monthly panel data over 1970-87 to find a very strong 'legislation' effect on days lost, a weaker effect on strike frequency, but none on workers involved. In both tests, the dummy was the usual time proxy for legal intervention. It captured the residual part of the downward shift in the pattern of strikes after 1979 that was unexplained by the other variables. Maybe the residual was the law, maybe not. Ingram *et al.* (1991: 15–16; 1993: 712) add precision by applying Freeman and Pelletier's 'legislation index' to the massive CBI Pay Data Bank's information on strikes during wage bargaining in manufacturing. They find that as the index becomes less favourable to unions, so strike incidence drops. They also employ a pre- and post-1984 dummy to capture the impact of the 1984 strike ballot law. They admit, however, that, although it proves significant in relation to the large fall in strike frequency in the second half of the 1980s (40 per cent less than previously (1991: 17)), the dummy might be capturing other factors. They mention product market competition (1993: 712). To this might be added the psychological damage done to the union movement by the Conservative election victories in 1984 and 1987 and, sandwiched between, the defeat of the miners' strike. Ingram *et al.*'s final judgement is therefore cautious: 'the evidence is consistent with the idea that changes in the law have reduced strike incidence, but we are not asserting that this has definitely occurred' (1991: 16).

Analysis of Economic Performance

We have said that the Hayekians anticipate significant economic benefits, if the law were able to curb union power. As the immunities still survive and industry is not union-free, they would scarcely expect all their hopes to be met. Nor, in the light of the previous section, would it be possible to give the law all the credit for any hoped-for changes that did occur. In the following segments on productivity, profits, pay, and jobs, we review the evidence. On each topic, the methodological problem is exactly the same and frustratingly familiar. Even though the statistical analysis is rigorous, the equations have no separate 'law' variable. Instead, a legislative effect tends to be inferred from a change in the impact of a 'union' variable. For brevity, we discuss this at length only in the next segment.

Labour productivity   Claims of a productivity miracle surfaced in the mid- to late 1980s. In the preceding two decades, the UK had been bottom of the growth league of the Big-7 OECD countries. During the 1980s, it moved to the top (Treasury 1989). This has been attributed to a more intensive use of labour, stimulated by greater product market competition and the shock of the deep recession in the early Thatcher years, both of which spread 'fear' among managers and workers (Metcalf 1989). Did legislation help too? Brown and Wadhwani propose the following test: 'if the legislation were to reduce the capacity of unions to sustain restrictive working practices, it should lead to a relative improvement in the unionised over the non-unionised sector in terms of labour productivity' (1990: 20).

Econometric evidence suggests that unionized areas did indeed improve their performance more than non-unionized in the early days of the Conservatives' programme. The 1984 WIRS2, for example, showed that unionized plants were, *ceteris paribus*, 17 per cent more likely to report changes in working practices not involving new machinery than those without recognized unions (Machin and Wadhwani 1989). Examination of company accounts by Nickell *et al.* (1992) found that total factor productivity growth in union-ized firms was 1 per cent lower p.a. than in non-union firms between 1975 and 1979, then switched to 2 per cent higher between 1980 and 1984. Inter-industrial evidence, summarized by Metcalf (1990), pointed in the same direction. Summing up, Oulton estimated that 'between a quarter and a half [of the labour productivity increase] is attributable to a decline in the disadvantages of unionisation' (1990: 84).

Such findings accord with the Brown–Wadhwani test. But, as the test itself seeks only to identify conditions from which we might infer that the law has had its intended effect, we are presented only with the possibility that the law has contributed. We can reasonably claim that it has done so, as when Oulton, say, surmises that 'the Thatcher government's programme of trade union reform should receive a share of the credit' (1990: 84). Yet, it is no more than conjecture. The equations root out a changing relationship between unions and productivity, not legislation and productivity.

To convince ourselves that the law did have an impact, we need to dismiss other explanations as less plausible. One such would be as follows. Take two hypothetical workplaces, Plant U and Plant Non-U. They are identical except that Plant U has a closed shop, organized stewards, and bargaining machinery, while Plant Non-U has none of these. Up to the beginning of the 1980s, Plant U's productivity growth was hampered by job controls, collectively won and defended. Plant Non-U's productivity growth was less restrained because, although job controls existed, they were pursued individually and spasmodi-cally, and were often short-lived because of weak collective resistance to managerial prerogative (for a detailed study of job control variation between unionized and non-unionized plants, see Edwards and Scullion 1982). After 1979 both plants are equally hit by business difficulties. Let us say that the two workforces feel equal fear for their jobs and the two sets of managers are equally driven to squeeze more productivity out of them. As a result, produc-tivity growth increases in Plant Non-U. But it increases even faster in Plant U. Why? An obvious answer is that workers in Plant U have more to give management in surrendering their greater job control, just as mugging someone with £100 in his pocket yields more than mugging someone with £10. The law need not enter into the picture.

However, the crucial question is whether Plant U workers will resist management initiatives more stubbornly because they have '£100' to lose. If so, does this mean that Plant U management comes more heavily armed to the mugging, brandishing anti-union law, than does Plant Non-U management?

The answer lies in the nature of the legal weapons available. Throughout the 1980s, and despite the narrowing of the immunities, it remained perfectly lawful for the unions at Plant U to negotiate and to strike over such job control issues as manning, breaks, finishing time, work study values, incentive pay-ment schemes, and labour flexibility. Admittedly, from 1984 such lawfulness depended on a ballot, if the strike were official. But the research quoted above shows that quicker productivity growth in unionized workplaces was well under way by 1984. Moreover, the tough measures against unofficial strikes, the traditional means of defending job controls, did not come in until 1990, outside the period under consideration. A stronger case can be made for the anti-closed shop legislation, especially where it helped erode those pre-entry practices underpinning the most restrictive job controls. Yet, its intervention became influential only later in the decade. In short, just how useful was the new legislation to management? It seems more plausible to suggest that economic circumstances, notably the crash in manufacturing employment at the start of the 1980s, which fell most heavily on unionized plants, shifted power on the shop-floor. This provided the initial impetus for productivity gains that infused the middle Thatcher years with economic optimism.

But what about later? We have seen in relation to strikes, the closed shop, and bargaining coverage, that changes in the industrial relations system became much more marked into the 1990s. Was the productivity momentum in unionized plants sustained as well? Indeed, with more law firmly entrenched, did the productivity momentum in unionized plants gather pace? The most recent evidence is a little contrary and requires careful reading.

One reading suggests that quite the opposite happened. The 'disadvantages of trade unionism' seemed to reappear. WIRS3 revealed that establishments with a strong union presence (a closed shop or management 'encouragement') tended to have had lower productivity growth between 1987 and 1990 (based on managers' estimates) than those that were less unionized or had no unions at all. Instead, improved performance was most frequently associated with sophisticated management techniques (Fernie *et al.* 1994). This need not dismay market liberals, however. The Brown–Wadhwani test presumes that the success of legal intervention is best calculated by looking at changes in the performance of unionized firms in comparison with non-unionized. From this angle, the Fernie *et al.* evidence would indicate that, in the longer run, the law has failed. Yet, if unionism continues to bring productivity disadvantages, market liberals would contend that the success of Conservative legislation lies in limiting the extent of collective bargaining by protecting non-union workplaces from unwanted union attention. In short, fewer firms suffer such disadvantages. And, bearing in mind the arguments in our Responsibility subsection, above, if employers continue to encourage or recommend union membership or continue to recognize the closed shop tacitly, then, according to market liberals, it is their free choice and they must bear the consequences. We can debate how necessary the legislation was in insulating firms from outside unions, but it is hard to deny the Conservatives their satisfaction that things have developed as intended.

Yet, that is not the whole story. Using an unbalanced NIESR panel sample of 328 private sector companies together with productivity measures calculated from company accounts, rather than subjective managerial judgements (as in WIRS3), Gregg *et al.* (1993) found no productivity growth differential between union and non-union firms between 1984 and 1987. These are precisely the years when we would expect the new legislation to have bitten. The differential did, however, reassert itself in 1988–9 (2.3 per cent higher in unionized companies, though not statistically significant). In this 'second surge' (1993: 895), which does not show up in the WIRS3 data cited above, the pattern offers somewhat mixed comfort to Hayekian market liberals. On the one hand, companies that had partially or wholly derecognized unions enjoyed the best results (5 per cent higher), which market liberals would regard as a vindication of the Conservatives' attempt to chip away at bargaining coverage. On the other, companies that repudiated closed shop agreements did no better than unionized firms generally. As market liberals see the closed shop as the major restrictive practice and as the law's impact on it can be pinpointed, the lack of additional productivity gain upon its disappearance would be a disappointment for them, although, to be fair, many repudiations had occurred too recently to have had an effect. It could be, however, that by 1990 the closed shop had lost its sting and its removal made no difference (see Profit and Union Mark-Up subsections, below).

Overall, Gregg and his colleagues's account of productivity growth downplays the influence of the law. They doubt its direct influence. Instead, they emphasize the reassertion of management prerogative, first, in the early 1980s when workers were rattled by recession and, second, at the end of the decade when greater product market competition gave managers in unionized companies a second wind in the drive for higher productivity. Derecognition, usually on quite a small scale, and the ending of closed shop agreements were seen merely as a management signal to the workforce of a fresh determination to push through more efficient working practices.

Profits   All nine studies of unions and financial performance in the early 1980s show a negative relationship (summarized by Metcalf 1993). The most recent, Machin and Stewart (1994, using WIRS evidence), reported that, measured by managerial estimates, unionized establishments were 9 per cent less likely to report above average financial performance than non-union equivalents in 1980 and 10 per cent less likely in 1984.

After a decade of rising aggregate profit margins, WIRS3 reveals a similar gap (8 per cent) still exists (Machin and Stewart 1994). But this hides an interesting change. The union–non-union difference has disappeared everywhere except where a closed shop survives or where management recommends or encourages union membership. *Ceteris paribus*, managers in such establishments were 12.6 per cent less likely to claim above average financial performance, much the same as 1984. Moreover, where this type of establishment has some product market power and its managers admit to union restrictions on their freedom, the likelihood of above average financial performance is 21 per cent below an equivalent non-union workplace.

Looking at their data overall (including likelihood of lower performance), Machin and Stewart estimate that the union effect on financial performance has halved since 1984. Good news for market liberals. In economists' terms, it appears that unions have become 'less successful at extracting a share quasi-rents for their members' (Machin and Stewart 1994: 29), except in those one in ten plants in the sample where the 'old industrial relations' endures. Here, managers seem less motivated to resist union restrictions, being able to shelter behind a degree of monopoly power, and more tolerant of union negotiators creaming off profit for pay.

How far can these changes be credited to legislation? The closed shop offers some evidence. Because far fewer establishments had closed shops in 1990, far fewer were reporting poor financial performance than in 1984. But, merely banning the closed shop did not automatically lead to better performance, because managerial encouragement of union membership, a kind of closed shop downgraded to comply with the law, had the same detrimental effect as the practice itself. Nevertheless, if the Conservatives' intent was to redistribute commercial rewards from workers to companies, from pay to profits (see Dowrick 1988), making the closed shop unlawful seems to have helped a bit.

Union wage mark-up and pay dispersion   Unionized workplaces still pay, on average, higher wages than otherwise comparable non-union ones, although this premium has fallen since 1984. For example, for skilled workers the mark-up dropped from 3.4 to 1.5 per cent by 1990 and for semi-skilled from 10.0 to 6.3 per cent (Stewart 1994 using WIRS data; erosion confirmed by Ingram 1991 (CBI Pay Data Bank) and Gregg and Machin 1992 (company data); for a summary see Metcalf 1994).

For our purposes, the important details are as follows. First, while the closed shop is still associated with a higher than average mark-up, the super premium that pre-entry arrangements once generated (estimated to be around 20 per cent in 1984) no longer exists. In fact, neither the pre-entry nor the post-entry shop are associated with significantly higher wages than those paid in workplaces where management encourages union membership, suggesting once again that outlawing the practice does not automatically reduce bargaining power. Second, union success in achieving above average mark-ups is linked, as with poorer financial performance, to product market power. Third, the price unions seem to have paid to gain recognition in new establishments has been to forego a premium for their members. Fourth, the decline in average union differentials hides a dramatic widening in the dispersion of earnings generally since 1980, a fifth of which (for semi-skilled workers) Gregg and Machin (1993: 25) attribute to the reduced influence of collective bargaining. The weakening of the quasi-collective bargaining of the wages councils had an impact here too, even before they were abolished in 1993 (1993: 27). Since then, initial research reveals an acceleration of the pay dispersion among the low paid (Cox 1994). All this adds up to progress towards the market liberal ideal: a lower union wage effect, fewer workers, indeed fewer union members, enjoying it, and a pay structure less flattened by institutional pay-fixing. Without trudging over the difficulties in measuring the law's contribution again, we can at least say that it has dovetailed neatly with the other factors that have 'freed up' the labour-market to produce these results.

Jobs   According to market liberal theory, union monopoly effects reduce the number of jobs in the unionized sector, displacing labour into the non-union job market so that people find it harder to find work there. This oversupply is not rectified by the market's downward pressure on wages because jobs at the bottom become unattractive relative to welfare payments. The result is greater unemployment than would exist in unions' absence (Minford (1982) estimated the job loss to be 1 m.). The productivity, profit, and wage changes described above would have been expected to alleviate this problem. Yet, whereas in the post-war heyday of union power unemployment never went above 1 m., since the early 1980s it has never been below 1.6 m. Superficially, therefore, we have no need to explore the impact of legislation in reducing unemployment because it never happened. The market liberals' fall-back argument is that the law has not gone far enough, nor has the welfare system been modified enough to give the market a chance. That may be so. Nevertheless, with such a stark decline in union influence, we would have expected at least a glimmer of evidence that jobs had become more plentiful as a result, at least in the union sector. Certainly, doubt is cast on Hayek's assertion, quoted earlier, about unions being the prime cause of unemployment. Moreover, events since 1979 would suggest that unemployment has been the medicine to cure unions, rather than union reform the medicine to cure unemployment.

Admittedly, Britain's enduring difficulties with the pay-jobs trade-off may well be rooted in the industrial relations system. International comparisons suggest that decentralized, heavily unionized systems like ours are less successful in sustaining a favourable pay-jobs trade-off than those, as in parts of Europe, that work on more centralized bargaining machinery. The logic is that where thousands of bargains occur each year, each one has trivial external consequences and bargainers have little incentive to consider the macroeconomy. But, in total, they are prone to be inflationary, especially because of copycat and leapfrog claims, something which Britain's multi-unionism is likely to exacerbate (Olson 1965). Centralized bargaining, by contrast, encourages unions to take more account of the national economy, partly because the government has more influence on the vastly fewer bargains and partly because large union alliances are more sensitive to such influence in so far as any adverse result of settlements falls directly on their mass membership (Calmfors and Driffill 1988; Bruno and Sachs 1985: summarized in Crouch 1993). The Labour Government tried this approach in the 1970s Social Contract and were successful for a while (1976–8). But such things are anathema to the Conservatives. So, they are stuck with pursuing decentralization and weakening unions as the solution. International comparisons have shown that this, too, can be successful if unions are sufficiently feeble. The trouble is that the Government has made most of the big legal moves to emasculate unions without achieving the necessary results. Realistically, more law does not seem to be the answer. And, ironically, if the market liberals' ultimate wish were to be somehow granted, the abolition of the remaining immunities would probably require a sustained period of high unemployment to suppress resistance.

5. Conclusions

When Brown and Wadhwani tried this exercise in 1990, one of their conclusions, we noted, was that the law's impact was to some extent perverse. The latest evidence denies such perversity. The industrial relations system and its economic effects seem to be going in directions that the Conservatives hoped the law would propel it. Even though extracting legislative influences from a complex of variables remains difficult, at least the law is part of the flow. Even the balloting provisions, which remain a risk for the Conservatives, have not had major perverse consequences. Whether the law's general impact continues to be limited, as Brown and Wadhwani also concluded, is open to doubt as well now. Since their work, WIRS3 has reported the closed shop's collapse and the near elimination of all kinds of secondary action. And other research indicates that unions have become very reluctant to disobey strike restrictions. Even so, when the steep institutional decline of the industrial relations is considered, the law assumes a more peripheral, or at most a less distinct, role as one element in the tide of change. Hard as we have tried, it has proved impossible to make a stronger case than that. A similar judgement seems inescapable when economic outcomes come under scrutiny. As Brown and Wadhwani implied, unemployment, including two deep recessions, and stiffer product market competition remain of paramount importance in weakening unions and stimulating management. True, the unions' effect on the economy is less prominent. This partly stems from the growth in the non-union sector and partly from the lesser drag on productivity and profits and the lower wage mark-up where unions exist. Yet, where we can pinpoint the law's impact, legislative intrusion does not automatically bring the expected economic changes. Notably, when management eliminated closed shops in favour of merely recommending union membership, some economic consequences of 'compulsory' unionism survived. Moreover, despite the tip in the balance of power towards management, the enduring wage-jobs trade-off problem persists for the government.

Finally, the law's drip-drip corrosion of trade-unionism is likely to continue until a change of government. The 1993 Act's rules on check-off, its removal of State funding for ballots, and its dispensation regarding less favourable treatment for union members have scarcely touched union organization so far. But, whether this will bring the 'salvation' of the British economy, as the Hayekians hope, seems dubious now. Hampering unions is no longer sustainable as the simple, populist answer to a complex problem. The very success of the legislation demonstrates that law is not enough. Add some or take chunks away, the economy will not feel much.

REFERENCES

ACAS (1990), *Annual Report* (London: HMSO).

Agence Europe (1994), *Europe Daily Bulletin and Supplement*, 6250 (13/14 June).

Ashenfelter, O., and Johnson, G. (1969), 'Bargaining Theory, Trade Unions and Industrial Strike Activity', *American Economic Review*, 59/1: 35–41.

Auerbach, S. (1990), *Legislating for Conflict* (Oxford: Clarendon).

Beaumont, P. (1987), *The Decline of Trade Union Organisation* (London: Croom Helm).

Booth, A. (1989), 'What Do Unions Do Now?', Discussion Paper in Economics 8903; Brunel University.

Brown, W. (1981), *The Changing Contours of British Industrial Relations* (Oxford: Blackwell).

—— and Wadhwani, S. (1990), 'The Economic Effects of Industrial Relations Legislation since 1979', *National Institute Economic Review* (Feb.), 57–69.

Bruno, M., and Sachs, J. (1985), *The Economics of World-Wide Stagflation* (Oxford: Blackwell).

Burton, J. (1978), 'Are Trade Unions a Public Good/"Bad"? The Economics of the Closed Shop', in L. Robbins (ed.), *Trade Unions: Public Goods or Public 'Bads'?* (Reading, 17; London: Institute of Economic Affairs).

Calmfors, L., and Driffill, D. (1988), 'Bargaining Structure, Corporatism and Macro-Economic Performance', *Economic Policy*, 6.

Certification Officer (1993), *Annual Report* (London: HMSO).

Claydon, T. (1989), 'Union Derecognition in Britain in the 1980s', *British Journal of Industrial Relations*, 27/2 (July), 214–24.

Cox, G. (1994), *After the Safety Net: A Study of Pay in Wages Council Sectors Post-Abolition*, (Manchester: Low Pay Network).

Cronin, J. (1979), *Industrial Conflict in Modern Britain* (London: Croom Helm).

Crouch, C. (1982), *The Politics of Industrial Relations* (London: Fontana).

—— (1993), *Industrial Relations and European State Traditions* (Oxford: Clarendon).

Department of Employment (1983), *Democracy in Trade Unions*, Green Paper, Cmnd 8778 (London: HMSO).

Disney, R. (1990), 'Explanations of the Decline of Trade Union Density in Britain: An Appraisal', *British Journal of Industrial Relations*, 28/2: 165–78.

—— Gosling, A., and Machin, S. (1994), 'British Unions in Decline: An Examination of the 1980s Fall in Trade Union Recognition', Discussion Paper W94/4, Institute of Fiscal Studies.

Dowrick, S. (1988), 'The UK Profits Boom and the Reserve Army of Labour', Australian National University, mimeo.

Dunn, S. (1985), 'The Law and the Decline of the Closed Shop', In P. Fosh, and C. Littler (eds.), *Industrial Relations and the Law in the 1980s* (Aldershot: Gower).

—— (1993), 'From Donovan to . . . Wherever', *British Journal of Industrial Relations*, 31/2: 169–87.

—— and Gennard, J. (1984), *The Closed Shop in British Industry* (London: Macmillan).

—— and Wright, M. (1993), 'Managing without the Closed Shop', In Metcalf and Milner (1993).

—— —— (1994).'Maintaining the "Status Quo"? An Analysis of the Contents of

British Collective Agreements, 1979–1990', *British Journal of Industrial Relations*, 32/1 (Mar.) 23–46.

Edwards, P., and Scullion, H. (1982), *The Social Organisation of Industrial Conflict* (Oxford: Blackwell).

Elgar, J. and Simpson, R. (1993a), 'The Impact of the Law on Industrial Disputes', in Metcalf and Milner (1993).

————— (1993b), 'Union Negotiators, Industrial Action and the Law', Centre for Economic Performance, Discussion Paper 171, LSE, Oct.

Employment Department (1991), *Industrial Relations in the 1990s*. Green Paper, Cm 1602 (London: HMSO).

————— (1994), 'Labour Disputes 1993', *Employment Gazette* (June).

Evans, S. (1985), 'The Use of Injunctions in Industrial Disputes', *British Journal of Industrial Relations* 23/1: 133–7.

————— (1987), 'The Use of Injunctions in Industrial Disputes May 1984–April 1987', *British Journal of Industrial Relations*, 25/3: 419–35.

Ewing, K. (1989), *Britain and the ILO* (London: Institute of Employment Rights).

Fernie, S., Metcalf, D., and Woodland, S. (1994), 'What Has HRM Achieved in the Workplace', *Economic Report* (London: Employment Policy Institute) (May).

Flanders, A. (1974), 'The Tradition of Voluntarism', *British Journal of Industrial Relations*, 12/3: 352–70.

Fosh, P., Morris, H., Martin, R., Smith, P, and Undy, R. (1994), 'Politics, Pragmatism and Ideology: The "Wellsprings" of Conservative Union Legislation (1979–1992)', *Industrial Law Journal*, 22/1: 14–31.

Freeman, R, and Pelletier, J. (1990), 'The Impact of Industrial Relations Legislation on British Union Density', *British Journal of Industrial Relations* 28/2: 141–64.

Gall, G. (1993), 'The Employers' Offensive in the Provincial Newspaper Industry', *British Journal of Industrial Relations*, 31/4: 615–24.

Gennard, J. (1984), 'The Implications of the Messenger Newspaper Group Dispute', *Industrial Relations Journal*, 15/3: 7–20.

Geroski, P., Gregg, P., and Desjonqueres, T. (1993), 'Did the Retreat of UK Trade Unionism Accelerate during the 1990–93 Recession', Discussion Paper, NIESR.

Gregg, P., and Yates, A. (1991), 'Changes in Wage Setting Arrangements and Trade Union Presence in the 1980s', *British Journal of Industrial Relations*, 29/2: 361–76.

————— and Machin, S. (1992), 'Unions, the Demise of the Closed Shop and Wage Growth in the 1980s', *Oxford Bulletin of Economics and Statistics* 54/1: 53–72.

————— ————— (1993), 'Is the UK Rise in Inequality Different?', Discussion Paper, NIESR, July.

————— ————— and Metcalf, D. (1993), 'Signals and Cycles? Productivity Growth and Changes in Union Status in British Companies 1984–9', *Economic Journal*, 103/419: 894–907.

Guest, D. (1987), 'Human Resource Management and Industrial Relations', *Journal of Management Studies*, 24/5: 503–21.

Hanson, C., Jackson, H., and Miller, D. (1982), *The Closed Shop* (Aldershot: Gower)

————— and Mather, G. (1988), *Striking Out Strikes* (Hobart Paper, 110; London: Institute of Economic Affairs).

Hayek, F. (1960), *The Constitution of Liberty* (London: Routledge & Kegan Paul).

————— (1984), *1980s Unemployment and the Unions* (Hobart Paper, 87; 2nd edn., London: Institute of Economic Affairs).

Hemingway, J. (1978), *Conflict and Democracy* (Oxford: Oxford University Press).

Hendy, J. (1989), *The Conservative Employment Laws: A National and International Perspective* (London: Institute of Employment Rights).

Ingram, P. (1991), 'Ten Years of Manufacturing Wage Settlements 1979–1989', *Oxford Review of Economic Policy*, 7/1: 93–106.

——Metcalf, D., and Wadsworth, J. (1991), 'Strike Incidence and Duration in British Manufacturing Industry in the 1980s', Discussion Paper 48, CEP, LSE, Aug.

—— —— ——(1993), 'Strike Incidence in British Manufacturing', *Industrial and Labour Relations Review*, 46/4: 704–17.

Kahn-Freund, O. (1959), 'Labour Law', In M. Ginsberg (ed.), *Law and Opinion in England in the 20th Century* (London: Stevens).

Kelly, J. (1990), 'British Trade Unionism 1979–1989: Change, Continuity and Contradiction', *Work, Employment and Society*, 4 (May) (special edn.), 29–65.

——and Bailey, R. (1989), 'British Trade Union Membership, Density, and Decline', *Industrial Relations Journal* 20/1: 54–61.

Kessler, S., and Bayliss, F. (1992), *Contemporary British Industrial Relations* (London: Macmillan).

Labour Research Department (1985), *Labour Research*, 74/10 (Oct.).

——(1993), *Labour Research*, 82/2 (Feb.).

Lash, S., and Urry, J. (1987), *The End of Organised Capitalism* (Cambridge: Polity).

McCarthy, W. (1964), *The Closed Shop in Britain*, (Oxford: Blackwell).

——(1992) (ed.), *Legal Intervention in Industrial Relations: Gains and Losses* (Oxford: BLackwell).

McConnell, S., and Takla, L. (1990), 'Mrs Thatcher's Trade Union Legislation: Has It Reduced Strikes?', Discussion Paper 374, Centre for Labour Economics, LSE, Jan.

Machin, S., and Wadhwani, S. (1989), 'The Effects of Unions on Organizational Change and Employment', *Economic Journal*, 101 (407), 835–54.

——and Stewart, M. (1994), 'Trade Unions and Financial Performance', mimeo, May.

McIlroy, J. (1991), *The Permanent Revolution? Conservative Law and the Trade Unions* (London: Spokesman).

MacInnes, J. (1987), *Thatcherism at Work* (Milton Keynes: Open University Press).

Marsh, D. (1992), *The New Politics of British Trade Unionism* (London: Macmillan).

Martin, R., Fosh, P., Morris, H., Smith, P., and Undy, R. (1991), 'The Decollectivisation of Trade Unions? Ballots and Collective Bargaining in the 1980s', *Industrial Relations Journal*, 22/3: 197–208.

Metcalf, D. (1989), 'Water Notes Dry Up: The Impact of the Donovan Reform Proposals and Thatcherism at Work on Labour Productivity in British Manufacturing', *British Journal of Industrial Relations*, 28/1: 1–32.

——(1990), 'Industrial Relations and the "Productivity Miracle" in British Manufacturing in the 1980s', *Australian Bulletin of Labour*, 16/2: 65–76.

——(1991), 'British Unions: Dissolution or Resurgence?', *Oxford Review of Economic Policy* 7/1: 18–32.

——(1993), 'Industrial Relations and Economic Performance', *British Journal of Industrial Relations*, 31/2: 256–83.

——(1994), 'Transformation of British Industrial Relations? Institutions, Conduct and Outcomes 1980–1990', in R. Barrell (ed.), *Is the British Labour Market Different?* (Cambridge: Cambridge University Press).

——and Dunn, S. (1989), 'Calm Wriggling', *New Statesman* (28 July) 22–3.

————and Milner, S. (1993) (eds.), *New Perspective on Industrial Disputes* (London: Routledge).

Michels, R. (1915), *Political Parties* (New York: Free Press).

Millward, N. (1994), *The New Industrial Relations?* (London: PSI).

————and Stevens, M. (1986), *British Workplace Industrial Relations 1980–1984* (Aldershot: Gower).

————————Smart, D., and Hawes, W. (1992), *Workplace Industrial Relations in Transition* (Aldershot: Dartmouth).

Minford, P. (1982), 'Trade Unions Destroy a Million Jobs', *Journal of Economic Affairs*, 2 (Jan.), 73–9.

————(1983), *Unemployment: Cause and Cure* (London: Martin Robertson).

Nickell, S., Wadhwani S., and Wall, M. (1992), 'Productivity Growth in UK Companies', *European Economic Review*, 36: 1055–99.

Olson, M. (1965), *The Logic of Collective Action* (Cambridge, Mass: Harvard University Press).

Oulton, N. (1990), 'Labour Productivity in UK Manufacturing in the 1970s and 1980s', *National Institute Economic Review*, 132 (May) 71–91.

Pencaval, J. (1970), 'An Investigation into Industrial Strike Activity in Britain', *Economica*, 37/147: 239–56.

Purcell, J. (1991), 'The Rediscovery of the Managerial Prerogative: The Management of Labour Relations in the 1980s', *Oxford Review of Economic Policy* 7/1: 33–43.

————(1993), 'The End of Institutionalised Industrial Relations', *Political Quarterly*, 64/1: 6–23.

Richardson, R. (1995), 'Freidrich Hayek, Social Philospher or Propagandist?', in S. Frowen, (ed.) *Hayek, the Economist and Social Philosopher: A Critical Retrospect* (London: Macmillan).

————and Rubin, M. (1993), 'The Shorter Working Week in Engineering: Surrender without Sacrifice', in Metcalf and Milner (1993).

Ross, A., and Hartman, P. (1960), *Changing Patterns of Industrial Conflict* (New York: Wiley).

Royal Commission on Trade Unions & Employers' Associations (1968), *Report*, Cmnd 3623 (London: HMSO).

Smith, P., and Morton, G. (1990), 'A Change of Heart: Union Exclusion in the Provincial Newspaper Sector', *Work, Employment and Society*, 4: 105–24.

————————(1993), 'Union Exclusion and the Decollectivism of Industrial Relations in Contemporary Britain', *British Journal of Industrial Relations*, 31/1: 97–114.

————Fosh, P., Martin, R., Morris, H., and Undy, R. (1993), 'Ballots and Union Government in the 1980s', *British Journal of Industrial Relations*, 31/3: 365–82.

Steele, M. (1990), 'Changing the Rules: Pressures on Trade Union Constitutions', in P. Fosh and E. Heery (eds.), *Trade Unions and their Members* (London: Macmillan).

————Miller, K. and Gennard, G. (1986), 'The Trade Union Act 1984: Political Fund Ballots', *British Journal of Industrial Relations*, 24/3: 443–67.

Stewart, M. (1994), 'Union Wage Differentials in an Era of Declining Unionisation', University of Warwick, mimeo.

Takla, L. (1988), 'An Empirical Study of Strikes in the UK', LSE, mimeo.

Taylor, R. (1993), *The Trade Union Question in British Politics* (Oxford: Blackwell).

Treasury (1989), *Autumn Economic Statement*, Red Book (London: HMSO).

Tur, R. (1982), 'The Legitimacy of Industrial Action: Trade Unions at the Crossroads', in K. Wedderburn and W. Murphy (eds.). *Labour Law and the Community: Prospects for the 1980s* (London: University of London, Institute of Advanced Legal Studies).

Turnbull, P., Wolfson, C., and Kelly, J. (1992), *Dock Strike: Conflict and Restructuring in British Ports* (Aldershot: Avebury).

Undy, R., and Martin, R. (1984), *Ballots and Trade Union Democracy* (Oxford: Blackwell).

Waddington, J. (1992), 'Trade Union Membership in Britain, 1980–1987: Unemployment and Restructuring', *British Journal of Industrial Relations* 30/2: 287–324.

Wedderburn, Lord (1991), *Employment Rights in Britain and Europe* (London: Lawrence & Wishart).

Weekes, B., Mellish, M., Dickens, L., and Lloyd, J. (1975), *Industrial Relations and the Limits of the Law* (Oxford: Blackwell).

Wilkinson, T. (1987), *Guide to Workplace Balloting* (London: IPM).

5

INDUSTRIAL RELATIONS AND PERFORMANCE SINCE 1945

Peter Nolan

1. Introduction

This chapter investigates the nature of the linkages between industrial relations and the character and performance of British industry since 1945. Countless studies of Britain's post-war performance record have cited industrial relations as a critical source of weakness. Employers, the argument runs, were prevented from organizing production efficiently by the adversarial production politics which allegedly inscribed workplace behaviour and bargaining systems in the three decades after 1945. Indeed, so commonly has this argument been advanced, and so rarely has it been challenged, that it has come to serve as a powerfully seductive conventional wisdom.

In the run-up to the 1979 General Election, Mrs Thatcher skilfully harnessed the conventional wisdom to win popular support for new measures to restrict trade unions. Her self-professed aim was to shift the balance of power in industry and restore management prerogative in the workplace. The extent to which her policies succeeded in transforming the character of production politics and industrial performance has been the subject of intense debate. One line of argument suggests that, in contrast to the Donovan reform strategy which failed to deliver significant performance gains in the 1970s, Thatcher's policies appear to have done the trick (Metcalf 1989). The potent combination of rising unemployment, tougher labour laws, privatization, and deregulation allegedly gave birth to 'new' industrial relations practices in the workplace and a corresponding improvement in productivity and competitiveness.

The analysis which follows challenges this perspective. It argues that the system of industrial relations and employment regulation which came to dominate key sectors of the economy after 1945 was not conducive to industrial modernization: not, it should be stressed, for the reasons cited by proponents of the conventional wisdom, but because the trade unions and other regulatory mechanisms were too weak to force firms to abandon progressively outmoded business practices. The presence of a relatively cheap, disposable, and malleable labour force inhibited the emergence of high wage, high productivity growth strategies and helped entrench a relatively low wage, low productivity industrial system from which it is now proving difficult to escape. This is the first sense in which I wish to invoke the legacy of the past.

There is also a second sense, which concerns the academic study of industrial relations and its relationship to economics. Much more so than in other European countries and the United States, there has been a sharp demarcation line in Britain between the study of the institutions of job regulation and the study of their economic consequences. This may seem an arid academic point, but it is not without consequence, for this unwelcome division of academic labour has served to impede theoretical innovation and entrench established ideas, particularly the conventional wisdom. This chapter draws out the significance of this point for the contemporary analysis of change and continuity in industrial relations. The argument commences with a brief review of the evidence on Britain's post-war industrial performance.

2. British Industrial Performance

It is relatively uncontroversial to note that in the three decades after 1945 British industrial performance exhibited significant deficiencies as compared to other leading capitalist economies. Relevant performance measures in this context include output and productivity growth rates, the balance of trade, and investment in technology, plant, and people. The evidence of British under-performance is most striking in the case of manufacturing.

Comparisons of output and productivity movements across time, sectors, and countries are fraught with measurement problems (see Nolan and O'Donnell 1995). Nevertheless, the evidence—whatever its shortcomings—reveals a substantial and enduring shortfall between Britain's record and that of other leading economies. Fig. 5.1 charts the movements in manufacturing output, and exposes a significant and growing gap between Britain and the other countries. For the period shown, domestic output has remained more or less stagnant.

Britain's productivity record reveals similar weaknesses. Table 5.1 compares labour productivity levels in manufacturing in the United Kingdom for selected years since 1960 with the United States and three other European countries. The differential with the United States, which currently stands in excess of 100 per cent, opened up early on this century. Within Europe, by contrast, Britain emerged from the Second World War as a relatively high productivity economy, yet within the space of two decades that position had been eroded. Britain's relative performance, as Table 5.1 confirms, deteriorated sharply in the 1970s, showed signs of improvement in the 1980s, but none the less continued to lag the performance of the other European countries by between 25 and 40 percentage points.

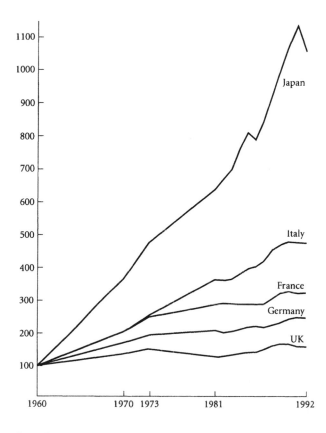

FIG 5.1.

How, given this shortfall in labour productivity, have British-based firms survived under competition? Part of the answer is provided by Table 5.2 which shows that labour costs in Britain are among the lowest of the advanced economies. In 1970 only Japan of the major industrial countries had lower

Table 5.1 Gross Value Added per person–hour in Manufacturing in the Netherlands, France, Germany and the USA as a Percentage of the UK, 1960–88, UK = 100

Year	UK	Netherlands	France	Germany	USA
1960	100	98.5	80.7	105.3	242.5
1970	100	124.8	111.7	133.1	223.7
1975	100	142.4	119.8	141.9	216.7
1980	100	173.5	144.2	164.3	227.2
1984	100	165.5	130.8	146.8	209.6
1988	100	144.1	125.5	136.8	207.0

Source: van Ark (1990)

Table 5.2 Manufacturing compensation per hour in current US dollars

Year	US	Germany	Japan	France	UK	Italy	Belgium	Netherlands
1960	2.66	0.85	0.26	0.82	0.84	0.63	0.81	0.67
1970	4.18	2.36	0.99	1.73	1.49	1.76	2.08	2.12
1976	6.92	6.73	3.30	4.70	3.17	4.41	6.90	6.90
1980	9.84	12.33	5.61	8.94	7.43	8.00	13.15	12.06
1986	13.21	13.35	9.47	10.27	7.50	10.01	12.35	12.24
1992	16.17	25.99	16.16	16.88	14.69	19.41	22.01	20.72

Source: US Bureau of Labor Statistics

labour costs, but by the mid-1980s Britain had fallen to the bottom of the international league table. Despite this cost advantage in respect of labour, the ratio of British manufacturing exports to imports has fallen sharply. Exports exceeded imports by a factor of three in the early 1960s, but by 1983 this substantial trade surplus had been eroded. Britain's trade balance has remained in deficit ever since.

In its investigation of the causes of this adverse trend in domestic manufacturing performance, the 1985 House of Lords Select Committee on Overseas Trade highlighted as critical sources of weakness the concentration of investment in low value-added, low research-intensive sectors and a more pervasive problem of underinvestment in manufacturing industry as a whole (House of Lords 1985). But the Report's findings and policy proposals were ignored, chiefly because they were published at a time of growing optimism, within the Government and economics community at large, about the underlying condition and future potential of British industry.

The economy had been through a very deep crisis in the early 1980s. Two million jobs and one-fifth of total output in manufacturing had been lost between 1979 and 1981. But by 1985, during Mrs Thatcher's second administration, the economy was apparently showing signs of renewal. Manufacturing output had more or less recovered to its previous peak of 1979. Employment in manufacturing did not recover—indeed it has continued to contract to this day—but there was a significant surge in measured productivity. There was also a very substantial rise in investment, output, and employment in services. The fact that the overwhelming majority of the new jobs in hotel and catering, retail, and the public sector were part-time, poorly paid, and insecure scarcely attracted any comment.

Instead the evidence of productivity gains reminiscent of the mid-1960s, and a seemingly flourishing service sector, was seized upon by Government ministers and a significant number of academic economists to justify their view that Britain was experiencing an economic miracle (e.g. Muellbauer 1986; Crafts 1988; Maynard 1988). Production organization and efficiency, it was said, had been lifted by Government policies which, directly and indirectly, hastened the collapse of many allegedly inefficient firms and industries. Conversely, with the consolidation of a new structure of power relations and politics in the workplace, surviving firms faced a bright future. With managers firmly 'back in the saddle', companies would be free to take steps to implement 'best practice' and secure international competitive advantage as recessionary conditions faded.

By the end of the 1980s, however, the mood was different. Recessionary conditions had returned after a brief interlude, and the legacy of underinvestment—in new technology, plant, and people—was becoming more evident. Numerous studies revealed a serious skills gap in domestic industry, as compared to the leading countries in Europe (Steedman and Wagner 1987 and 1989; Finegold and Soskice 1988). Other research findings demonstrated, in line with the House of Lords Report, that industry was becoming increasingly skewed towards the low skill, low value-added end of the technological spectrum (Porter 1990; Archibugi and Michie 1995). Far too many firms, it transpired, had failed to upgrade their products and processes and break with the past practice of importing high value-added intermediate products for assembly and subassembly domestic production. The telling conclusion of one recent study of international productivity comparisons accordingly suggests that the raw figures greatly flatter Britain's relative position by neglecting crucial variations in the quality of produced goods (Mason *et al.* 1994).

With mounting evidence of enduring weaknesses in British industry, some commentators who had previously stressed Mrs Thatcher's achievements revised their views. Crafts, for example, roundly condemned her Governments for what he now judged to be their scandalous neglect of training and technology provision (Crafts 1991). Others accepted that they had previously overstated the gains as new (econometric) evidence revealed that the 1980s had merely reinstated the trends of the 1960s (Darby and Wren-Lewis 1988). In a reworking of the productivity statistics, using the method of double deflation accounting, Stoneman and Francis (1992) thus found for 1979–89 that the official estimates (based on single deflators) significantly overstated the true position at 51 per cent as compared to their own estimate of 34 per cent.

Yet there was to be no recantation on the key policy issue of industrial relations. The Government's record in this respect continued to attract the unqualified support of most economists. Crafts, for example, suggested that the productivity gains of the 1980s may yet prove sustainable 'if the bargaining power of workers over manning levels remain[ed] weak' (Crafts 1991). Numerous other writers echoed this conclusion, and insisted that Thatcher's success in taming the unions has been her single greatest achievement. Two questions are thus relevant in this context. Why are economists instinctively committed to the principle of management prerogative, and why is unionism automatically connected to problems of economic inefficiency?

3. Conventional Economic Analysis

Strictly speaking, in its most refined forms, economic theory has little or nothing to say about the functions, processes, and prerogatives of management. As any student of the subject would explain, it is the market mechanism which governs the selection and deployment of factor services in production. Managers are mere ciphers, prisoners of underlying market and technological forces.

In practice, however, most economists tend to deviate from this highly abstract view, which after all amounts to a denial of one of the most salient institutions of modern capitalism. Relying more on pragmatic judgement than the underlying theory, they would argue that the management hierarchies and authority structures which dominate social relations in modern organizations developed as an efficient response to prevailing deficiencies in the utilization of information, technology, and productive resources. Were this not the case, the argument runs, they would not have survived in the face of competition from superior organizational forms (e.g. Williamson 1980; Landes 1986).

Unions are treated far less generously. Denigrated as monopoly sellers of labour, they are accused of distorting markets, generating technical inefficiencies in production, and pursuing sectional gains in the political arena at the expense of the common good.

The analogy with monopoly producers is misleading. As intermediary organizations, unions do not sell labour services nor do they pursue profit-maximizing objectives, yet such details are ignored in neo-classical theory. What matters, we are told, is that unions interfere with the free play of market forces with necessarily damaging consequences for their members and the social welfare of the community at large. Attempts by unions to lift their members' wages above prevailing competitive rates will prompt employers to substitute alternative inputs (e.g. physical capital) for relatively expensive unionized labour and cut output in order to balance costs with anticipated revenues. Initially confined to unionized establishments, these price and scale effects will be amplified throughout the economy as displaced unionized workers are gradually re-employed at lower wages in relatively labour-intensive, low productivity jobs in non-unionized firms. In aggregate the economy will tend to exhibit significant structural imbalances with too much (physical) capital absorbed by the unionized sector and too much labour power employed within non-union firms.

The role and impact of unions in production are less clearly specified, but since Rees's seminal study (Rees 1963) their activities are none the less thought to be damaging to productivity. Starting from a theoretical position which treats production as a technical relationship between inputs and outputs, economists judge attempts by unions to influence the level of work effort and choice of technique as an unwarranted interference with firms' optimizing decisions in the face of given technological and price constraints. Interruptions to production through strikes and other 'hostile' practices (e.g. work to rules and overtime bans) are cited as further evidence of unions' adverse effects.

Finally, it is claimed that unions may inflict additional damage by attempting on behalf of their members to influence the character and scope of government economic policy. Neo-classical theory advances a very limited view of the legitimate role of government, effectively restricting it to the tasks of controlling the money supply, safeguarding the law of contract, and limiting the distortions from externalities and natural monopoly. From this standpoint, it follows that if governments extend their activities, for example by pursuing an active industrial policy in response to pressure from unions or other organized sectional interest groups, economic efficiency may be impaired.

Like the treatment of management in orthodox theory, the above propositions about unions should be treated with considerable caution. For they are derived from a model of the economy which is highly abstract, ahistorical, and preoccupied with static, allocative questions. The method of neo-classical theory construction involves, in the first instance, the elaboration of the allocative and distributive properties of a perfectly competitive economy. Prominent institutional features of actual economies, including firms and unions, are ruthlessly excised. Then, by taking the individual as the basic unit of analysis and assuming away all transactions costs, the theory is able to demonstrate the existence of an equilibrium price vector which allows all mutually beneficial trading opportunities to be fully exploited.

Exponents of this approach, of course, readily concede that the model is merely an ideal type, a device to better understand the workings of the real economy. But, in practice, the real economy is judged against the properties of the model rather than the other way round. This can clearly be seen in the case of unions, which are inserted into the analysis as imperfections and then found to be an impediment to the achievement of a Pareto efficient resource allocation. It is then but a short step to the policy conclusion that unions should be rooted out to facilitate a movement towards the first best world of perfect competition. This result, it should be stressed, does not derive from dispassionate empirical investigation, still less an analysis of the dynamic properties of the capitalist economy. What are the sources of economic change, and what role do historically forged collective institutions play in the developmental process? Questions such as these were once central concerns of political economy, but are sidelined by modern analysts.

Nor is there any serious attempt to understand the root causes of interest conflicts in production. Evidence that such tensions predated the formation of unions, indeed that they helped spur the growth of worker combinations, is swept aside. Classic studies by Commons (1904) and Mathewson (1931), and more recent empirical research, have stressed the salience of conflict in the employment relation irrespective of whether unions are present, yet economic analysis continues to treat the non-union firm as the benchmark for socially optimal production. Far easier, the cynic might observe, to ascribe to unions the blame for strikes, wages struggle, and associated industrial relations difficulties than to concede that conflicts in production are an intrinsic feature of the wage–labour relationship, a product of the fact that wages are a claim on human capacities and not some pre-specified quantity of performed work. What has academic industrial relations contributed to this debate?

4. The Contribution and Limits of Industrial Relations Research

To answer this question properly it is necessary to return to the 1960s, which have come to be seen retrospectively as the beginning of the golden age of academic industrial relations. The 1960s brought urgent new pressures for expansion. The conduct of workplace collective bargaining had become a central focus of public policy debate, yet the established social sciences (economics, sociology, and politics) were ill-situated to provide the detailed insights into the distinctive character and consequences of production politics demanded by the policy-makers of the day.

The new research agenda was shaped by a developing consensus in government and industry that disorder on the shop-floor was a direct and major cause of Britain's deteriorating industrial performance. These concerns were reflected in the writings of the Oxford School, notably Hugh Clegg, Alan Flanders, and Alan Fox, which had a profound influence on the policy recommendations of the Royal Commission on Trade Unions and Employers' Associations, established under Lord Donovan in 1965 by the then Labour government.

Much of the research conducted for the Commission reinforced the prevailing view that there was a direct link between the industrial relations system and industrial performance. The Commission argued that the decaying national and industry-wide system of collective bargaining had allowed disorder and informality to flourish in the workplace. Restrictive practices, unconstitutional and unofficial strikes, degenerate piecework payment systems, and associated wage drift were held to be the most salient manifestations of the problem. On the issue of restrictive practices, one of the key research papers published in 1967 contained the following evaluation of the problem by Hugh Clegg, the principal architect of the final report:

Under employment of labour is one of the major scandals of the British economy. There may be few workers—outside the newspaper industry—who are paid to do nothing at all, but throughout British industry there must be hundreds of thousands of workers who are paid to do nothing for a considerable part of their working time . . . Then there are the new machines and changes in technology—many of them in use in other countries—which would be introduced here but for the limits placed by workers on their output

In the event, however, the Commission did not lay the blame for disorder at the feet of the unions. The argument was more subtle. Senior management were held culpable for neglect, and for being too ready to allow foremen and supervisors to enter into covert and cosy deals with the rapidly expanding ranks of shop-floor trade union representatives. Stressing that management alone could put the situation to right, the Commissioners argued for comprehensive factory agreements, the formalization of industrial relations procedures, and the proper integration of shop stewards into the revamped machinery of collective bargaining. The remaining details need not concern us now.

The point to stress is that the Donovan Commission was a crucial turning-point in the development of the subject. It took as its basic problematic the connections between industrial relations and economic performance, and argued for an extensive programme of institutional reforms to help promote industrial productivity and competitiveness. But at no point did it attempt to unravel the complex causal connections. There is no doubt that the leading scholars and practitioners believed there were crucial connections. But the linkages were assumed rather than demonstrated, thought to be too obvious to warrant further investigation.

Such weaknesses were evident at the time. Turner (1968) spoke of the Commission's ignorance of economics, and Crossley (1968) lamented the poverty of the historicist method which underpinned the Donovan Report, while Reid (1968), in an important but sadly neglected paper, took issue with its central thesis. In his view the origins of workplace disorder were to be traced to economic rather than institutional structures and constraints: disorder had become a feature of workplace relations, he argued, not because of the existence of the 'two systems' but because 'in the post-war conditions of the British economy no-one worried too much about disorderly pay structures' (1968: 306).

Reid's analysis of the roots of disorder was suggestive rather than decisive: it pointed to the need for further investigation into the connections between workplace relations and the wider set of economic and social structures that were propelling Britain along the path of a low wage, low productivity, and low skill economy. But his argument failed to redirect the focus of debate. In the years that followed researchers in industrial relations failed to construct a research agenda that was sufficiently broad to allow for the generation of major insights into the complex connections between industrial relations and economic development.

Thus it was that this critically important terrain of analysis became the province of economics. When the Government in 1979 set about the task of promoting a revival of domestic industry by waging an offensive against trade unions, there was no developed body of theory or empirical evidence to counterbalance the perspective from economics. The result, not immediately obvious but now plainly so, was that academic industrial relations had allowed itself to become marginal to the key debates about the role of unions and workplace industrial relations in the developing underperformance of the British economy.

Lessons from Abroad

The conventional wisdom may be deeply entrenched, but it is a poor guide to past and present developments in the British economy. Since 1979 union membership has halved, and the role of collective bargaining in the determination of employees' pay and conditions has been severely curtailed, yet the symptoms of weakness which characterized earlier phases of domestic industrial development have endured. Manufacturing output and investment have been stagnant, despite the gains in profitability achieved in the 1980s, and the

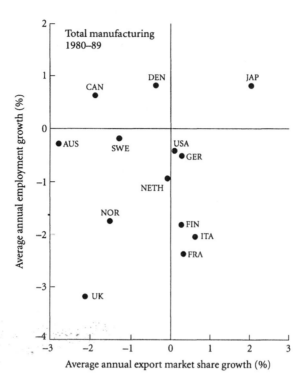

Fig. 5.2.

data continue to confirm previous adverse trends in Britain's international trading position (House of Commons 1994). Fig. 5.2, which compares the growth of exports and employment in the advanced economies in the 1980s, confirms the relative underperformance of UK manufacturing. While such evidence does not, in and of itself, decisively refute the commonplace allegations about unions' deleterious economic effects, it is indicative of a more complex set of connections between labour–market institutions, workplace behaviour, and performance outcomes. Can the elements of a more adequate theorization be derived from research on unions and economic performance in other countries?

Two perspectives are pertinent in this context. The first derives from the work of American economists at Harvard University, particularly Freeman and Medoff (1979 and 1984), which has attempted to empirically investigate the effects of unions in production. Why is it, they ask, that unionized firms in the United States, which typically pay a wage premium to their workers, none the less appear able to compete with their low wage, non-unionized counterparts?

Reviving the insights of an earlier generation of institutional economists (e.g. Slichter *et al.* 1960), the Harvard studies highlight two faces of unionism:

the monopoly face uniquely stressed by the orthodoxy and a positive face associated with the institution of collective voice. 'Voice' and 'exit' are counterposed as alternative methods of conflict resolution. 'Exit' implies a decision by disaffected workers to quit and seek alternative employment, whereas 'voice' describes the efforts by incumbent workers to secure material improvements in their terms and conditions by organizing and mobilizing within the workplace. The Harvard economists argue that unions are a necessary precondition for effective voice for two reasons. First, unions are said to reduce the risk of management reprisals against workplace activists. Secondly, by socializing the costs and benefits of collective action, unions limit the scope for free-riders and thus help create a more united and motivated workforce. One consequence may be reduced levels of labour turnover and absenteeism. Another may be increased internal flexibilities and higher levels of productivity.

In addition, the Harvard research suggests that unions may spur management into organizing production more efficiently. In non-unionized enterprises, there is a tendency for actual and feasible production levels to diverge because it is possible for such firms to compete on the basis of lower wage costs. By striving to close off this option unions serve as a disciplinary force within the enterprise in an analogous way to the effects of inter-firm competition. Empirical support for the above claims is provided in a series of industry, sector, and company level studies which show that unionized enterprises on average tend to have lower rates of turnover and absenteeism, and higher levels of productivity, than their non-unionized counterparts (see Freeman and Medoff 1984).

Such results have been strongly contested by defenders of the conventional wisdom (e.g. Addison 1985). Said to be flawed theoretically and empirically, the Harvard research has been attacked for failing to explain why firms in the absence of unions fail to operate at peak efficiency; for ripping unions from context and treating them as an independent positive force for productivity rather than one element in a more complex, simultaneously determined system; and for major sins of omission in respect of the collection of adequate time series and cross-section data. Some of these criticisms have force, to be sure, but they must be seen in context. The tradition of detailed empirical research on workplace unionism in the United States had waned by the early 1960s, only to be replaced by the formalistic and arid theorizing of neo-classical economics which, as indicated, sees unionism as an unwelcome departure from the ideal of competitive equilibrium. The motivation for the Harvard studies is different: labour-market institutions are treated not as imperfections but as historically forged social entities whose effects in the economy should be analysed in their own right.

A similar orientation is evident in the institutional–sociological research on unions which arguably has succeeded rather better than the Harvard studies in conceptualizing their social practices as but one of a number of social, economic, and technological forces in production. Streeck's work is a paradigm case (e.g. Streeck 1991). Issues of power and conflict are allowed to surface, as are detailed questions about the social purpose and dynamic effects of rules, hierarchies, and other institutional constraints on management.

Streeck's research focuses on the institutional conditions of the relatively successful West German manufacturing system. Inverting the logic of economic theory, Streeck argues that the high quality, high value added production system—what he calls 'diversified quality production'—emerged precisely because of the existence of powerful and binding 'institutional constraints'. Especially significant, he argues, was the presence of strong trade unions with the organizational capacities to force companies to pursue a strategy of continuous modernization and improvement. Other vital ingredients which he lists include: a system of 'rigid' wage determination, which forced employers to 'adapt their product range to non price competitive product markets capable of sustaining a high wage level'; a legally enforceable system of employment protection that promotes internal flexibilities and a commitment to invest in training and retraining; and 'a set of binding rules' compelling employers to consult with their employees 'and seek their consent above and beyond what many or most would on their own find expedient' (Streeck 1991).

As indicated, exponents of the conventional wisdom would instinctively condemn such rules as a fetter on economic efficiency. Streeck, by contrast, argues that their net effect has been to induce 'a virtuous circle of upmarket industrial restructuring'. By blocking quick-fix solutions and inefficient, low wages routes to profitability, this framework of rules and institutions has 'forced, induced and enabled' managements to pursue more imaginative production and employment strategies.

5. Historical Case Studies

Recent historical case study research for Britain exposes a similarly dense and complex interplay of social, economic, and technological relationships in production. Crucially, for the present argument, what emerges from such studies is a far richer understanding of the ways in which the pattern of industrial restructuring and the outcomes of production are shaped by shifting structures of power and the politics of cooperation, conflict, and compliance in the workplace.

Consider first the case of the Lancashire cotton spinning industry, which experienced rapid decline in the last quarter of the nineteenth century in the face of the superior competitive challenge from American producers located in the New England district. Lazonick, the American business historian, has shown that American cotton textile companies were spurred by a configuration of tight labour-markets, high wages, and industrial concentration to innovate and produce with the latest 'ring spinning' machines. Lancashire cotton firms, however, struck compromises with the accommodating mule spinners' craft union to increase work effort and lower unit costs on existing machines by following the practice of 'bad spinning', that is using low grade but cheaper counts of yarn. The deal effectively sealed the long-term fate of the British industry (Lazonick 1981).

According to Lazonick, efforts by the skilled textile workers to maintain their relatively privileged position in the hierarchical division of labour led them to agree to an intensification in the pace of work, as well as a reduction in the quality and cost of inputs. But by making existing machines more cost-effective in the short run, the mule spinners removed the incentive and pressure on employers to innovate.

In the British coal industry, three decades later, colliery owners achieved a decisive victory over the highly fragmented Federated Miners' Union of Great Britain. The conflict, which culminated in the General Strike of 1926, had been precipitated by wage cuts and work intensification as ailing colliery companies sought to cut costs in order to compete in international markets with coal producers from Germany and elsewhere.

With the union in disarray, and with the threat of increased foreign competition, the colliery owners had both the power and incentive to moder-nize methods of production. Instead, they opted to take advantage of their situation by further degrading wages and working conditions. Productivity and profitability levels were thus lifted in the short run through pay cuts and enforced extensions in the working day, while investment in new methods and machinery stagnated. By 1938, as a result, mechanized coal cutting accounted for only 55 per cent of output in Britain, as compared with 97 per cent in Germany, 98 per cent in Belgium, and 88 per cent in France (Fine, O'Donnell, and Prevezer 1985). By 1945 the industry had become moribund.

Both studies highlight the limitations of short-term, quick-fix strategies to boost productivity and profitability. Moreover both studies confound com-mon-sense views about the universal desirability of worker cooperation or compliance in production. In textiles, investment in new methods was post-poned not out of fear of resistance from a hostile union, but because the dominant craft union cooperated with management in raising the short-term competitiveness of existing methods. In the coal-mines, a defeated and demoralized labour force was unable to prevent opportunistic colliery owners from raising profits and productivity while eschewing investment in the new mechanized mining techniques commonly deployed elsewhere.

Moving forward three decades, to the years in which union power allegedly reached intolerable levels and Britain's strike-torn car industry was rarely out of the news, contemporary research exposed a strong, 'clear but inverse connection between striker days and production' (Turner, Clack, and Roberts 1967). Turner and his colleagues claimed their findings provided clear evidence that management had used strikes as a way of regulating output in an industry subject to acute seasonal shifts in demand. Re-examining the evidence some twenty years later, Tolliday noted that the 'interruptions of production due to disputes do not seem to have had very serious effects on car makers' performance' (Tolliday, n.d.). 'By the 1960s the . . . manufacturers' main problem was not inadequate volumes of production but being able to sell the cars they made at a profit and "beneficial strikes" could avoid the pile-up of unsaleable cars.' On the question of the impact of workers' job controls on productivity, he concluded that 'under piecework the pace and intensity of work were generally high'. But the low levels of pay in the industry 'made it less attractive' for the manufacturers 'to invest in capital intensive methods' (Tolliday n.d.). The eventual consequence was technical stagnation in the industry.

6. Performance and the 'Old' Industrial Relations

Of course it would be quite misleading to suggest that the case study evidence for the cotton, coal, and car industries is sufficient to clinch the argument. There may well be compelling evidence for other industries which points, on balance, in favour of the view that employers in Britain had been seriously hamstrung by workers' job controls in production. This is the more common perception to be sure, and it is one shared by commentators of differing political hues.

Indeed one of the clearest expressions of this position is provided by Kilpatrick and Lawson (1980), two economists writing from a position some considerable way to the left of orthodoxy. Concluding that workers in Britain were better placed than their overseas counterparts to resist cost-cutting changes in production, Kilpatrick and Lawson identify three distinctive features of British industrial relations—what we might for present purposes call the 'old' system—which militated against the construction of a more dynamic domestic industrial base.

First, the early acceptance of the principles of collective organization before the turn of the twentieth century facilitated the 'growth of real power by workers to resist changes and to defend standards . . . [particularly craft] customs and norms which existed before the introduction of mass production techniques' (1980: 87). Second, in contrast to the autonomous unions of Spain, Italy, and Germany for example, British unions were not subject to political repression by an authoritarian state. Third, Britain's decentralized structures of collective bargaining enabled work-groups to exert leverage precisely at the points at which their power was concentrated. In consequence, they were able to delay 'the adoption and diffusion of new techniques and [lift] staffing levels above what they would otherwise have been' (1980: 86).

Kilpatrick and Lawson, it should be stressed, do not condemn workers and their unions for adopting a defensive posture towards production reorganization. Workers' resistance to change, in their view, is an expression of their subordinate and insecure position within the workplace. Nor, moreover, do they blame management for failing to eliminate outmoded practices in production. The 'conciliatory' stance of employers towards established custom and practice reflected Britain's peculiar structural position in the international economy. In particular, according to Kilpatrick and Lawson, 'the existence of formal and informal imperial markets' gave domestic firms easy access to semi-captive markets and thus 'reduced the necessity for prolonged confrontation with workers over the restructuring of work (1980: 89). While such insights are a welcome corrective to the more common search in the literature for a scapegoat for Britain's industrial weaknesses, there are problems with the argument none the less.

First, as Hyman and Elger (1981) observed, it tends to over-romanticize the strength of workgroup power and resistance. Hyman and Elger mobilized evidence from four industries (steel, railways, cars, and print) to show that, at decisive moments, unions capitulated to offers of enhanced pay in return for concessions over staffing levels, work organization, and technology. Second, the evidence adduced by Kilpatrick and Lawson to support their case, for example Lazonick, is not always consistent with their emphasis on workers' blocking power. Lazonick, as noted above, showed how technological innovation was inhibited by a historical compromise between craft union and bosses to increase the pace of work and cut costs on existing machines. Third, as Coates (1994) notes, there is a lack of attention in their analysis to the details of the ebb and flow of trade union power. Is it really plausible, Coates asks, to suggest that unions offered such effective resistance after the employers' offensive against trade union rights in the 1890s? Would the organizational capacities of unions at workplace level have survived the force of mass unemployment in the inter-war years? If not, was their strength such in the aftermath of the Second World War that they could be held to account for the sluggish performance of the 1950s?

This question is addressed directly in a recent study of the impact of workers' job controls in production in the 1950s by Tiratsoo and Tomlinson (1994). Their work reviews the contemporary academic literature and the results of hitherto neglected findings from three surveys by the British Employers' Confederation on behalf of the NJAC. The academic reports include those by Zweig (1951), Andrews and Brunner (1950), and Carter and Williams (1957).

Zweig examined five sectors (cotton, engineering, iron and steel, printing, and civil engineering) and aimed to discover whether or not managers felt that they had been prevented from lifting productivity by the restrictive controls of trade unions. He found evidence of such restrictionism in the printing industry but not elsewhere. Moreover, as Tiratsoo and Tomlinson note, Zweig was careful to 'record his belief that the overall position was gradually improving' (1994: 70). Similar conclusions were reached by Andrews and Brunner, who found no evidence of resistance by workers to the introduction of new machinery, and Carter and Williams (1957), who claimed that 'hindrances caused by labour . . . cannot be regarded as a major determinant of the speed of scientific advance . . . in the period 1945–1956'.

The surveys by the British Employers' Confederation are a particularly rich source of evidence. The final study carried out in 1957/8 was the most comprehensive. It embraced 112 industries and sought to partition them into three categories: those reporting that they had experienced no problems in regard to the efficient utilization of labour; those that had set up machinery to deal with such problems; and those that had not yet succeeded in tackling the issue. On the basis of the responses received, the NJAC determined that sixty-four industries fell into the first category, forty-two into the second, and only six in the third. The NJAC reported that the majority of industries 'were meeting no real difficulty in their effort to ensure that manpower [sic] was efficiently used'.

Tiratsoo and Tomlinson are careful to note that it may have been in the interests of senior management in the industries concerned to report that they were firmly in control of the organization of work. Yet, as the authors stress, 'it is reasonable to believe that when employers spoke of restrictive practices in the 1940s and 1950s, they knew what they were talking about. After all, it was they who had to deal with the problem from day to day' (1994: 78). Furthermore, the open-ended nature of the questions posed to the employers in the surveys under consideration were, as Tiratsoo and Tomlinson suggest, more rather than less likely to elicit evidence of adverse labour practices if they had in fact existed.

Put together with other recent surveys of the relevant evidence for the post-war period (see Nichols 1986; Noland and O'Donnell 1995), these results are suggestive of a far more accommodating and flexible trade union movement and labour force than supporters of orthodoxy would care to concede. There are also strong theoretical reasons for questioning the conventional wisdom.

Attempts to explain domestic underperformance with reference to the structural characteristics of Britain's old system of industrial relations, and more particularly trade union obstructionism, fail to make clear how, over the course of many years, highly fragmented and often fragile workplace-based union organizations were able to defy the forces of competition. At issue here is not whether institutions are able to modify and shape market pressures, for they most certainly are. But given that the coverage of unions was uneven, and that the strength of particular work-groups varied considerably, one might reasonably and logically anticipate that those firms with weak (or no) unions would have pushed through changes in production and outcompeted firms constrained by 'belligerent' unions. Competition should have had the effect of pushing back the frontiers of unionism, yet the record of union membership gains before and after 1945 exposes a more complex picture.

It is indicative, first and foremost, of the urgent need for a reappraisal of the conventional wisdom. Is the standard characterization of the old system, which is an essential reference point for contemporary analyses of the effects of the restructuring of industrial relations since 1979, securely based? The force of the above comments is that it is not. The standard characterization of the old system's material consequences for the development of the industry in Britain is at worst highly misleading, at best based on very little, if any, evidence at all. The historical record, moreover, indicates that previous attempts to analyse the effects of unions in production in abstraction from the wider forces of competition are inadequate. Yet such is the enduring influence of the systems' perspective, which treats industrial relations as a more or less autonomous set of social relations, that the development of a more integrated perspective must remain a long-term aspiration.

7. Back to the Future?

Strongly influenced by contemporary events in the car industry, the Donovan Commission, as noted above, argued for fundamental institutional reforms in the collective bargaining system. What it did not consider, however, was the deeper structural context in which the bargaining relationships of the day were fashioned. It thus failed to note that the car industry, in common with many other industries, was characterized by low wages. True, the Commissioners did note that capital–labour ratios were low, but they failed to forge a link between labour-intensive work methods, overmanning, and the existence of low wages. In short what they overlooked was the powerful presence in many branches of industry of high exit barriers for inefficient firms. Low wages, in effect, provided relief for those companies that sought to compete on the basis of outmoded techniques and effort intensive systems of work organization.

Following the election of Mrs Thatcher in 1979, the Government sought to escape from the past legacy of industrial failure by eroding unions and other regulatory mechanisms in the labour-market. What followed was a surge in manufacturing productivity and profit levels, but investment, as noted, stagnated. Economic commentators have had difficulty in accounting for this curious combination of events. Some, for example Crafts (1991), sought to blame the Government for failing to underwrite investment in people and technology. Others argued that the reform of industrial relations remained incomplete, and that union power had still not been comprehensively dismantled (Hanson and Mather, 1988). Both arguments lack a historical perspective.

For what we have witnessed is, in crucial respects, a rerun of the past. The incentives for businesses to seek competitive advantage by upgrading product, process, and labour force skills have been seriously undermined by policies which have entrenched inherited weaknesses in the labour-market and labour force of this country. Yet how, it might reasonably be asked, does this argument square with the evidence of rapid productivity growth in the 1980s, which after all formed the basis for the claim that there had been an industrial miracle?

The central issue here is the difference between short-term and long-term advances (Nolan 1989). The gains of the 1980s were not rooted in a fundamental structural transformation of the supply side conditions of production, but derive from three interlinked factors: labour shedding; incremental changes in production organization; and what some analysts have referred to as the 'fear' factor, the central idea being that the threefold increase in unemployment in the early 1980s made employees more likely to acquiesce to new and more intensive (but not necessarily more efficient) work routines. These three elements interacted to produce a series of step-by-step increases in productivity, rather than a fundamental and sustainable transformation of industrial performance.

Reviewing the evidence for Britain for the 1970s and early 1980s, Metcalf reported that there was little support for the Harvard proposition that unions are good for productivity. 'The weight of the evidence suggested that union presence is associated with lower labour productivity' (Metcalf 1989*b*). But more recent studies have contradicted his conclusion. Nickell, Wadhwani, and Wall (1989) and Wadhwani (1990) looked at the impact of unions on rates of productivity growth. Using data culled from the accounts of 124 manufacturing companies between 1972–86, they were able to track changes in productivity during the second half of the 1970s (a period of relative union strength) and the first half of the 1980s (a period of union weakness). Wadhwani found that unions in the 1970s, and the pro-union legislation of that period, did not discourage investment or inhibit productivity growth; while both studies noted that unionized firms in the first half of the 1980s experienced faster productivity growth than their non-unionized counterparts.

These results are open to different interpretations. Unionization and productivity growth may have been positively correlated in the first half of the 1980s, not because of unionization *per se* but because of other external forces. It is also possible, as the authors note, that the faster rates of growth were the product of the removal of obstacles to work reorganization. Perhaps wisely, Wadhwani, and Nickell *et al.*, concluded that 'there is no simple association between unionism and productivity growth . . . Contrary to what is alleged, unions do not consistently reduce productivity growth' (Nickell *et al.* 1989: 21, 29). Indeed, according to Wadhwani, 'there is no evidence here for the view that unions reduce productivity growth' (1990: 382).

The most recent evidence for the first half of the 1980s presents a similar picture. Machin and Wadhwani (1991) report a 'positive association between unionism and organizational change' for the period 1981–4. Organizational change is defined as 'substantial changes in work organization or work practices not involving new plant, machinery or equipment'. Their study focused on 721 private sector establishments of which 27.2 per cent had experienced some form of organizational change. Machin and Wadhwani interpreted their results in two ways. On the one hand, the higher incidence of change in unionized establishments may have reflected the removal of restrictions on managerial discretion. On the other hand, it is possible that union voice effects, by improving communications in the workplace, may have encouraged organizational change. Noting that there is evidence for both explanations the authors 'incline towards the view that *both* the above channels combine to give us a positive association between unionism and organizational change' (1991: 852).

8. Conclusions

The evidence for the period since 1979, like the findings for the 1950s highlighted above, does not conclusively show that the orthodox case is wholly without substance, but it does go some way towards undermining the cosy consensus behind the conventional wisdom. The Thatcher Governments sought to engineer a major restructuring of industrial relations, and such has been the impact of these policies that it has become increasingly commonplace to refer to the emergence of a new industrial relations system in Britain.

Attempts to theoretically and empirically substantiate the dichotomy between the old and new invariably make reference to the material outcomes of the two systems. What has been argued above is that the conceptualization of the old is not securely rooted. The search for substantive evidence connecting workplace behaviour and institutions with the ailing performance of British-based industry in the post-war period yields few positive leads. Indeed, it is hard to escape the conclusion that the conventional wisdom, which is so crucial to recent attempts to posit a structural break in the character and outcomes of industrial relations, is based more on prejudice than hard evidence. It has been argued, moreover, that the policies of the 1980s have served to consolidate, rather than eliminate, the sources of underperformance by reinforcing the pressures on firms to compete on the basis of low wage, low skill, and effort-intensive systems of production.

REFERENCES

Addison, J. (1985), 'What Do Unions Really Do?', *Journal of Labor Research*, 6/2: 127–46.

Andrews, P. W. S., and Brunner, E. (1950), 'Productivity and the Business Man', *Oxford Economic Papers*, 2: 197–225.

Archibugi, D., and Michie, J. (1995), 'Science and Technology, R & D and Innovation', in D. Coates (ed.), *Economic and Industrial Performance in Europe* (Aldershot: Edward Elgar), 153–201.

Ark, B. van (1990), 'Comparative Levels of Manufacturing Productivity in Postwar Europe: Measurement and Comparisons', *Oxford Bulletin of Economics and Statistics*.

——— (1992), 'Comparative Productivity in British and American Manufacturing', *National Institute Economic Review* (Nov.), 63–74.

Broadberry, S., and Crafts, N. (1990), 'Explaining Anglo-American Productivity Differences in the Mid-Twentieth Century', *Oxford Bulletin of Economics and Statistics*, 52/4: 375–402.

Carter, C. F., and Williams, B. R. (1957), *Industry and Technical Progress*.

Clegg, H. (1964), 'Restrictive Practices', *Socialist Commentary*, cited in *Productivity Bargaining and Restrictive Labour Practices* (Research Paper, 4, Royal Commission on Trade Unions and Employers' Association; London: HMSO, 1968).

Coates, D. (1994), *The Question of UK Decline: The Economy, State and Society* (Brighton: Harvester Wheatsheaf).

Commons, J. R. (1904), 'Trade Union Regulation and Restriction of Output', *Eleventh Special Report of US Commissioner of Labor.*

Crafts, N. (1988), 'The Assessment: British Economic Growth Over the Long Run', *Oxford Review of Economic Policy*, 4/1: i–xxi.

——— (1991), 'Reversing Relative Economic Decline? The 1980s in Historical Perspective', *Oxford Review of Economic Policy*, 7/3: 81–98.

Crossley, J. R. (1968), 'The Donovan Report: A Case Study in the Poverty of Historicism', *British Journal of Industrial Relations*, 6/3: 296–302.

Darby, J., and Wren-Lewis, S. (1988), 'Trends in Manufacturing Labour Productivity', (National Institute of Economic and Social Research Discussion Paper, 145).

Fine, B., O'Donnell, K., and Prevezer, M. (1985), 'Coal Before Nationalisation', in B. Fine and L. Harris (eds.), *The Peculiarities of the British Economy* (London: Lawrence & Wishart).

Finegold, D., and Soskice, D. (1988), 'The Failure of Training in Britain: Analysis and Pescription', *Oxford Review of Economic Policy*, 4/3: 21–53.

Freeman, R. B., and Medoff, H. (1979), 'The Two Faces of Unionism', *Public Interest*, 57: 69–93.

——— ——— (1984), *What Do Unions Do?* (New York: Basic Books).

Hayek, F. (1980), *Unemployment and the Unions* (London: Institute of Economic Affairs).

House of Lords (1985), *Report from the Select Committee on Overseas Trade* (London: HMSO).

Hyman, R., and Elger, T. (1981) 'Job Controls, the Employers' Offensive and Alternative Strategies', *Capital & Class*, 15: 115–49.

Kilpatrick, A., and Lawson, T. (1980), 'On the Nature of Industrial Decline in the UK', *Cambridge Journal of Economics*, 4/1: 85–102.

Landes, D. (1986), 'What Do Bosses Really Do?', *Journal of Economic History*, 46: 585–623.

Lazonick, W. (1981), 'Production Relations, Labor Productivity and Choice of Technique', *Journal of Economic History*, 41: 491–516.

Machin, S., and Wadhwani, S. (1991), 'The Effects of Unions on Organisational Change and Employment', *Economic Journal*, 101/3: 835–54.

Mason, G., van Ark, B., and Wagner, K. (1994), 'Productivity, Product Quality and Workforce Skills: Food Processing in Four European Countries', *National Institute Economic Review*, 147: 62–83.

Mathewson, S. B. (1930), *Restriction of Output among Unorganised Workers* (New York: Viking Press).

Maynard, G. (1988), *The Economy under Mrs Thatcher* (Oxford: Blackwell).

Metcalf, D. (1989a), 'Water Notes Dry Up: The Impact of the Donovan Proposals and Thatcherism at Work on Labour Productivity in British Manufacturing Industry', *British Journal of Industrial Relations*, 27/1: 1–31.

——— (1989b), 'Trade Unions and Economic Performance: The British Evidence', *LSE Quarterly*, 3: 21–42.

Muellbauer, J. (1986), 'The Assessment: Productivity and Competitiveness in British Manufacturing', *Oxford Review of Economic Policy*, 2/3: 1–25.

Nichols, T. (1986), *The British Worker Question: A New Look at Workers and Productivity in Manufacturing* (London: Routledge & Kegan Paul).

Nickell, S., Wadhwani, S., and Wall, M. (1989), 'Unions and Productivity Growth in Britain 1974–86: Evidence From Company Accounts Data' (Centre for Labour Economics Discussion Paper, 353 (Aug.); London School of Economics).

Nolan, P. (1989a), 'The Productivity Miracle?', in F. Green (ed.), *The Restructuring of the UK Economy* (Brighton: Harvester), 101–121.

——— (1989b), 'Walking on Water? Performance and Industrial Relations Under Thatcher', *Industrial Relations Journal*, 20/2: 81–92.

——— and Marginson, P. (1990), 'Skating on Thin Ice? David Metcalf on Trade Unions and Productivity', *British Journal of Industrial Relations*, 28/2: 227–47.

——— and O'Donnell, K. (1995), 'Industrial Relations and Productivity', in P. K. Edwards, (ed.), *Industrial Relations: Theory and Practice in Britain* (Oxford: Blackwell), 397–433.

Porter, M. (1990), *The Competitive Advantage of Nations* (London: Macmillan).

Rees, A. (1963), 'The Effects of Unions on Resource Allocation', *Journal of Law and Economics*, 6/2: 69–78.

Reid, G. (1968), 'Economic Comment on the Donovan Report', *British Journal of Industrial Relations*, 6/3: 303–15.

Slichter, S. H., Healy, J. J., and Livernash, E. R. (1960), *The Impact of Collective Bargaining on Management* (Washington: Brookings Institution).

Steedman, H., and Wagner, K. (1987), 'A Second Look at Productivity and Skills in Britain and Germany', *National Institute Economic Review*, 122: 84–95.

——— ——— (1989), 'Productivity, Machinery and Skills: Clothing Manufacture in Britain and Germany', *National Institute Economic Review*, 128: 40–57.

Stoneman, P., and Francis, N. (1992), 'Double Deflation and the Measurement of Productivity in UK Manufacturing 1979–1989' (Warwick Business School Discussion Paper).

Streeck, W. (1991), 'On the Institutional Conditions of Diversified Quality Production', in E. Matzner and W. Streeck, *Beyond Keynesianism: The Socio-Economics of Production and Full Employment* (Brighton: Edward Elgar).

Tiratsoo, N., and Tomlinson, J. (1994), 'Restrictive Practices on the Shopfloor in Britain, 1945–1960: Myth and Reality', *Business History*, 36/2: 65–84.

Tolliday, S. (n.d.), 'High Tide and After: Coventry Engineering Workers and Shopfloor Bargaining, 1945–1980', in B. Lancaster and T. Mason (eds.), *Life and Labour in a 20th Century City: The Experience of Coventry* (Coventry: Cryfield Press), 204–43.

Turner, H. A. (1969), 'The Donovan Report', *Economic Journal*, 79/1: 1–10.

——— Clack, G., and Roberts, G. (1967), *Labour Relations in the Motor Industry: A Study of Industrial Unrest and an International Comparison* (London: Allen & Unwin).

Wadhwani, S. (1990), 'The Effects of Unions on Productivity Growth, Investment and Employment: A Report on Some Recent Work', *British Journal of Industrial Relations*, 28/3: 371–85.

Wells, J. (1989), 'Uneven Development and Deindustrialisation in the UK since 1979', in F. Green (ed.), *The Restructuring of the UK Economy* (Brighton: Wheatsheaf).

Williamson, O. (1980), 'The Organisation of Work', *Journal of Economic Behavior and Organisations*, 1/1: 5–22.

Zweig, F. (1951), *Productivity and Trade Unions* (Oxford).

6

PUBLIC SECTOR INDUSTRIAL RELATIONS

Rachel Bailey

1. Introduction

In recent years organizational change in the public sector has been unprecedented in its scope and speed of introduction. It has not only focused on alternative methods of service delivery, but has put industrial relations firmly in the spotlight, both as a necessary partner in service reforms, and as a focus for reform in its own right. The changes have all affected the way in which the employment relationship in the public sector is managed, both at the collective and individual levels. How this relationship has been affected, and with what actual and potential consequences provide the two main themes of this chapter. What has been the rationale for the changes which have occurred over the last decade or so, and do they reflect a substantial shift in what is considered important in the employment relationship by public sector managers, unions, and employees?

In seeking to answer these questions, we concentrate on the most important developments of the 1980s and 1990s, analysing different aspects of the management of industrial relations. Section 3 focuses on the collective, formal organization of industrial relations, with particular reference to pay determination mechanisms. In Section 4, a partial assessment of these arrangements is given by looking at two key industrial relations outcomes, pay and strikes. We then look at some of the main tools used in the management of human resources, such as pay and grading structures (Section 5), to understand what is happening to the employment relationship at the individual level. Throughout, it should be borne in mind that where changes are noted, they should not be viewed as departures from some neat model of the 'old' public sector employment relationship. The sector is not, and has never been, homogeneous in terms of its industrial relations, with each service or industry

The author would like to thank the editor of the *British Journal of Industrial Relations* for their kind permission to use some of the material from Bailey (1994).

developing its own characteristics at its own pace. But over time certain general features have prevailed, and it is departures from these which are of concern here. No attempt is made to compare what is new in public sector industrial relations with its private sector equivalents. Before turning to the first of these topics, a brief overview of the sector is given, in terms of its chief employment characteristics.

2. The British Public Sector

Employment

The employment data given in Table 6.1 point to several conclusions about public sector employment. Figures for 1979 are included by way of comparison, and while together they point to an overall picture of considerable decline, they do not by any means support the impression often given of a sector axed to the bone. Figures for 1992 are given in detail, but public sector employment has continued to show a considerable stability on into the mid-1990s, with at least half of the decline in the public sector workforce of 0.5 m between 1993 and 1994 being due to reclassifications of data (arising mainly from service reorganizations), a notional rather than real cut in employment, (Central Statistical Office 1995).

While the privatization of certain nationalized industries clearly took its toll on aggregate public sector numbers, it must be recognized that much of this decline was due to the reclassification of some industries and utilities, rather than to a real fall in employment. If these areas are excluded from the calculations, public sector employment has remained broadly constant since its heyday of the late 1970s. Furthermore, some categories of public sector employment have actually expanded. The police have seen a steady increase in numbers throughout the period, as have other local government groups. For example, employment in the social services has increased by about one-third. While the overall numbers of local government clerical and manual staff have remained broadly constant at 0.8 m. over the period, there has been a sizeable increase in white-collar employment within this: the proportion of non-manual to manual local government employees rose by 13 percentage points between 1979 and 1992, from 37 per cent to 50 per cent. In part this was due to the contracting-out of local authority services where manual employment had been high, such as refuse collection.

The figures for central government also reveal mixed developments. Civil service statistics for 1992 indicate an overall decline in numbers employed by government departments (excluding the industrial civil service) of just over one-fifth (23 per cent) to almost 0.6 m., but within that, employment in some departments has soared. For example, Home Office numbers have increased by 57 per cent. Casting off 0.3 m. civil servants to executive agencies has also done

Table 6.1. Public sector employment 1979–1992

	1979 (millions)	1992 (millions)	% change
Total public sector employment	7.4	5.8	−22[a]
Nationalized industries and public corporations	1.8	0.9	−50
Central government[b]	0.9	0.8	−11
NHS[c]	1.2	1.2	—
Local authorities[d]	1.3	1.3	—
Education[e]	1.5	1.4	−7
Police[f]	0.18	0.2	+11
Armed Forces[f]	0.31	0.29	−6

Source: Central Statistical Office (1993).

Note: All figures refer to headcount, and apply to mid-1992.

[a] Universities, polytechnics, Higher Education colleges, and grant-maintained schools are no longer classified in the National Accounts as part of the public sector. If numbers employed in these sectors are added to the total for 1992 to allow a more accurate comparison with 1979, the figure becomes 6.2 m., representing a decline of 16 per cent.

[b] Central government numbers exclude the NHS and the Armed Forces.

[c] Numbers for the NHS and for NHS Trusts are classified separately in the official figures, but have been combined here.

[d] Local authority numbers exclude the police and education. In both 1979 and 1992 about 0.8 m. were classified as 'other' employees, i.e. largely clerical and manual workers, and in 1992 there were 0.4 m. employed in social services, up from 0.3 m. in 1979, an increase of one-third.

[e] See note [a]. Separate figures for numbers employed in grant-maintained schools are not given, so the figure given here slightly exaggerates the decline in this sector. DFE figures for Jan. 1992 for England and Wales only indicate that of the 0.4 m. school teachers employed, about 7,000 were in grant-maintained schools.

[f] Most figures are rounded up to 1 d.p., except where so doing would imply no change in the numbers employed, as for the police and armed forces.

little to cause a real reduction in numbers. In its analysis of employment in the twenty-eight oldest agencies, the *Financial Times* (1993) highlighted a 12 per cent increase in staffing levels since their inception during 1988 and 1989.

It remains to be seen in which direction the extension of compulsory competitive tendering in local and central government, and in the NHS, will take the numbers. Applied since around the mid-1980s to a number of manual occupations such as refuse collection and NHS laundry and cleaning services, compulsory competitive tendering has now been extended to white-collar functions such as office services. In the past, where tenders have been won in-house, compulsory competitive tendering has been associated more with reduced earnings for those concerned than with job losses. In fact, in the short run the advent of a tendering process appears to increase white-collar employment, as extra numbers are taken on to manage it (e.g. in the Civil Service). However, the future is uncertain in terms of the impact of compulsory competitive tendering on public sector employment, as tendering procedures are in part on hold, due to the confusion surrounding Transfer of Undertakings (Protection of Employment) (TUPE) legislation of 1981. Where these regulations apply, the successful bidder for the service must take over the workforce on their existing terms and conditions. When TUPE, the British enactment of an EC Directive, first came into being, the Government confined its applicability to the private sector. But recent case law here and in the European court has overruled tis narrow definition. TUPE can now apply to the public sector, and although not every case has been won by the union presenting it, sufficient apprehension exists to stall private sector bids, and put on hold action by public sector managers.

The employment data put a question mark over one long-standing feature of public sector employment, namely relatively high levels of job security. At first sight, this does not appear to have been diluted to anywhere near the extent that some public sector unions would claim. While hard to quantify in financial terms, the benefits of job security were used by managers and the government in the past as arguments to justify relative pay differentials with the private sector. The employment numbers suggest that this may still be the case. But the existence of job security is not a given as it once was, and in the end it is likely that employee *perceptions* of insecurity over the longer term outweigh the facts, and may serve to damage workplace relations and performance as increasing levels of distrust emerge. Because recent proposals to cut numbers have focused as much on senior managerial levels as on lower organizational levels (e.g. the 1994 and 1995 central government Fundamental Expenditure Reviews), performance implications may be considerably greater than the actual numbers of employees suggest. Recent analysis of the industrial relations climate of 1990, using WIRS data, finds a worse climate in the public sector than in the private (Fernie and Metcalf 1993).

If this is so, this has implications for unions, but in which direction depends on the causes of those poor industrial relations. Are employees disillusioned more with employer–management behaviour, or with union inability to prevent some of the changes, or at least use them to employee advantage? Some unions clearly have been successful in altering government plans (e.g. in education), but not all. While union membership remains relatively strong, as the following subsection indicates, employee as well as management attitudes towards unions need to be borne in mind.

Public Sector Unions

The most important point to note here is the healthy state of public sector union density levels relative to those of the private sector. There are several sources of information on union membership across the economy as a whole (WIRS, the Labour Force Surveys, and the Certification Officer's returns), and a variety of methods for calculating density (see Kelly and Bailey 1990). But where separate figures for the public sector as a whole have been collated, they are not completely up to date, although they are sufficient to give a clear indication of the nature of public sector unionism.

The WIRS3 data on the public sector (which excludes coalmining from its sample) gives a density figure for workplaces with more than twenty-five employees of 72 per cent, down from 80 per cent in 1984. Waddington (1992)[1] calculates a figure of 82 per cent for 1987 (the latest year in his series), down from 84 per cent in 1979. Metcalf (1991) averages several other sources (1987–9) of public–private sector density to come up with an implied density split of 63 per cent and 28 per cent respectively. Recalculation of his results using the two additional sources alters the numbers only marginally.

As with the employment data, the aggregate public sector density figures hide considerable variation across different services. Data for 1992 show that railways retain the highest level of density at 90 per cent, largely unchanged over recent years, while hospitals have one of the lower rates at 60 per cent (Department for Education and Employment/Central Statistical Office 1993), still well above the private sector average. It remains to be seen whether the new public sector 'superunion' UNISON, created in July 1993 from the merger of NALGO, NUPE, and COHSE can increase some of the lower levels of density.

But the apparent rosiness of the picture may in part be cosmetic. Overall, Waddington notes that the decline in public sector union density between 1979 and 1987 was caused by a lower rate of membership increase compared with the increase in employment, and only one public sector union has bucked that trend spectacularly (the RCN has almost tripled its membership since the early 1980s, to hit 300,000 by the end of 1993, a density figure of 80 per cent amongst qualified nurses). So unions have failed to capitalize fully on the areas of employment growth noted earlier, and any increases appear to be at the expense of fellow unions.

We do not know why. Is it to do with ineffectual union organization, individual reluctance to belong to a union, or management policies which discourage membership? It is only in isolated cases that the government itself has taken direct steps to weaken or marginalize a union, as in the early 1980s with GCHQ's derecognition of the union, in the mid-1980s with the National Union of Miners, and in its recent attempts to dispute the legitimacy of the Prison Officers Association's union status. Management policies to offer employees individual contracts, often on more attractive terms, are likely to have something to do with it. Certainly, this last development will be true of a number of managers themselves, amongst whom union membership was previously high relative to their private sector counterparts, but who have been increasingly offered different terms of employment on individual bases (e.g. in the NHS).

This reflects a crucial shift in attitudes. As with the issue of job security, positive attitudes towards union membership by public sector management have been a long-standing feature of public sector employment. This may now be under threat. While national forms of pay determination remain in place,

---

[1] Waddington's 'Density B' measure is given here, which uses as its denominator all employees in employment, rather than the total workforce.

the impact of this trend may be muted, but if it continues or gathers pace as national arrangements start to come under fire, a system of industrial relations in which a central assumption has long been the existence of highly organized labour may face dramatic changes in the longer term.

The opportunities and constraints offered to unions by the different public sector pay determination mechanisms will also play an important role in shaping what happens to unions. We turn now to an analysis of those institutions and criteria used in setting the pay of five million public sector employees.

3. Public Sector Pay Determination

About three-quarters of public sector employees still have their pay and conditions determined by collective bargaining (Millward *et al.* 1992), while the rest are covered by some kind of third-party intervention, either in the form of independent review bodies or by indexation mechanisms. In other words almost the whole of the public sector is still covered by collective arrangements. But how has the nature of this collective approach changed? The following subsections discuss this issue first in the context of collective bargaining, and then in relation to other types of arrangements.

Collective Bargaining

Whitleyism   The greater part of collective bargaining arrangements in the public sector take the form of what has long been termed 'Whitleyism'. The general principles of Whitleyism, which takes its name from the chairman of a series of committees set up between 1917 and 1918 to look at ways of organizing post-war management–worker relations, are well known: they emphasized the need for negotiations between employer and employee representatives at a jointly agreed level; joint agreements between the two sides; and formal conciliation and arbitration procedures. In practice, over a number of decades this configuration resulted not only in national level processes, but also in pay and grading structures with national applicability to the occupational groups concerned.

By the time the successive Conservative Governments of the 1980s came to demand decentralization of bargaining, Whitleyism had become for unions (and some managers) all that was good and fair about public sector industrial relations. For government ministers and some senior public service managers (such as Eric Caines, former director of personnel in the NHS), Whitleyism does not allow pay to respond to service needs, leading in some cases to underpayment of employees, but (so runs the implication) to overpayment in many instances.

Such polarization muddies the waters, so much of this chapter aims to consider the arguments on both sides. As a starting-point, it is useful to look back briefly at the origins of Whitley almost eighty years ago. The authors of the several reports made a fundamental assumption that collective representation of workers and management was the most likely means by which the transition to peacetime production could be managed with maximum cooperation and minimum industrial action—a wholly pragmatic approach, rather than one based on value-driven principles, and one reinforced by the widespread strikes of 1917. In order to be effective, 'well-organized' industries were required, meaning those with high levels of employee collective organization. Whitley principles were thus intended to apply first to such industries as shipbuilding and engineering. Recommendations to extend them to State and municipal authorities came in a second report, which argued that State intervention was probably necessary to support their application until those sectors became well organized (Sheldrake 1988).

Union responses to Whitley in the years immediately following the First World War are interesting. Where strong unions already existed, for example in engineering and shipbuilding, there was opposition, based essentially on the view that too much cooperation with employers would weaken unions. But second-tier unions, such as those representing particular occupations rather than industries, saw Whitley as a route to greater influence. This is instructive in the light of the historical experience of some particularly powerful public sector unions such as the British Medical Association and in the 1980s the RCN, who have become strong advocates of alternatives to collective bargaining as the means by which pay and conditions are set (i.e. the review body system). The historical evidence suggests a paradox. Where unions are powerful enough to win the formal institutions and processes of collective bargaining in the first place, it may be that (other things being equal) these are in fact less advantageous to the exercising of that power than alternative industrial relations mechanisms.

The varied union responses of 1918–19 have been reflected subsequently in the coverage and nature of the Whitley principles across different parts of the public sector, which have developed at different rates and in different ways. For example, in the NHS they were more comprehensively entrenched in a series of Whitley Councils at an earlier stage than in the water industry, where it was only by the late 1970s that all the main Whitley features were in place (Ogden 1993)—less than a decade before privatization pressures caused some water authorities to pull out from the system, causing its total collapse. Thus not all sectors have experienced decade after decade of stability and consistency in the formal organization of industrial relations, with some more accustomed to change than others.

The Whitley debates raise the question of the kind of arrangements most likely to ensure that it is in unions' interest to cooperate in ongoing relations with management, and vice versa. The Whitley formula makes some heroic assumptions about the routes to cooperation, and the likely consequences of that cooperation. Analysis of the conditions under which cooperation evolves has been extensive in other disciplines (see e.g. Self 1993), but is less frequently applied to industrial relations. Metcalf (1989) makes a useful attempt to do so in his analysis of British productivity growth in the 1980s. Three general sets of conditions for cooperation are identified. First, relationships between specific individuals involved in the process should be frequent and lasting. Second, there should be a relatively small number of participants. The third set of factors refer to the nature of the 'game' or exchange between the parties: to what extent can it be enforced, how often is it to be repeated, to what extent do participants value present compared to future potential gain, and how great are the costs of non-cooperation?

Whitley recommendations were not analysed or formulated in this way, but it can be inferred from them that their authors intended close interaction between the two sides, and emphasized future benefits over short-term gain. For the Committee, the costs of non-cooperation were extreme: industrial relations anarchy. Instead, over time, Whitleyism would make participants better off (or at least they would believe themselves to be so) than under an alternative system, both financially and in relation to other employment conditions. But, as Section 4 indicates, this may not always be the case: indexation formulas and review bodies have been of considerable benefit to those covered.

The Committee's recognition of existing representative organizations, and its desire to encourage their development in other sectors of the economy, ignore the issue of the number of participants on each side. Either this was a pragmatic acceptance of reality at the time, or no thought was given to the fact that the greater the numbers involved in the bargaining game, the harder cooperation might be to achieve. It is noteworthy that where decentralization of bargaining has occurred in both the private and public sectors over the last decade or so, and where managers have had a choice, the number of unions recognized for bargaining purposes has been reduced.

This raises the question of the link between bargaining level and cooperation. Why should cooperation at national level foster cooperation locally, more than local management–union dialogue or direct management–employee relations? If one condition for cooperation is frequent and lasting interaction between participants, this is at least likely, if not more so, at local level.

But this point begs the question of 'cooperation in what'? The aim in 1918 had been to ensure that the transition to peacetime would allow the economy to grow, undisturbed by industrial action such that both sides gained from the resulting economic prosperity. Yet the transplantation of Whitleyism to what became the public sector diluted this objective. In part, this was inevitable, given the fact that in some parts of the public sector beneficial productivity gains are either hard to achieve, or do not allow the same kind of redistribution of 'economic rent' as in the private sector. But it is also the case that in some sectors it seems that cooperation became focused on maintaining the national level industrial relations status quo of Whitley pay determination arrangements. As studies of BR (Pendleton and Winterton 1993), the PO (Lucio 1993), and the Electricity Supply Industry (Messenger 1993) show, national bargaining bought peace in the 1960s and 1970s in part because of a mutually beneficial cosy relationship between managers and unions, which ignored the operating costs of their respective service, but gave both sides the terms and conditions of employment and industrial peace that were wanted.

Ironically, such consequences seem to be in the Whitley tradition of pragmatism. The Committee's reports had little to say, as we have seen, on fairness. Cooperation would occur because the system provided the incentives to participants to do so. This is a wholly logical approach, and flies in the face of some academic research in the field of social psychology (e.g. Cropanzano and Folger 1991) which indicates that a distinction should be made between processes and outcomes: if the former are considered to be fair, individuals will cooperate despite unfavourable outcomes. It is highly unlikely that any process producing consistently unfavourable results over time to one or more partici- pants would be labelled fair for long by the losers. This fact is borne out by the way in which initial cries of 'unfair' from some public sector unions in the context of the creation of review bodies for nurses, and subsequently for schoolteachers (see Table 6.2), faded rapidly as the alternative pay determina- tion process began to deliver the goods for their members.

It must, therefore, be the case that the perceived fairness of a given process and satisfaction with results are over time one and the same. A system that will engender long-term cooperation will be one that recognizes the power of participants, and gives them the opportunity to exercise it (or produce the same results as if they had exercised that power). The alternative will be conflict or compliance, each costly in its own way. If analysed in this way, the original Whitley formula was a recognition of a certain power distribution between employers and workers at a given point in time. That does not mean its assumptions were valid either across different sectors, or for different periods.

Why then did it endure for so long? Was it because alternative means of determining pay were considered too risky (i.e. potentially high gains, but also severe losses), since neither side could predict what action the other would otherwise take (the classic prisoners' dilemma). This was the situation in 1918. Or was it the case that as Whitleyism became entrenched in the public sector over the years, it embodied so strongly the conventional industrial relations wisdom that few thought to question its relative costs and benefits? Given that the dominant industrial model in the private sector in the 1970s was also one of centralized collective bargaining, the lack of an alternative role model may have reinforced this.

None of this is meant to imply that the Whitley system was without its critics before the Conservative Governments of the 1980s and 1990s. Its faults have been noted on previous occasions (e.g. McCarthy Committee on Whitleyism in the NHS, see McCarthy 1976). But remedies always focused on reform around the edges, tinkering with the situation rather than transforming it. Likewise, the option to pass on costs to the customer and taxpayer meant that there was little incentive to question the system from within. Governments had the incentive, but for political reasons did not act.

Whether the survival and extensive coverage of Whitley was a matter of rational self-interest by participants, or of tradition (and perhaps it was a blend of both, one shaping the other), for well over a decade now it has been questioned and doubted in an unprecedented manner by moves towards decentralization, and by moves away from collective bargaining. For the public sector at least, claims about the relative costs and benefits of the different forms of collective industrial relations have not yet been researched. Section 4 gives some pointers in this direction, but it must be recognized that at the moment no full evaluation of the various forms exists. First, however, the nature of the developments themselves is looked at.

Decentralization   While the private sector trend towards decentralized bargaining arrangements has not escaped the public sector, its incidence is for the moment relatively patchy, although the rate of coverage is beginning to increase, particularly in Executive Agencies and the NHS. Differential rates of progress are only to be expected, as the fragmentation of arrangements inherent in decentralization occurs. Opponents of the Government argue that this is because the rationale of decentralization is fundamentally flawed in the context of the public sector, and is now showing itself to be so. A more neutral stance might argue that it is simply too early to tell: the limited and irregular coverage of decentralized arrangements is as likely to be the result of the time needed to make such major changes. The following paragraphs summarize the extent to which employees have their pay and conditions determined at the level of their organizational unit (e.g. an NHS Trust, a school, a water company). Greater detail can be found in Bailey (1994) and Pendleton and Winterton (1993).

In central and local government, moves to link pay issues more closely to the level of financial responsibility gathered momentum in the late 1980s. In central government, large-scale change was triggered by the Government's 'Next Steps' report (Ibbs 1988) on the way in which the civil service was organized. It pointed to the incompatibility of a policy-oriented focus with the efficient management of service delivery, recommending the restructuring of civil service departments into a series of executive agencies to overcome this imbalance. By autumn 1993 about 60 per cent (350,000) of all non-industrial civil servants were employed by ninety-one agencies and a further sixty-four executive units and offices within Customs and Excise and the Inland Revenue.

Initially, most agencies established their own Whitley councils, with the Treasury retaining tight control of wage bills and pay structures, an indication that the decentralization of service delivery does not automatically mean that industrial relations issues are decentralized in any substantive way. But since 1990 the trend has been towards a greater degree of actual decentralization. The first agency to pull out from national bargaining and adopt its own pay and grading system was HMSO in 1990. A number of other agencies have followed suit, minimizing the role played by Whitley procedures and pay structures, but generally retaining collective bargaining, even if it runs in tandem with employee involvement techniques such as team briefings, and even if agency 'framework' documents refer only to 'consultation' with unions rather than negotiation.

Two developments during 1992 and 1993 have suggested that the retention of traditional industrial relations forms may be weakening. At the end of 1992 legislation on civil service management was enacted. The Civil Service (Management Functions) Act allows the Treasury and Cabinet Office to delegate their responsibility for setting civil servants' pay and conditions to the agencies. In part this simply reflects formalization of the existing situation, but it empowers agencies and departments to set a wider range of their staff's pay and conditions (IRRR 1993). However, the Treasury retains the right to alter conditions, and to revoke delegated authority, as well as maintaining overall budgetary control. In addition, agencies are now also subject to market-testing for some of their functions, and in some cases full-blown privatization is in the pipeline. In many instances, privatization has had a significant effect on industrial relations, but in a variety of ways (see below), so its consequences for parts of the civil service are as yet unclear.

Elsewhere in the public sector the numbers affected by decentralization are still relatively small. However, for the NHS, the evidence suggests that decentralization of industrial relations will extend in practice over the next few years as the organizational changes take root, and as government policy adds increasing pressure to Health Service managers to pursue decentralized pay determination (as seen in the half-way house achieved by the 1995 pay settlement). It was only in 1990 that the National Health Service and Community Care Act allowed hospitals to apply for Trust status, with subsequent 'waves' of applications to do so. This was in the context of the changeover to a service organized along purchaser–supplier (Health Authorities–hospitals) lines. With Trust status goes responsibility for the pay and conditions of all staff within each Trust. In practice relatively small numbers of Trusts have taken advantage of the opportunity to launch wholescale local pay bargaining and remuneration packages (see, for example, an IRS survey in April 1993 of thirty-three first- and second-wave Trusts (IRS 1993)). Trinder (1993) estimates that about 50,000 staff are covered by some form of local bargaining, less than 10 per cent of the NHS workforce eligible for such coverage. It should be noted, however, that all staff in post at the time of the transfer to Trust status are permitted to retain pre-Trust Whitley terms and conditions until Spring 1995, so long as they remain in the same job. Limited local measures by management may simply be a matter of time.

While the balance of the evidence still suggests a 'wait and see' approach to pay determination, it should be remembered that the NHS situation is complicated by the fact that currently over half of NHS staff (doctors, nurses, midwives, and other medical professions) have their pay determined by independent review at national level. These staff will not lightly accept any Trust refusal to honour the recommendations of this review process, although already in 1995 the RCM were prepared to deal separately with NHS management in trading off grading concessions for an element of local pay determination. Unlike most of the rest of the public sector, the process of decentralization in the NHS started with the brakes on.

The main features of developments in the Civil Service and the NHS highlighted above are in part repeated in the local government sector, and in particular local authority clerical and professional staff, and school teachers. The latter are discussed later, as their pay is set nationally by independent review, although they are employed by LEAs. The former, known as 'APT and C' staff (local government administrative, professional, technical, and clerical employees) have retained a broadly Whitley-based system.

Recent research (Jackson *et al.* 1993) calculated that only about thirty authorities had adopted local bargaining for their APT and C staff by the early 1990s—well under 10 per cent of all authorities in England and Wales. The vast majority of them were in South-East England, and they acted to meet vacancy rates of up to 35 per cent for certain categories of employee such as engineers and computer staff. While national agreements were only framework agreements beyond which authorities could apply some discretion in the use of pay scales, incremental points, and annual increases (upwards), this was inadequate in the South-East in terms of resolving relative pay problems. National bargaining had been ineffective, as most annual increases negotiated by NALGO tended to benefit their lower-paid members, rather than professionals. UNISON may face a similar problem of trying to get the best deals for very different categories of employee membership.

Amongst the privatized industries, and those next in line for privatization, the picture is somewhat different, with decentralized bargaining arrangements being in general more extensively developed. This raises the question of whether this is due simply to longer timescales: the pressures to decentralize have existed for longer in sectors such as steel, water, or BR than in health or education. Or is it due to the suitability of the particular sectors in terms of the transition to decentralized arrangements, and of their benefits? A full discussion of these issues is not possible here, but some brief points can be made.

First, a comparison of the history of industrial changes over the last two decades or so across the different sectors suggests that the ease with which changes occurred, and the extent to which a truly decentralized system operates is a function of the sector's financial or commercial status, and its industrial relations traditions or culture. For example, by the late 1970s and into the 1980s, BS faced an increasingly saturated world market, hampered by significant levels of underinvestment and by a government hostile to any State handouts to save the situation. Survival pressures and a history of relatively amicable industrial relations, with a tradition of workplace productivity deals negotiated locally, combined to facilitate the decentralization of industrial relations to product divisions. While national bargaining was not abolished until privatization in 1988, decentralized arrangements over working practices and bonuses were already well developed. Decentralized industrial relations can be as much a factor contributing to the benefits of privatization, as a consequence of it.

By way of contrast, developments in both BR and the PO (both candidates for privatization in the near future) have evolved in a much more tortured fashion, as financial pressures have taken longer to bite, as monopoly positions (for BR and for Royal Mail at least) have afforded some protection for both unions and management, and as unions have hung on for dear life to extensive job controls. It is worth noting that the entrenched nature of these in comparison to the relative flexibility of working practices in, say, steel has been in part a consequence of relatively poorer pay in BR and the PO. While bargaining has been decentralized to different functions (e.g. Royal Mail and Counter Services) within the two sectors, decentralization has not gone much lower than this, beyond local agreements on working practices already in existence for some years. Changes have occurred, and concessions have been won by management on working practices, but more so in divisions which are less liable to disruption from industrial conflict, such as the non-mail parts of the PO. The process has been more piecemeal than in steel or, for that matter, the utilities.

In the water industry, for example, certain authorities unilaterally broke away from the national agreement in the run-up to privatization (1989), causing the whole structure to collapse relatively quickly and individual water company arrangements to be made. This suggests a second factor which might predict the transition to decentralization: the quality and objectives of management. Again, a clear distinction can be drawn between, for example, the water industry and BR. In the former, chief executives were often recruited from the private sector to bring financial discipline to bear. By contrast, BR managers (usually long-service, dyed-in-the-wool BR employees) responded to pressures in the early 1980s by trying to improve the industrial relations status quo to give to a government hell-bent on privatization the impression of managing, rather than by actually tackling, some of the main issues (Pendleton 1993).

These few examples of decentralization of collective bargaining in the context of privatization suggest its public service counterparts will reflect great variation as they develop. Where service delivery pressures (e.g. financial survival needs vs. the need to maintain 'production') force action by management and unions, the transition may be smoother and faster. But in services such as health, the issues may not be so clear-cut, and developments will continue to be fragmented.

Conclusions   What conclusions can be drawn from the myriad decentralization processes described above? It was argued earlier that for reasons of self-interest and habit, no real alternative to Whitleyism with the potential to cover the majority of the public sector emerged until the early 1980s. Yet how different is the alternative of decentralized bargaining? The evidence to date suggests some continuity with the past. Where decentralization has occurred, it retains many Whitley features, and it should be remembered that the Whitley principles stated only that bargaining should be at an agreed level, with which representatives from both sides were content. But are its consequences different?

First, can decentralization be equated with weaker unions? There is no clear answer to this, as there are arguments in both directions. The fact that pressures to decentralize have forced both industrial relations managers and unions to reorganize may mean that on both sides there is both the need and the ability to justify respective existences, and this will itself sustain more traditional forms of collective organization, even if the outcomes are different.

It is also wrong to assume that because unionism is positively associated with workplace size any measures that reduce size through reorganization are likely to threaten union organization (Corby 1993). While this association is found in the private sector, it does not appear to hold for much of the public sector (WIRS3, see Millward *et al.* 1992), suggesting that continued unionization is in part also a function of organizational factors such as the type and quality of previous union organization and management attitudes towards union presence. It is only if these kinds of factors can be explained satisfactorily by workplace size that the reorganization threat holds.

But certain other factors point to a picture of considerable change, at least for inter-union relations. In the NHS, for example, as Buchan (1992) comments, UNISON creates an organization with the potential to represent all employees within an employing unit, thus raising the possibility of single union deals being struck. This could threaten with marginalization some of the smaller professional unions, such as the Royal College of Midwives, but does not automatically mean better wage and employment outcomes for UNISON.

Such developments could lead to a significant shift in the balance of power not only between the unions themselves, but between unions and management. From the management perspective, for example, the change in union composition in the NHS leads to the risk of pressure to bring the earnings of lower-paid Health Service workers closer to the levels of professional staff. Because of the bargaining power of some of these professional groups, such a move could then lead to the entire pay structure being shifted upwards. Decentralization could well lead to larger, not smaller, wage bills, unless funding is simply not available or a trade-off with employment is made.

The counter-argument to this lies with the substantive demands now being made of bargaining arrangements. These include changes in some of the key tools of the management of human resources, such as grading structures, and appraisal and reward systems, such as the introduction of performance-related pay, seen particularly in the agencies and local government, but also now in the NHS and education. A further discussion of these developments concludes this chapter, but it is important to note here that their introduction represents the main rationale for decentralization, in line with private sector developments.

In his review of decentralization developments in private sector bargaining in a number of countries, Katz (1993) assesses three different hypotheses which have been used to explain moves towards decentralization. First, it is argued that it represents the natural response of managers now that the balance of power lies with them: national bargaining, however organized, dilutes the control they want over their businesses. Second, the opportunity to reorganize work at operational level is hypothesized to be the key determinant of moves away from centralized arrangements. Finally, it is claimed that industrial relations arrangements have simply followed corporate restructurings which have favoured decentralized business units. Clearly, the three predictions are not mutually exclusive, but Katz finds that the evidence most strongly supports the second hypothesis. This would also seem to be true of the British public sector: service restructurings have provided the catalyst to review arrangements, and in many cases the balance of power appears now to lie with management, but where managers have pushed for local responsibility for employee pay and conditions it has been primarily with a view to obtaining benefits from reshaping these to fit local requirements.

Yet the benefits will not necessarily be solely for management. Katz also argues that the reason we have not yet seen a reversion to centralized arrangements once workplace changes are in place is because both sides gain from them. While it is too early to test this statement in the public sector, it seems highly plausible: the interdependence of unions, employees, and managers is much more apparent at local level, thus creating a much wider range of issues over which trade-offs can be made. Some evidence of this emerged in the context of the 1.5 per cent annual pay increase imposed by the Government for the 1993 pay round. For example, the average pay rise for about 25,000 middle-ranking civil servants was 3.5 per cent, yet the cost to the Treasury came in at 1.25 per cent, just below the 1.5 per cent ceiling. This was achieved by unions accepting that no automatic incremental increases would be given, and that performance-related increases would be awarded instead. While an imposed pay norm is not compatible with real decentralization, responses to it indicate that trade-offs even in the context of financial stringency can be of benefit to all. Where unions may suffer is where the trade-off is one of pay for jobs, rather than just changing the composition of rewards. Katz's arguments apply only to the survivors.

All-round benefits may also only occur where union–management relations deliver the goods. It is possible that managers will choose to deal direct with employees, particularly where some form of national bargaining remains, and their hands are partly tied. It may also be the case that direct contact facilitates organizational change. With regard to attempts in the PO to become more efficient, Lucio (1993) comments that if more attention had been paid to management–employee relations, rather than to formal arrangements, less hostility and demotivation might have occurred.

To conclude, decentralization may allow a return to one of the original Whitley aims, namely that cooperation between employers and employees should be channelled towards making the changes required to make everyone better off, and rewarded accordingly, rather than shying away from change. It may be that what is emerging keeps the best of both worlds, and that where decentralization has taken root, participants have avoided throwing out the baby with the bath water. But a similarly incremental response to service reforms may be less feasible where the collective organization of the employment relationship has little or nothing to do with formal collective bargaining arrangements, as the next subsection discusses.

Indexation and Independent Review

Despite the dominance of collective bargaining in the public sector, a surprisingly large minority of employees here have little or nothing to do with it in the setting of their pay. If the old nationalized industries and utilities are excluded, the pay of one-third of public sector employees is determined either by indexation or third-party review.

Over 200,000 employees have their annual increase determined by indexation. This allows automatic increases in line with the chosen index, while other terms and conditions remain the subject of collective bargaining. Police (since 1979) and firefighters (since 1977) are subject to this process. For the former, wage increases until 1994 were linked to the annual underlying increase in whole economy average earnings. In that year the index was changed, and one based on the median increase in private sector non-manual settlements is now used. Firefighters' pay is linked to the top quartile of male manual earnings.

For the remaining 1.4 m. employees not covered by collective bargaining, a system of independent, third-party reviews, known as review bodies, applies. To these, evidence supporting desirable pay settlements is presented by service managers, employee representatives, and the Treasury. Drawing on this, and their own evidence, review body members then make recommendations to the Prime Minister on the annual increase. While only accorded the status of advice, rather than a binding settlement, the recommendations have rarely been rejected outright, but awards are often staged throughout the year to meet expenditure constraints. Table 6.2 gives review body numbers.

The rationale for indexation and the review system has been slightly different in each case, but a common theme has been the perceived need to find arrangements appropriate for groups who voluntarily (some nurses and a minority of teachers) or by law (the armed forces, police) do not have the right to strike. In the cases of nurses, the review body was seen as a means of rewarding and encouraging the RCN's no-strike ruling (itself thrown into question during the 1995 pay round). The nurses' review body was seen very much as a victory for the RCN, with the two other unions, NUPE and COHSE, being strongly opposed to the loss of bargaining rights.

In contrast, the teachers' review body emerged from the Interim Advisory

Table 6.2. Public sector review bodies

Review body	Date of establishment	Nos. covered (1991 or 1992)
Doctors and dentists[a]	1962	121,000
Armed Forces[b]	1971	280,000
Top salaries[c]	1971	2,000
Nurses, midwives, and professions allied to medicine	1983	527,000 (wte)[d]
School teachers	1991	442,000 (wte)[e]

Sources: *Review Body Reports* 1993, HMSO: London.

Note: wte = whole-time equivalent, defined differently in different services.

[a] Doctors covered by the Doctors' and Dentists' Review Body number about 94,000, 60,000 of whom work in NHS hospitals. There are about 20,000 dentists.
[b] Armed Forces figures exclude the reserve army.
[c] Members of the judiciary constitute 61 per cent of the Top Salary groups, with senior civil servants amounting to 31 per cent.
[d] Of the figure given for nurses etc., 483,500 wte are nurses and midwives. The numbers refer to Sept. 1991.
[e] For teachers the numbers refer to Jan. 1992. Their review body followed four years of pay determination by an interim advisory committee (1987–91). Their situation is slightly different, in that the review body is a statutory body set up to fulfil the requirements of the 1991 School Teachers' Pay and Conditions Act, which include consultation with 'certain interested parties' (STRB 1993: para 2). Unlike the other review bodies, the STRB's remit is not limited only to pay: it also covers all conditions of service relating to teachers' professional duties, which permits some trade-off between pay increases and other elements of the wage bill.

Committee (1987–91) set up when bargaining rights were withdrawn by way of punishment for extensive industrial action in the mid-1980s. But whether through positive or negative reinforcement, indexation and review are intended to provide the means by which the client groups feel that they are getting a fair deal, and in return at least tacitly renounce the strike weapon.

Non-collective bargaining forms of pay determination have thus become much more visible and high profile since the late 1970s. Do they represent a real redefinition of how industrial relations is viewed in the public sector? From the fuss that COHSE and NUPE made in the early 1980s when the RCN was offered and accepted a review body for nurses (a similar response was made by some teacher unions in the mid-1980s), it would appear that they do—and to the disadvantage of unions and employees. Yet much about them suggests otherwise.

Their very existence clearly reflects the collective strength and degree of formal organization of the occupations concerned. No government can rely on the third party being a political poodle, and has to assume that the costs of making such a concession will not outweigh the gains. In practice, as Section 4 indicates, in some cases this hope has not been entirely fulfilled, as shown by earnings data.

These alternative systems maintain the 'old' industrial relations assumption that nationally determined aspects of public sector employment are not necessarily at odds with the local management of industrial relations. There is some truth in this. Managers can just as easily use indexation or review as a scapegoat for unpopular pay settlements as collective bargaining. It is also now the case that review bodies have begun in recent years to play a substantial role in reward policy development, affecting what happens locally. The 1993 STRB report, its second, contains detailed analysis and recommendations of changes in the pay scale for State school teachers, and in the range of incentive allowances available on individual bases.

The STRB recommendations are of a similar nature to the steps taken by the nurses' review body in 1988 to introduce a new pay and grading system for nurses. The RCN in particular had been pushing for this for many years, but had failed to achieve it through the collective bargaining process. It appears that a third party is able to take existing views and evidence on rewards and act on them in a way that the process of negotiation cannot so readily do, at least in the short term. How beneficial this is to the service in question is a separate issue, but it revives the notion that national level processes can at least take operational issues and run with them, refuting criticisms of remoteness.

Where indexation and review may differ in the approach to industrial relations which they represent is in the degree of cooperation they are able to elicit. Because of their status as an exchange for industrial peace, they have provided clear-cut actual, and therefore potentially ongoing, benefits for those covered. This keeps the parties tied in, even in the 'bad' years. For example, in the context of the 1.5 per cent imposed settlement for 1993, clearly incompatible with indexation and independent review, the union response was one of virtual quiescence. Most striking was the response of the firefighters. In order to preserve their valuable indexation link, they accepted an increase of 1.4 per cent—the amount dictated by the link with male manual earnings. Their action represents the highly unusual step of a union accepting a settlement below the offer, but a step that can be understood as taking a small short-term cost for longer-term gain.

The question then remains as to whether cooperation should be bought in such an explicit manner, and whether these alternative mechanisms result in greater rigidities in managing industrial relations than collective bargaining. The costs as well as the benefits of indexation and review need to be reassessed in the light of government statements on productivity. The police and firefighters are in effect at least in part benefiting from private sector productivity gains, without having to make their own. This is of course true of certain private sector groups too, and has historically been the case for much of the public sector. But in the context of the productivity criterion likely to apply to all public sector pay settlements in the foreseeable future, indexation affords these two groups a degree of protection now being withdrawn from many of their public sector colleagues.

It should be noted that this point assumes that the application of productivity criteria is feasible in the first place. While much more attention is now paid to such measures (e.g. via Audit Commission and National Audit reports, as well as within organizations themselves), there is much debate about how meaningful they can be in certain contexts, and how little they may say about quality versus quantity. In addition, there is the question of how changes in performance indicators, say, at service or unit level (e.g. school, hospital, Police Force) should translate into pay increases even if they do manage to capture qualitative improvements as well as quantitative ones. This issue is further complicated by the question of the level of pay settlements: do productivity gains have to be service-wide or at some lower level? Even where the impact of improvements can be quantified (e.g. an increased number of university students taught by the same number of lecturers) can such a change be costed, and the savings translated into pay increases? Difficult in itself, this assumes too that the funding would be made available to meet any savings made.

Review bodies have not tended to tackle the productivity question head-on, and still place great emphasis on ensuring that relative earnings with relevant private sector groups are 'fair', again giving some degree of protection, albeit in a weakened form. Review body reports indicate due regard for other criteria too, which have become common parlance in the 1980s: in the famous words of the Megaw Inquiry into civil service pay (Megaw 1982: para. 91, p. 24), pay levels should be sufficient to 'recruit, retain and motivate', taking into account affordability. Clearly attention to relative earnings is part of the Megaw trinity, although not in quite the same way as the 'comparability' criterion, the dogma of the 1970s. In other words, review bodies can if they wish place considerable emphasis on the general principles of performance and productivity in a way indexation formulas cannot. But in the end the review process lacks the remit to turn principles into practice. Collective bargaining, by contrast, allows the trade-offs between pay settlements and pay structures to be much more easily made, permitting the language of Megaw to be put into practice.

With regard to the internal pay structures which flow from the various mechanisms, the problems vary, but suggest a tension arising from nationally conceived structures. Indexation means that internal relativities within the two services cannot be readily shaped to fit changing circumstances and avoid cases of over- or underpayment. If pay levels can be adjusted through alternative means, such as more flexible pay scales or performance-related, as being suggested for the police in the 1993 Sheehy Report (see Section 5), the costs of indexation may gradually be reduced.

With regard to review bodies, less rigidity is inherent in the system with respect to pay and grading structures, but in practice there is the problem of the coexistence of review bodies with decentralized employing units. For NHS Trusts, the issue has not yet been tackled, but in education the problem can be severe. Since the Education Reform Act of 1988 introduced the concept of 'Local Management in Schools' (LMS), responsibility for school budgets, and thus the teaching wage bill, has rested with head teachers. The accompanying funding formula allows schools money calculated according to the cost of an 'average' (in terms of age and grade) teacher's salary. No allowance is made where 'above average' staff profiles exist. Schools must implement the STRB's recommendations within these budgets.

Does this mean that the problems are caused by the hybrid of centralization and decentralization, rather than one form of pay determination versus another? Review body proposals on reward structures allow some local pay flexibility (e.g. the teachers' 1993 grading structure and incentive allowances), but evidence suggests that in this instance head teachers have chosen to make cost savings by other means (Sinclair *et al.* 1993), viewing pay flexibility as destructive in terms of a spirit of collegiality. But even if nationally determined flexibility options were adopted, over time this would cause pay increase recommendations to have an increasingly differential impact, and would weaken the relevance of the review process.

Yet for the moment evidence suggests that service managers prefer to run with hybrid forms. As a recent analysis of nurses' pay (Buchan 1992) found in a series of interviews with managers in twenty-three Trusts, most preferred a cooperative route to determining the pay of their staff. They believed that to break from the review body system would lead to 'anarchy', a level of conflict not outweighed by potential gains. More precisely, this implies managerial compliance with the review process, but with a view to clawing back 'losses' through local flexibility measures, which they considered adequate within the existing system, a comment very much in line with Whitley arguments. But whether the happy coexistence of national and local arrangements can survive the expenditure constraints and demands of service reforms in the 1990s must be open to question.

Which form of pay determination provides the required amount of flexibility at an acceptable cost is now being tested, and we do not yet have the answers. We can go some way, however, towards a more concrete, albeit partial, evaluation, by looking at two other outcomes, public sector pay and industrial action.

4. Public Sector Pay and Strikes 1979–1993

Pay

The predominant concern of public sector union leaders, past and present, has been the pay of their members relative to either the private sector as a whole, or to sections within it. Real wage level concerns are usually subsumed within this focus on relative pay, although the 1.5 per cent imposed increase for 1993 brought the point to the fore again. In terms of real wages, few public sector workers have seen a decline since 1979, unless they have remained in the same job, on the same grade, with no increases through grade increments: the wage rates for some job grades (e.g. some manual NHS grades) have not increased in line with inflation. It may also be the case that those who received only the 1.5

per cent in 1993 (i.e. without additions from incremental pay points or bonuses) have suffered a decline in real wages in 1993.

The pay data presented here concentrate on relative earnings for the sector as a whole, and for certain groups. Results vary according to the type of data used (essentially, earnings or wage rates attached to a particular job grade, such as police constable), the year taken as the point of comparison and the comparator group (see Brown and Rowthorn (1990) for a fuller discussion). Fig. 6.1 shows what has happened to public sector earnings relative to the economy as a whole since 1979. If the numbers are calculated for public service earnings only relative to the whole economy, the results are closely similar up until the mid-1980s, but then diverge as public service relative earnings catch up with whole economy earnings.

The differential earnings pattern within the public sector suggested here is reinforced if the earnings of selected public sector groups are analysed (Figs. 6.2–6.5). The comparator groups chosen reflect those groups with whom nurses, teachers, police, and local authority white-collar staff are most commonly compared. The figures are not directly comparable with those of Fig. 6.1, as the former refers to weekly rather than hourly earnings. The graphs point clearly to a healthy pattern of relative earnings for police, nurses, and midwives.

For the police (Fig. 6.2), the indexation link has kept them comfortably ahead of levels of male non-manual earnings for most years (except 1989 and 1990). For nurses (Fig. 6.3), the remarkable increase in relative earnings has in

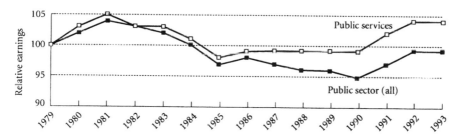

Fig. 6.1. Public sector: Changes in relative earnings 1979–1993

Sources: New Earnings Survey (1994) This reports the earnings of those affected by a listed major collective agreement, and these earnings are then assigned to the sector in which the agreement mainly operates. Earnings data for 1979–82 use separate adult male and female earnings, with a weighted average calculated from the following male and female employment data: Whole economy—UK employees in employment for June 1981, Dept. of Employment (1981). Public sector—UK headcount figures for mid-1981, Central Statistical Office (1983).

Notes: Figures refer to average gross weekly earnings excluding overtime for full-time male and female adults for the public sector as a whole, and public services alone, relative to all industries and services.

Key: Public sector (all): Central government (mainly national government services + the NHS; the Armed Froces are not included); Local government (local government services + education + police); Public corporations (excluded once privatized); Utilities (excluded once privatized). Public services: Central government + local government as defined above.

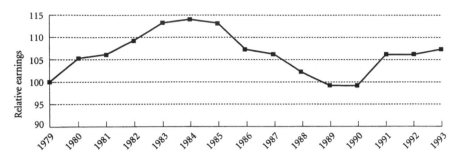

FIG. 6.2. Changes in police relative earnings 1979–1993 as a percentage of male non-manual earnings

Source: New Earnings Survey (1994). By national agreement.

Note: Figures refer to average gross hourly earnings excluding overtime for full-time adult male police relative to full-time adult male non-manuals.

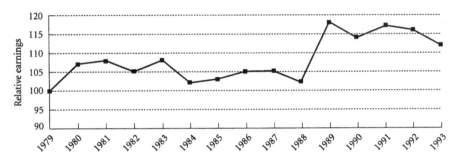

FIG. 6.3. Changes in nurses' and midwives' relative earnings 1979–1993 as a percentage of whole economy female non-manual earnings

Source: New Earnings Survey (1994). By national agreement.

Note: Figures refer to average gross hourly earnings excluding overtime for full-time adult female nurses relative to full-time adult female non-manuals.

These data include the earnings of unqualified nurses. If these are excluded, larger increases would be observed. Buchan (1992) notes an earnings ratio of 1.44 for the earnings of qualified : unqualified nurses in 1990, compared to a ratio of 1.23 in 1983.

large part been due to the fact that for almost all of this period nurses' pay has been the subject of some form of independent review. In 1980 they were one of the many groups under the remit of the Clegg Comparability Commission, and by 1984 their review body was in place. From then until 1988 a slow but steady increase can be seen, followed by a large one-off increase, the carrot for the introduction of a new clinical grading structure. While the higher level has not been fully maintained, nurses' relative earnings in 1993 show an increase since 1979 greater than any other public service group. If compared with male non-manual earnings (not shown here) an even higher set of increases emerges.

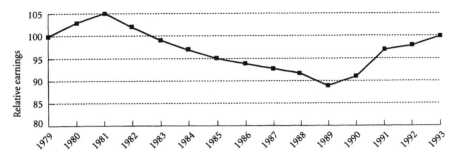

FIG. 6.4. Changes in APT and C staff relative earnings 1979–1993 as a percentage of male non-manual earnings

Source: New Earnings Survey (1994). By national agreement.

Note: Figures refer to average gross hourly earnings excluding overtime for full-time adult APT and C staff relative to full-time adult male non-manuals.

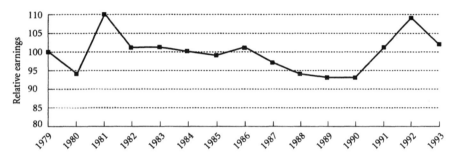

FIG. 6.5. Changes in schoolteachers' relative earnings 1979–1993 as a percentage of whole economy male non-manual earnings

Source: New Earnings Survey (1994). By national agreement.

Note: Figures refer to average gross hourly earnings excluding overtime for full-time adult male schoolteachers' relative to full-time adult male non-manuals.

The remaining figures only serve to reinforce the apparent costs to individuals of having their pay determined by collective bargaining under Conservative governments. Male white-collar staff in local government and male manual workers in the NHS have seen their relative earnings dip throughout most of the 1980s, although gradually begin to climb again by 1993 (Fig. 6.4). The same has been true for male schoolteachers (female teachers earn less on average, because they are concentrated in the primary school sector or in more junior secondary school positions), and again with the advent of a review body, their relative situation has improved (Fig. 6.5).

Clearly, factors other than the institutional form of the pay determination machinery influence earnings. Indeed, the very existence of indexation or a review body is in part caused by the need to reward these groups more highly, either as compensation for not striking or to get through major reforms, as in the case of education. But there seems to be no doubt that as far as review bodies are concerned, there appears to be an element of 'capture' by the client group of the institution's members, with arguments tending to favour employees rather than management.

The earnings data presented here raise the important point about the price being paid for winning union and employee cooperation. The strike data in Table 6.3 indicate that alternatives to collective bargaining do buy peace, at least in terms of formal industrial action. But could this peace have been won in ways other than that which increases the public sector wage bill?

Strikes

Two facts stand out from the 1992 figures used here on labour disputes in the United Kingdom. One is that 0.5 m. working days were lost, the lowest calendar year total ever recorded since records began in 1891. The second is that almost 60 per cent of these occurred in the public sector, and more specifically in public administration, education, and sanitary services (mainly local government council workers). Again, this is the highest proportion recorded, if coal disputes are excluded. As Table 6.3 shows, as the total (all industries, excluding coal) number of working days lost began to fall in the 1980s, the proportion of days lost in the public services (the former nationalized industries and corporations are excluded) tended to rise.

Between 1970 and 1979, disputes with more than 5,000 working days lost did not occur every year in the public services and utilities. When disputes of this magnitude did occur, an annual average of 5.6 per cent of total working days lost was attributable to these parts of the public sector. The equivalent figure for 1980–9 is 14 per cent. In both decades almost all disputes were over pay issues, a feature that appears to be changing according to the reasons for strikes given in Table 6.3. Job security appears to be the real fear of the early 1990s, suggesting that for the time being, preferential awards to buy peace are less necessary. While this is clearly linked to recession and to further public sector reforms, it may also reflect the fact that lower rates of wage increases in the private sector have improved the relative pay position of many public sector employees.

To understand whether the public sector is becoming more strike-prone relative to the private sector, analysis is needed taking into account strike activity per employee, and in particular per union member. This should also take into account the fact that around three-quarters of a million union members cannot strike by law or because of union regulations. Dickerson and Stewart (1993) analyse different data sources to answer the question of whether the public sector is more strike-prone than the private sector. They conclude that even when (by the late 1980s) strikes per union member were lower in the private than in the public sector, this was the result of the

Table **6.3** Major public service strikes 1980–1992

Year	Group	Reason	WDL per cent of total	total (millions)[a]
1980	Schoolteachers	Pay claim	0.8	11.9
1981	Civil Servants	Pay claim	20	4.3
1982	NHS nurses and ancilliaries	Pay claim	15	5.3
1983	Electricity, gas, water	Pay claim	20	3.7
1984	Schoolteachers	Pay claim	5	4.7
1985	Schoolteachers	For independent pay review	33	2.4
1986	Schoolteachers	Review and pay claim	16	1.9
1987	Schoolteachers	Pay claim and terms and conditions	4	3.5
1988	Civil servants	Trade union membership	3	3.7
	Nurses/ancillaries	Privatization	6	
	Postal workers	Casual labour	27	
1989	Local government	Pay claim	49	4.1
	Ambulance crews	Pay claim	12	
1990	Schoolteachers	Pay claim	2	1.9
	Civil servants	Staffing levels	5	
1991	Civil servants	Pay claim	10	0.8
	Civil servants	Safety issues	6	
	Council workers	Redundancies	14	
	Treasury staff	Redundancies	10	
	Social workers	Pay claim and grading	5	
1992	Electricity, gas, water	Safety issues	4	0.5
	Council workers	Redundancies	36	
	Civil servants	Safety issues and London weighting	4	
	Admin. and clerical	Pay parity	7	
	Lecturers	Pay claim	4	
	Social workers	Pay claim	7	
1970–9[b]				5.6
1980–9[b]				14

Source: Dept. of Employment, *Employment Gazette*, annual surveys.

Note: WDL = working days lost.
Major strikes are those with > 5,000 WDLs.

[a] WDLs lost in the coal dispute of 1984–5 have not been included. 'Total' refers to all industries, excluding coal, not to the whole of the public sector.
[b] Annual average for major disputes.

dramatic decline in the former. The greater visibility and dramatic rhetoric of public sector strikes should not mislead. In fact, it is noteworthy that the year of the 1.5 per cent increase saw no major backlash: most unions rolled over and accepted with little more than a whimper.

Such facts should not be taken to signify the dawning of a new age of harmony, but one based on compliance in the face of employment uncertainty, and, for some groups, the desire not to rock the pay boat in case the consequences are even more costly (i.e. loss of indexation or review privileges). In addition, much is happening at the level of individual employee–management relations which is producing tensions that may not necessarily find expression in collective action, but none the less can lead to covert conflict. To control public sector expenditure, and to achieve the array of service reforms now under way, the Government is dependent on the successful application of a number of changes in working practices. In the final section of this chapter, we look at some of the ways in which public sector employees are now being managed.

5. Managing Human Resources in the Public Sector

It has already been noted that the language of performance has permeated the formal institutions and processes of public sector industrial relations, even if its practical realization is somewhat hindered where indexation and review pay determination mechanisms exist. The issue of performance has been given more direct expression in the way in which employees (including managers) are now being managed, and in particular through their reward systems and employment patterns. By altering the bases of exchange in the public sector employment relationship, such moves can affect the individual's implicit contract, both with the particular service and with the sector as a whole. It was noted earlier that the changing reality and perceptions of job security has undermined one former important expectation about public sector employment. We do not know what effect that has had, but it may be that lower ability employees have been attracted to the public sector by a level of job security which protects poor performers. They have accepted the lower pay in return for this. Other things being equal, will less job security now lead to higher wages and cause higher performers to join the sector?

We also know relatively little about the impact of changes in working practices towards greater flexibility (however defined). This has been much more prevalent in the privatized industries, such as BS, but has also been of relevance to areas of manual employment subject to competitive tendering, and to BR and the PO. The latter's attempts to reduce overtime by introducing casual workers on shift bases met with strong resistance in the late 1980s, but the same was not true of BS's reshaping of production teams which gave greater skill flexibility, but reduced the former, more hierarchical, promotion ladder. A greater understanding is therefore needed of the circumstances under which people's expectations and motivations do or do not adjust when faced with different demands and rewards.

A little more is known about reactions to reward systems in the public sector. Two types of changes have been most common. First, there are those which entail the simplification of grading hierarchies through the reduction of pay points into one general pay spine, as has happened in parts of the Civil Service, such as the Inland Revenue, and schools. In all cases, the aim has been to use the simplified pay spine more flexibly, slotting in employees at levels which reward their own individual contributions, be they in the form of actual performance, or particular skills or experience.

Second, and often in conjunction with grading changes, has been the introduction of performance-related pay. For senior managers in services such as the civil service, local government, the NHS, and BR, this has been around for some years, at least since the mid-1980s. For the public sector as a whole, the proportion of workplace establishments covered by any form of incentive pay is lower than for all industries: WIRS3 data indicate that in 1990 31 per cent of public sector establishments had some employees covered by such schemes, compared to 52 per cent of all establishments (Millward *et al.* 1992). For public servants lower down the organizational hierarchy, it is a relatively new experience (e.g. Inland Revenue clerical staff), and for still others it is a form of reward still under debate, and subject to pilot studies (e.g. schoolteachers). Both grade restructuring and performance-related pay formed part of the proposals of the Sheehy Report into police rewards and responsibilities (Sheehy 1993), but moves towards performance pay appear in the main to have been put on ice.

The one major exception to the trend indicated by these changes was the clinical grading structure introduced for all NHS nurses up to management level in 1988, designed to encourage nurses to stay in clinical nursing rather than move on into management or nurse education. While it reduced the number of pay scale points available from around one hundred to about half that number, and kept the number of nursing titles the same, it increased the number of grades into which these titles could be slotted. Allocation of a particular grade is a function of a range of job-related criteria: the skills, experience, level of responsibility, etc. required by a specific job. Individual qualities, such as performance level, are explicitly omitted from the allocation process, at least if the official guidelines are followed.

With the exception of nurses, these changes reflect two major assumptions. First, the shift from the rate for the job to individual contribution redefines notions of equity in a manner quite alien to most public sector workers. Second, they all point to a policy of targeting incentives at the point of service delivery—a development which in theory at least fits well with the 1990s focus on 'customers', as manifested in the expanding number of citizens' charters.

What are the consequences of such a radical set of changes? There is a growing body of evidence about the effects of performance-related pay, not all of which points in the same direction. My own research into the consequences of clinical grading indicates a certain ambiguity on the part of nurses about the role to be played by rewards for individual contributions. Attitudes towards performance-related pay in general were largely negative. But when asked about the grading criteria in general against which they wished to be rewarded, it was clear from the results that those nurses who felt that they had been unfairly graded in the new structure, often resented the lack of recognition for their own performance.

Other studies of performance-related pay in the public sector (Marsden and

Richardson 1991; Thompson 1993) have indicated that although those affected were not against the principle of PRP, its application often seems flawed. Yet a recent American study (Ballou and Podgursky 1993) of teachers' attitudes to performance-related pay found a slight majority in favour of merit pay, and no significant hostility to such schemes from those who had worked under one compared to those who had not.

Clearly, no one strand of human resource management policy is likely to work in isolation. For example, Sheehy recognizes perhaps more explicitly than is seen in other parts of the public sector that performance-related pay forms only one part of paying for performance: jobs have to be graded correctly first, to ensure basic rates match the scope of the job. But the requirements of the job must match service demands. What the Sheehy Inquiry has also done is highlight the growing tension between rewarding the front line, while needing quality management to meet expenditure constraints. Most of the recent changes in public sector reward systems have tried to ensure those at the front line are rewarded more highly relative to management. Yet in much of the public sector, management appears to be a growth industry, particularly in the Civil Service and NHS (*The Economist*, 1993), while administrative tasks for non-managerial staff (e.g. nurses and teachers) are also increasing. If this is seen as necessary to implement service reforms, then inevitably it will be rewarded accordingly. In the context of tight controls on public expenditure, attempts to reward the actual job of teaching, nursing, or policing may in practice be swamped if the greater rewards and promotion opportunities continue to lie in management.

Such anomalies are perhaps inevitable in the context of rapid change, but some of the pitfalls involved in introducing so many changes could be avoided if a better understanding of how they worked and their intended costs and benefits could be gained. In this chapter the aim has been to discuss such issues, to question some of the conventional wisdoms of public sector industrial relations, and to assess how far developments reflect a radical redefinition of the public sector employment relationship at both the collective and individual level. While much remains that points to continuity with past practices, the conclusion must be that the demands being made on those practices point to a gradually weakening rationale for national collective structures, and a rewriting of what it means to be employed as a public servant.

REFERENCES

Bailey, R. (1994), 'Annual Review Article 1993', *British Journal of Industrial Relations*, 32/1: 113–35.
Ballou, D., and Podgursky, M. (1993), 'Teachers' Attitudes Toward Merit Pay: Examining Conventional Wisdom', *Industrial and Labor Relations Review*, 47/1: 50–61.

Blyton, P. (1993), 'Steel', in A. Pendleton and J. Winterton, (eds.), *Public Enterprise in Transition* (London: Routledge).

Brown, W., and Rowthorn, R. (1990), *A Public Services Pay Policy* (Fabian Tracts, 542; London: Fabian Society).

Buchan, J. (1992), *Flexibility or Fragmentation? Trends and Prospects in Nurses' Pay*, (Briefing Paper, 13; King's Fund Institute).

Central Statistical Office (1983), *Economic Trends* (Feb.).

—— (1993), 'Employment in the Public and Private Sectors', *Economic Trends*, 471 (Jan.).

—— (1995), 'Employment in the Public and Private Sectors', *Economic Trends*, 495 (Jan.).

Certification Office (1993), *Annual Report of the Certification Officer 1992* (London: Certification Office for Trade Unions and Employer Associations).

Corby, S. (1993), 'One More Step for the Civil Service', *Personnel Management* (Aug.), 30–1.

Cropanzano, R., and Folger, R. (1991), 'Procedural Justice and Worker Motivation', in R. Steers and L. Porter (eds.), *Motivation and Work Behaviour*, (New York: McGraw-Hill International).

Department of Employment (1981) *Employment Gazette* (June).

—— (1993), *Employment Gazette* (May).

Dickerson, A., and Stewart, M. (1993), 'Is the Public Sector Strike Prone?', *Oxford Bulletin of Economics and Statistics*, 55/3: 253–84.

The Economist (1993), *The Economist* (9 Oct.).

Fernie, S., and Metcalf, D. (1993), 'Climate of Industrial Relations 1990', CEP, LSE mimeo.

Financial Times (1993), *Financial Times* (8 Feb.).

Ibbs, R. (1988), *Improving Management in Government: The Next Steps* (London: HMSO).

IRRR (1993), *Industrial Relations Review and Report* (Pay and Benefits Bulletin, 328) (May).

IRS (1993), *Industrial Relations Services Employment Trends*, 537 (June).

Jackson, M. P., Leopold, J. W., and Tuck, K. (1993), *Decentralisation of Collective Bargaining* (London: Macmillan).

Katz, Harry C. (1993), 'The Decentralisation of Collective Bargaining: A Literature Review and Comparative Analysis', *Industrial and Labor Relations Review*, 47/1: 3–22.

Kelly, J., and Bailey, R. (1990), 'An Index Measure of British Trade Union Density', *British Journal of Industrial Relations*, 28/2: 267–70.

Lucio, M. (1993), 'The Post Office', in Pendleton and Winterton (1993), ch. 2.

McCarthy, W. (1976), *Making Whitley Work: A Review of the Operation of the NHS Whitley Council System* (London: HMSO).

Marsden, D., and Richardson, R. (1991), *Does Performance-Related Pay Motivate?* (London: LSE).

Megaw, J. (1982), *Inquiry into Civil Service Pay* Vol. 1, Cm. 8590 (London: HMSO).

Messenger, S. (1993), 'The Decentralisation of Collective Bargaining in the Electricity Supply Industry', M.Sc Diss., LSE.

Metcalf, D. (1989), 'Water Notes Dry Up', *British Journal of Industrial Relations*, 27/1: 1–31.

—— (1991), 'British Union Membership: Decay or Resurgence?', *Oxford Review of Economic Policy*, 7/1: 18–32.

Millward, N., Stevens, M., Smart, D., and Hawes, W. (1992), *Workplace Industrial Relations in Transition*, the ED/ESRC/PSI/ACAS Surveys, Dartmouth, USA.

New Earnings Survey (1994), *New Earnings Survey, Pt. A. 1979–1993* (London: HMSO).

Ogden, S. (1993), 'Water', in Pendleton and Winterton (1993), ch. 6.

Pendleton, A. (1993), 'Railways', in Pendleton and Winterton (1993), ch. 3.

—— and Winterton, J. (1993) (eds.), *Public Enterprise in Transition* (London: Routledge).

Self, P. (1993), *Government by the Market? The Politics of Public Choice* (London: Macmillan).

Sheehy, P. (1993) (chair), *Inquiry into Police Responsibilities and Rewards*, i, Cm 2280 (London: HMSO).

Sheldrake, J. (1988), *The Origins of Public Sector Industrial Relations* (Aldershot: Avebury, Gower Publishing).

Sinclair, J., Ironside, M., and Siefert, R. (1993), 'The Road to Market: Management and Trade Union Initiatives in the Transition to School Level Bargaining under Local Management of Schools', Paper presented at the BUIRA conference, York.

STRB (1993), *Second Report*, Cm 2151 (London: HMSO).

Thompson, M. (1993), 'Pay and Performance: The Employee Experience', *Report* no. 258. Institute of Manpower Studies: University of Sussex, Falmer.

Trinder, C. (1993), *Public Sector Pay over the Medium Term* (Working Paper, 44; London: Public Finance Foundation).

Waddington, J. (1992), 'Trade Union Membership in Britain, 1980–1987: Unemployment and Restructuring', *British Journal of Industrial Relations*, 30/2: 287–324.

7

UNION DERECOGNITION: A RE-EXAMINATION

Tim Claydon

1. Introduction

The last fifteen years have witnessed the erosion, some might say the collapse, of the industrial relations framework of the 1970s (Purcell 1993). However, due to the piecemeal and multi-faceted nature of the processes by which this has come about, there are no newly predominant arrangements for employment regulation which define the 'new' industrial relations (Beardwell 1992). Nevertheless, a major strand linking the various changes over the period has been a decline in trade union representation and influence at all levels. Since the mid-1980s it has become increasingly apparent that this decline does not simply reflect structural change in the economy and the growth of unemployment, but also the conscious intent of key industrial relations actors, notably the State and employers, to exclude unions from control of the employment relationship. The ultimate expression of this tendency is the termination of collective bargaining arrangements and the effective derecognition of trade unions by employers.

While union derecognition remains limited in its incidence and scope, there can be little doubt that it has become considerably more widespread since the mid-1980s. So far, there has been little attempt to assess its significance in terms of its distribution across industries and occupations, nor the extent to which derecognition is part of a long-term attempt by managers to restructure industrial relations on an organization-wide basis (Claydon 1989; Smith and Morton 1990). This chapter examines recent developments in union derecognition in Britain within the context of recent literature concerning the likelihood of a concerted movement towards union exclusion (Smith and Morton 1993). The basis for analysis is recently published survey data, original survey data, and interview material gathered during 1987–93, and published details of derecognition cases which have appeared in the press and periodical literature.

Union derecognition began to attract the attention of academics and practitioners during the late 1980s. While cases of derecognition remained rare, they did become more numerous particularly in publishing and shipping.

Signs of heightened trade union concern over derecognition became apparent during 1988. In April of that year the Labour Research Department reported that trade unions tended to dismiss cases of derecognition as 'one-offs' of little significance. (Labour Research Department 1988[a]). By July, however, derecognition was identified as a threat by the TUC Special Review Body, and the AEU submitted a motion to Congress calling upon it to recognize 'the slight but nevertheless significant trend to union derecognition and the growth of non-union workplaces' (TUC 1988: 33). In September a survey of union officials and managers conducted by the EPIC Communications Group found that nearly half of union officials and over 60 per cent of managers expected derecognition to become more widespread during the 1990s (*Financial Times* 1988). Finally, in its report for 1987, ACAS noted several examples of deunionization and derecognition. Although it regarded them as exceptional, ACAS observed that 'many managements were re-examining their relationships with trade unions' (ACAS 1988: 16–17).

Early academic research confirmed the limited extent of derecognition while at the same time noting a sharp increase in its incidence during 1987–8, mainly in publishing and transport, especially shipping. Outside these sectors derecognition was extremely rare (Claydon 1989). Claydon's study concluded that most derecognitions during 1984–8 were opportunist responses to union weakness, and that they were usually limited to workers in supervisory, professional, or managerial grades. Employers who derecognized trade unions had not usually adopted an articulated non-union approach to industrial relations for the organization as a whole. On this basis it was argued that, while derecognition would become more common, it would continue to be limited, piecemeal, and possibly temporary. It was seen as a fringe phenomenon, 'an extreme reflection of a much wider shift in the frontier of control within collective bargaining rather than a sign of a systematic movement for its rejection' (Claydon 1989: 222). However, it seems pertinent to re-examine these conclusions in the light of more recent survey work and the developing thesis concerning union exclusion. Recent survey-based studies have revealed that by 1990 derecognition was more widespread than had previously been recognized (Gregg and Yates 1991; Gregg and Machin 1991). Furthermore, detailed research into derecognition and deunionization in newspaper publishing revealed a greater degree of strategic intent and planned implementation than had been uncovered in earlier, more general studies of derecognition (Smith and Morton 1990).

2. The Incidence and Pattern of Derecognition: Survey Evidence

As a first step in analysing the development of derecognition, we examine published data relating to the incidence of derecognition, its distribution across industries, and across establishments and firms of different size. The form of derecognition, i.e. the categories of employees involved within organizations and the degree of union exclusion, is also examined. We then go on to discuss how this data might be interpreted in terms of what it reveals about the significance of union derecognition in the 1990s.

A number of surveys carried out in the late 1980s and early 1990s provided data on the incidence and pattern of derecognition over the period 1984–90. Gregg and Machin surveyed 279 firms during 1984–8. Of the unionized firms, 17 per cent had derecognized unions in 'some or all of their establishments in the mid to late 1980s' (Gregg and Machin 1991: 606). Gregg and Yate's 1990 survey of 558 firms found evidence of derecognition in 13 per cent of those which had recognized trade unions during 1984 (Gregg and Yates 1991). The much larger-scale Third Workplace Industrial Relations Survey (WIRS3) produced somewhat ambiguous evidence on the extent of derecognition. Cross-sectional data from the main survey indicated that both derecognition and new recognition were extremely rare, albeit with a substantial concentration of derecognition cases in 1989. However, data from the panel sample showed that almost 20 per cent of panel workplaces which had recognized trade unions present in 1984 reported having none in 1990 and that '9 per cent indicated that derecognition had occurred' (Millward *et al.* 1992: 75). The authors of the survey report prefer the panel data to the cross-sectional data, mainly on methodological grounds. They argue that retrospective questions, such as those asked of respondents in the main survey concerning union recognition, yield unreliable responses and the panel sample is therefore a more reliable guide to the extent of changes in recognition.

Another large-scale survey, the Warwick CLIRS2, also provides information on derecognition. This study, based on a representative sample of large companies, found that over the period 1987–90, 19 per cent of large firms had withdrawn recognition partially or wholly on sites which were in operation at the beginning of the period (Marginson *et al.* 1993). Survey data therefore suggests a significant incidence of derecognition, most of which has taken place since 1987.

The surveys also shed some light on the pattern and form of derecognition. Both the WIRS3 and CLIRS2 found a concentration in engineering, which the WIRS authors attribute to the termination of the national engineering agreement in 1989. In addition, CLIRS found the 'other manufacturing' and distribution sectors to be heavily represented. Further information on the pattern across sectors is provided by ACAS, which found cases of derecognition in the water industry, publishing and communications, chemicals, and financial services (ACAS 1992).

The relationship between size of organization and derecognition is worth exploring in the light of Smith and Morton's suggestion that large companies with substantial financial and managerial resources will be more likely than smaller concerns to be able to bear the costs of union derecognition, e.g. those of overcoming union and employee resistance (Smith and Morton 1993).

Unfortunately, the published data does not provide clear evidence on whether a relationship between size and derecognition exists. The establishment-level WIRS3 survey found that, in manufacturing, derecognition appeared to be concentrated in 'quite small establishments' (Millward *et al.* 1992: 75). The Warwick CLIRS2 found that among its sample of large organizations, it was the largest and most diversified firms that were most commonly associated with derecognition. This raises two possibilities. One is that WIRS3 picked up developments in smaller, independent companies that were not covered by the CLIRS2. If so, this would suggest that there was a similar incidence of derecognition across both large and small firms. Alternatively, it could be that both surveys picked up the same phenomenon, namely derecognition in some of the smaller plants owned by large companies. If so, this would give support to the argument put forward by Smith and Morton.

Regarding the form of derecognition, Claydon (1989) proposed a typology of derecognition based on the dimensions of 'breadth', i.e. the extent to which recognition was generalized throughout an organization or specific to certain groups of workers within it, and 'depth', representing the degree to which the derecognized unions were excluded from their erstwhile representational role. The significance of derecognition cases could then be considered in terms of breadth and depth variables. Briefly, it was argued that the greater the breadth and depth of derecognition, the greater was its impact on the totality of unionized relationships within organizations, and hence the greater was its significance. The broadest form of derecognition would be general derecognition across the organization which withdrew collective bargaining rights from all employees. Narrower forms comprised 'grade-specific' derecognition, i.e. withdrawal of bargaining rights from certain grades of employee only, and 'plant- or site-specific' derecognition, involving withdrawal of bargaining rights from all unions at some but not all plants in a multi-plant organization. A fourth possibility is a combination of grade- and site-specific derecognition, involving withdrawal of collective bargaining rights for some grades at some, but not all, sites. The depth categories range from partial derecognition, where unions retain some negotiating rights, e.g. over non-pay issues, to 'complete' derecognition, where they retain only the basic right to provide legal support to individual members. Indeed, one or two companies have set up their own systems of legal provision for employees in dispute with the company in an attempt to exclude derecognized unions even from this role.[1]

The published survey evidence, together with the reports of ACAS, provides information which can be analysed in terms of the categories above to build up a picture of the form of derecognition. Gregg and Yates's survey (1991) found that company-wide derecognition was rare. This was supported by CLIRS, which found that 75 per cent of cases of derecognition involved withdrawal of bargaining rights at some sites only, and at all or most sites in just 25 per cent of cases. ACAS reported that most cases of derecognition involved

---

[1] Tioxide and Unipart are two companies which have done this.

technical, professional and supervisory grades (ACAS 1992). There appear therefore, to be limits to the breadth of derecognition within organizations. In terms of depth, Millward found that unions retained a 'limited representative role' in only 13 per cent of workplaces where they had been derecognized, indicating that derecognition usually implied a complete rejection and exclusion of the union by management (Millward 1994: 33).

3. Interpreting the Surveys: The Union Exclusion Thesis

How should these survey findings be interpreted? What, specifically, do they suggest concerning possible changes in the significance of derecognition during the late 1980s and the 1990s? Both WIRS3 and CLIRS found derecognition in the private sector to be associated with low and/or sharply declining union density. CLIRS indicates that, for the most part, derecognition has been limited to a minority of sites or plants within large organizations, and WIRS3 suggests that it has been small establishments which have been most affected. Furthermore, ACAS reports suggest that derecognition has been most common among white-collar workers. It is possible that many of the small establishments affected by derecognition were those in which most employees were in technical, professional, or managerial roles. As far as the public sector is concerned, WIRS3 found that virtually all cases of derecognition were accounted for by the withdrawal of teachers' pay bargaining rights in 1987. In this case, although derecognition affected the majority of employees in the occupation, the termination of pay bargaining has not meant that teachers' unions no longer play a significant role in influencing teachers' terms and conditions of employment.

It is possible to conclude from this that, although derecognition may have been more widespread by 1990 than it was in 1987, it was still primarily an opportunist response to union weakness, directed mainly at the margins of the unionized workforce. Consequently, it could be argued that derecognition has had very little quantitative or qualitative impact on the totality of unionized industrial relations and remains a phenomenon of minor significance. On the other hand it is clear that the incidence of derecognition has grown substantially since the mid-1980s. Moreover, WIRS3 suggests that the substantial decline in union recognition and collective bargaining coverage in the late 1980s could not be explained simply or even mainly in terms of shifts in the composition of workplaces, as had been the case during 1980–4. Rather, it more probably reflected 'weakening support for trade unionism among employees, various government measures . . . and antipathy amongst a growing number of employers' (Millward *et al.* 1992: 102). This raises the possibility that as union density declines further and the number of non-union workplaces continues to grow, there may be increasing pressures and incentives which lead managers to consider derecognition and its extension to more categories of employee. Thus the CBI's Director of Employment Affairs has written: 'collective bargaining no longer presents itself as the only or even the most obvious method of handling relations at work; and fewer employees— and employers—feel the need of union mediation in their dealings', (Gilbert 1993: 252).

The possibility of a cumulative trend towards derecognition was implicit in some industrial relations analysis during the mid-1980s. Bain and Price (1983) argued that government, by withdrawing support for unions and imposing legal curbs on industrial action, had given employers an opportunity to challenge union organization and recognition. Brown and Sisson (1984: 33) saw management shifting towards unitarist policies and suggested that 'fragmented, shop-steward-led bargaining' could be a source of weakness when faced with a hostile management. Poole (1984: 62) foresaw that 'managerial strategies in industrial relations will focus more on individual employees and less on shop stewards and other union representatives than was the case in the 1970s'.

More recently, Smith and Morton (1993, 1994) have shown how, since the late 1980s, the government has acted with increasing confidence to implement a strategy of union exclusion. The main elements of this strategy are to enlarge the area of economic activity dominated by market forces; to withdraw political legitimacy from the unions while at the same time reducing their power and rejecting any proposals for codetermination in the workplace; to reduce the rights of individual workers *vis-a-vis* their employers; and to deinstitutionalize collective bargaining and industrial relations. These elements have been progressed through a variety of means. At the policy level, the virtual abandonment of tripartism has excluded unions from policy-making almost entirely. In the public sector, the programme of privatization and compulsory competitive tendering has had as one of its purposes the weakening of union influence over pay and working practices. Most crucially, successive Conservative governments have developed a legislative programme which has outlawed the closed shop, imposed increasingly onerous restrictions on industrial action, reduced trade unions' authority over their members, and also removed support for the extension of union recognition, reduced employees' protection against unfair dismissal, and dismantled machinery for setting minimum wages.

Smith and Morton see the 1990 Employment Act and the 1993 Trade Union Reform and Employment Rights Act as marking 'a significant escalation' of the legal assault on trade union power. The 1990 Act narrowed even further the scope for lawful industrial action and completed the outlawing of the closed shop. It also drove a further wedge between unions and their members through its provisions concerning union liability for unofficial industrial action. The 1993 Act imposed extra procedural burdens on unions wishing to organize industrial action, and empowered any individual to take legal action against apparently unlawful acts commited by trade unions or their representatives. It has also furthered the deinstitutionalization of industrial relations by subjecting 'check-off' arrangements for collecting union subscriptions to reapproval by secret ballot every three years, promoting inter-union competition by outlawing the 1939 Bridlington Agreement, removing the promotion of collective bargaining from the terms of reference of ACAS, and, through a literally reactionary amendment, allowed employers to discriminate against trade union members in respect of terms and conditions of employment (Smith and Morton 1994).

The government has thus withdrawn political and legal support for trade-unionism and has pursued labour-market policies which have reduced unions' organizational power. As Brown has observed, this has made unions 'more dependent on management for legitimacy and other resources' (1993: 196). At the same time, employers have been encouraged and enabled to withhold those resources. Hence Smith and Morton see government legislation combining with employer policies in a 'synergistic project to create a potent gradualist route to union exclusion' (1993: 100).

This synergy can be illustrated by drawing on a model developed by Poole (1986). The key measure of union strength is its 'manifest power', i.e. its ability to exercise control over the employment relationship. This is reflected in the union's procedural status at national and organizational level, and in its ability to achieve goals which compete with those of management. Manifest power is largely dependent upon the strength of the 'latent power resources' available to the union; in particular, membership size, positional power of the member-ship, and its 'willingness to act' in support of the union and its demands. These factors are in turn influenced by the wider political economy within which industrial relations are conducted. This includes the ideology and values of management. These values may themselves be malleable, interacting with broader ideologies and societal culture, and with the material features of capitalist competition and exploitation of labour. Importantly, one such feature is the extent of manifest union power. There is thus a reciprocal interdependence between variables which implies that, while there may be strong forces for stability, changes in union power, once initiated, will be cumulative unless arrested and reversed by some shock.

The dynamics of union exclusion as laid out by Smith and Morton can be explicated in terms of this model. Government policy, operating directly on industrial relations through legislation, and indirectly through its contribution to changes in the industrial relations environment, has weakened the latent power of trade unions at the level of the employing organization, thereby undermining the basis for their ability to exercise control within the employ-ment relationship. At the same time, government has sought to influence managerial values by promoting an ideology of individualism and entrepre-neurialism which challenges a trade union-centred approach to industrial relations. Furthermore, the weakening of unions' ability to contest and share in the control of the employment relationship which has resulted from the reduction in their latent power resources has encouraged managements to adopt more unitarist values and withdraw legitimacy and other resources from unions, thus further reducing their manifest power. Consequently, there has been created the potential for a fission-type reaction between the weakened manifest power of unions within organizations and a growing reluctance among management to support that which remains.

In practice, however, the question of how widely and how far employers will move down the road to derecognition remains a complex one. Dunn (1993) has argued that the 1980s saw a reversal of the 'unionization' of management thinking which had been a feature of the 1970s. However, Poole and Mansfield (1993) report that changes in managerial attitudes and behaviour altered rather less during the 1980s than might have been expected given the radical changes in the industrial relations environment. They found that 'the institutions of collective bargaining have remained more or less intact even though the actual influence of trade unions on outcomes has diminished considerably' (1993: 31). While the findings of WIRS3 must be seen as casting doubt on the continued stability of collective bargaining institutions, there are good reasons for thinking that the extent of actual union derecognition might remain limited compared with that which has theoretically been made possible over the last decade.

It has been argued that in the absence of 'corporate institutional constraints' and in 'conditions of continued economic decline', managers may come to see self-restraint in their dealings with unions as less and less rational (Streeck 1987: 292). Even so, 'strategic uncertainties' mean that an attack on union status and organization will not be an inevitable outcome. Such an attack might still be seen as involving unacceptable risks, particularly where productivity improvements are dependent on the cultivation of employee cooperation and the maintenance of 'legitimate governance structures' within the workplace (Streeck 1987: 292).

A similar point is made by Smith and Morton (1993), who argue that the decision whether or not to derecognize is essentially a practical one. Employers must assess the savings in unit labour costs against possible costs of disruption and 'the resources required to overcome union collective power' (1993: 101). Moreover, the potential costs and benefits must be compared with those arising from other ways of reducing unit labour costs. As a consequence of this type of calculation, managements in many cases see policies of 'partial exclusion', aimed at marginalizing union influence, as a less risky, and therefore preferable, alternative to attempted derecognition. This may result in 'the formal organisational indices of union representative structures [remaining] intact or . . . even . . . enhanced . . . while employers attempt to demobilise workers' collective power through joint consultation, direct communication and involvement, performance-related pay, and fragmentation of common employment' (1993: 102). However, if the union 'becomes sufficiently marginal, then it may be displaced altogether' (1993: 102).

What does this analysis imply for the relationship between government policies of union exclusion and union derecognition by management? Are they complements or substitutes? The absence of wider derecognition has generally been attributed to the relative strength of British trade-unionism (Purcell 1991). For Smith and Morton this means that employers have turned to partial exclusion as a lower-risk alternative to derecognition. Yet if government policies are successful, they could lead to either of two outcomes; derecognition as the culmination of a process of progressive exclusion, or continued formal recognition with little or no effective union participation in job regulation. Government policy has made it easier to derecognize trade unions (Metcalf 1991) but at the same time, by weakening union power, it may also have reduced the incentive to do so. Moreover, competitive pressures on organizations may have also reduced union power and/or engendered more cooperative, less adversarial industrial relations. Thus the escalation of the legal assault on union power noted by Smith and Morton cannot simply be assumed to lead straightforwardly to more widespread derecognition.

4. Union Derecognition: Developments in the 1990s

In examining developments in derecognition since the late 1980s we focus on the following questions. First, is derecognition becoming more generalized within those industries in which it began to take root during the 1980s, and is it being extended significantly to others? Secondly, has the predominant form of derecognition changed? Thirdly, have derecognitions which were initially limited in terms of their breadth and/or depth within organizations subsequently been extended to affect more employees and/or deepened so as to exclude unions more fully from influence over the employment relationship? Finally, what is the relationship between union strength and the growth of derecognition, and how might trade unions respond to the threat of it?

The following analysis seeks to present an up-to-date picture of derecognition and its significance by examining data for the early 1990s and making comparisons with the late 1980s. The analysis is based on the results of a postal questionnaire survey of full-time union officers carried out during 1992–3, information gathered from research interviews with managers and union representatives carried out during 1987–8, and published reports of cases of derecognition covering the period from 1984 to 1993. Where possible, questionnaires were sent to district or regional officials in the expectation that they would be more aware of developments occuring at the level of the employing organization than would national officers. However, this was inappropriate for some unions because of their size or the nature of their collective bargaining arrangements, and here responses were obtained from national officers. Respondents were asked whether any employers had withdrawn collective bargaining rights during the previous five years. Where bargaining rights had been withdrawn, respondents were asked to identify the organizations concerned, the grades or occupations affected, and to state whether, in the case of multi-site organizations, bargaining rights had been withdrawn in all sites or more than one site. They were also asked whether withdrawal of bargaining rights was preceded or accompanied by particular personnel policies associated with human resource management, i.e. individual performance-related pay, single staff status arrangements, team briefing, quality control circles, company councils, profit-sharing or employee share ownership schemes, flexible working practices, and an increase in the proportion of part-time and/or temporary workers. Finally, they were asked whether they or other officials had been consulted in advance of the decision to derecognize and, if so, what steps they had taken to resist derecognition and whether they were successful.

A total of 141 responses were received, covering thirty-one trade unions. Because not all unions responded to the questionnaire, and some were over- or under-represented relative to their size, the results could not be taken as representing accurately the overall incidence of derecognition or its distribution across sectors and occupations. Therefore the questionnaire data was supplemented by monitoring secondary sources. A total of 170 cases of derecognition was identified, plus a further eleven cases in which attempts at derecognition were successfully resisted by the unions. In counting cases, newspaper companies presented a problem, since in many cases a number of titles, sometimes having the status of legally independent companies, were owned by the same organization. The issue was whether each title should be counted as a separate case, or as an outcome of a single, wider derecognition carried out by the parent company. It was decided that, where derecognitions occurred simultaneously across a number of such titles, they would be counted as a single case of derecognition. This reflected the purposive, coordinated approach of the large companies and also made for consistency of measurement in relation to other multi-site or multi-plant organizations. Given the concentration of ownership in the newspaper industry this has the effect of reducing what has sometimes been seen as the overwhelming predominance of newspapers in derecognition.

A second difficulty was that it was not possible to date precisely every case of derecognition that was identified. In fifty-five cases the precise year in which derecognition occurred is unknown, although it is clear that they took place after 1988. These cases were distributed equally across the years 1989–93. On this basis the distribution of identified cases across the period was as shown in Table 7.1.

Clearly, a step increase in derecognition occurred during 1987, but there is no evidence of any continued upward trend. Particularly interesting, in the light of WIRS3's finding of an upsurge of derecognition in 1989, is that this is reflected in the data in Table 7.1, but is not continued into the 1990s. If all of the undated instances are allocated to the years 1990–3, there is some indication of a further small-step increase from 1989, but no strong, continuing upward trend.

A comparison of the distribution of derecognition by sector during 1984–8 and 1989–93 is presented in Table 7.2. This suggests that new concentrations emerged during the latter period. Publishing continued to account for the

Table 7.1. Annual incidence of completed derecognitions

Year	No. cases[a]	No. Cases[b]
1984	4	
1985	2	
1986	8	
1987	22	
1988	20	
1989	29	
1990	22	24
1991	18	21
1992	22	25
1993	23	26

[a] Undated cases allocated equally across 1989–93
[b] Undated cases allocated equally across 1990–3

largest proportion of the total, with derecognition extending more widely into book and magazine publishing and the national press. Petroleum and chemicals accounted for a significant proportion of the total during both periods. In line with the findings of WIRS and CLIRS2, the metal, engineering, and vehicles sector, and wholesale and retail distribution emerged as new areas in which derecognition was concentrated. The share of health and education also rose, and there are indications that withdrawal of pay bargaining, if not complete derecognition, may be becoming more common in this sector as hospital trusts develop their own approaches to industrial relations. Only half of the thirty-three respondents in a 1993 survey of first- and second-wave trust hospitals reported that they had signed pay bargaining agreements with trade unions (IRS 1993). Ports, shipping, and transport accounted for a smaller proportion of cases during 1989–93 than in the earlier period. This appears to have been because of the timing of derecognitions of the TSSA by a number of privatized service organizations previously operated by London Transport.

It can therefore be seen that derecognition has taken root in one or two industries in particular and that it may be extending to one or two others. Publishing is the best-known case, where, in certain sectors of the industry, such as provincial newspapers, derecognition of the National Union of Journalists is almost universal and that of the Graphical, Paper, and Media Union widespread. The other industry in which derecognition has emerged on a significant scale is petroleum and chemicals. This is of considerable significance, since derecognition has taken place in 'blue chip' companies having a long history of well-developed collective bargaining arrangements and which were seen as examples of a 'sophisticated modern' style (Fox 1974: 302; Purcell and Sisson 1983: 114–16) of industrial relations management. Morever, derecognition has involved unions of manual workers with high membership density.

Turning to the form of derecognition, Claydon's study in 1988 obtained details of the form taken by thirty-six cases. Twenty of these were grade-

Table 7.2 Percentage distribution of derecognition cases by industrial sector

	1984–8[a]	1989–93[b]
Water, gas, and electricity	0.0	3.5
Publishing, paper, and print	20.7	22.9
Broadcasting and communications	10.2	2.6
Ports, shipping, and transport	19.0	5.3
Petroleum and chemicals	10.2	13.4
Metal, engineering, and vehicles	6.9	14.0
Food manufacture	10.2	4.5
Other manufacturing	1.7	0.9
Hotel, catering, and leisure	8.6	2.6
Wholesale and retail distribution	0.0	13.2
Banking, insurance, and finance	5.2	4.5
Miscellaneous services	0.0	0.9
Health and education	3.4	9.6
Central government	3.4	1.8

[a] n = 58
[b] n = 112

specific and directed at white-collar workers in every case. Ten more were general, and six plant-specific. In terms of depth, twenty-nine were either complete or collective derecognitions. While their predominance indicated a strong rejection of union representation by management for the group of employees affected, the high incidence of grade-specific derecognition, and the fact that it was confined to white-collar workers, often with low membership density, suggested that derecognition was of limited significance. It was frequently a case of management picking off weakly organized groups, often following a change of ownership or senior management.

As shown above, the evidence from WIRS3, CLIRS2, and ACAS appears to be consistent with this pattern having been maintained since 1988. However, analysis of ninety-four cases during 1989–93 suggests that it has changed somewhat. In particular, the relative incidence of general derecognition increased compared with 1984–8. General derecognitions accounted for 27 per cent of the total cases during 1984–8 which were analysed by Claydon but 50 per cent of those identified during 1989–93. The proportion of grade-specific derecognitions fell from 55 per cent to 39 per cent. During 1984–8 the remaining 18 per cent of cases were plant-specific. In the latter period 11 per cent of cases were both plant- and grade-specific. There was an even greater predominance of collective and complete derecognition during 1989–93, with these two categories accounting for 90 per cent of all cases as against 80 per cent during 1984–8. Morever, relatively more companies in these categories derecognized unions completely, withdrawing from all formal agreements, during 1989–93.

The increased incidence of general derecognition, taken in conjunction with the findings of Gregg and Yates and CLIRS2 that general derecognition across multi-site companies is rare, suggests that derecognition is not confined to large organizations and that it has become more common among small and medium companies. This casts some doubt on the generalizability of Smith and Morton's assertion, based on a study of newspaper companies, that derecognition is mainly confined to large organizations and that large resources are needed to overcome resistance to derecognition. As will be shown below, much depends upon the balance of power resources within the organization and, hence, the circumstances in which derecognition is attempted.

The main significance of the increased incidence of general derecognition lies in the growing extent to which production workers, particularly in manufacturing, have come to be affected. During 1984–8, 11 per cent of derecognitions involved craft, process, and production workers in manufacturing. During 1989–93 this proportion rose to almost 25 per cent. Taken together with the increased incidence of derecognition generally, it can be seen that 'classic' union organization has become increasingly vulnerable to derecognition.

It is this development in particular which suggests that a cumulative trend towards derecognition might be emerging. In some cases the organizational power of manual workers' unions has been reduced to the point where they can offer little resistance should management decide to derecognize. It also appears that more managements have been ready to attempt derecognition in these circumstances. Our own survey data suggests that derecognitions on grounds of low membership have been most common in retail and wholesale distribution, but there is also some evidence from engineering. Here, it seems that the derecognized unions' ability to claim a share in job regulation rested upon the status conferred on them by the national engineering agreement rather than organizational power and managerial legitimacy in the workplace. The termination of the agreement in 1989 led managements to move from multi-employer bargaining to unilateral determination of terms and conditions of employment. In view of this it is unclear whether the increase in derecognitions in engineering during 1989–90 which was identified in WIRS3 will be maintained and extended to larger workplaces where domestic bargaining is well established.

More ominous from the trade union point of view are developments in the petroleum and chemicals sector. It is here that gradualist strategies of union exclusion leading ultimately to general derecognition of unions are exemplified most clearly. Specifically, what appeared to be grade- and plant-specific derecognitions during the mid-1980s have since revealed themselves to have been the first steps in a longer-term project to deunionize industrial relations throughout some of the most important companies in the industry. This is particularly significant because it has been directed at skilled and semi-skilled manual workers in plants with high union density, well-developed shop steward organization, and long-established collective bargaining agreements.

Within this sector, step-by-step dismantling of collective bargaining has been carried out by management at Esso, BP, Shell, and Mobil, and at Tioxide

UK, Scottish Agricultural Industries, and Pfizer. The process of derecognition has exhibited a broadly similar pattern across companies, centring on the transfer of successive groups of workers from collectively bargained to staff status based on individual contracts. Furthermore, there is evidence that, over time, managements have acted with increased aggression and confidence in implementing such changes.

Ahlstrand (1990) encapsulates the process with great clarity in his study of Esso's Fawley refinery. He reveals that as early as 1970 Fawley management made a strategic choice that it would seek to shift industrial relations onto a non-union basis by transferring employees to staff status (1990: 161). In line with the analyses of Streeck (1987) and Smith and Morton (1993), certain groups, namely process operators, were seen as being 'too large and unlikely to move to staff status' (Ahlstrand 1990: 161). Therefore moves to staff status were directed initially at craft maintenance workers. Even here, it was recognized that difficulties would be experienced, so a long-term approach was adopted in which successive subgroups were targeted rather than management attempting to end collective bargaining for craftsmen across the board.

The first group to be targeted by management were warehousemen. Ahlstrand identifies a number of reasons for this: they were a small, self-contained group who comprised only a small fraction of their union's membership at the site, and they were also seen as occupying 'a strategic position in the event of a dispute' (1990: 162). The transfer to staff status was opposed by the TGWU, but nevertheless achieved by 1974. Following the termination of collective bargaining for warehousemen, other groups were similarly identified on the basis of their size and their strategic position in the production process. Thus instrument fitters were taken out of bargaining in 1979, followed by the boilermakers in 1982. In 1983 management attempted to extend staff status to welders, but at this point union-led resistance involving industrial action put a halt to the process. In reporting this, however, Ahlstrand observed that this was almost certainly a temporary respite for the unions, as 'there is no indication that the plan has been set aside permanently. Staff status is seen as a realistic strategy to pursue, one that will need time and money to implement' (1990: 167).

This judgement has been borne out by subsequent developments within the company. In 1989 the remaining refinery craftsmen were transferred to staff status, and in 1993 the process was completed when the TGWU's bargaining rights on behalf of 700 process operators at Fawley were withdrawn. Esso maintained membership check-off arrangements, and unions retain the right to represent individual members in discipline and grievance proceedings. They have, however, ceased to have a role as collective representatives of the Fawley workforce (IDS 1993*a*). At the same time, moves to end collective bargaining have been extended to other areas of Esso's operations. Airport technicians employed by Esso were transferred to staff status in 1989, and in 1991 tanker drivers were similarly transferred and the TGWU derecognized for collective bargaining (IDS 1991).

The most suprising aspect of Ahlstrand's findings is how far back in time this strategy came to be formulated. Esso's productivity agreements at Fawley during the 1960s were presented as an example of pluralist industrial relations management (Flanders 1964), and this has coloured subsequent views of management's industrial relations style in the petro-chemicals sector (Purcell and Sisson 1983). Yet plans to dismantle collective bargaining were being formulated during this supposedly pluralist phase at Fawley.

A second example of a gradualist approach to derecognition is provided by BP. The first reported instance occurred at a chemical plant at Barry in South Wales in 1985. In this case, all bargaining groups were transferred to staff status at once, thereby derecognizing the AEU, EETPU, TGWU, and ASTMS. The unions were, however, offered a procedural agreement allowing for annual consultation meetings with management (TGWU 1988).

It was some time before the initiative at Barry was repeated at other BP plants. While some managers were keen to extend staff status more widely, it was felt that the Barry site possessed particular features which had eased the path to derecognition. A key factor was a massive reduction in the workforce during the early 1980s as BP divested itself of its PVC production capacity at the site and also stopped production of polyester resin. Consequently the size of the workforce plummeted from 2,000 in 1981 to 300 by the end of 1984, a process which involved large-scale compulsory redundancies. This was accompanied by a reorganization of the site into two businesses, each led by a business manager and a small group of executives (*Financial Times* 1984; IRS 1986).

In 1992, however, again on the back of job cuts, collective bargaining was ended at BP's plant at Baglan Bay, also in South Wales, and employees were transferred onto staff contracts. This did not, however, prevent the subsequent closure of the plant at the beginning of 1994 (*Financial Times* 1992a, 1992b, 1994). During 1993 BP Oil also began to transfer workers to staff status, beginning with eighty oil terminal operators hitherto represented by the TGWU. In the same year, collective bargaining was ended at BP Oil's Llandarcy site (IDS 1993a, 1993b).

Similar developments got under way at Shell during 1992–3. In June 1992, 520 employees in the trading, supply, and distribution division of Shell UK Downstream Oil, 400 of whom were tanker drivers, were moved to staff status and the collective agreement with the TGWU terminated (IDS 1992a). Shortly afterwards, administrative and craft workers were put on staff contracts at Shell refineries at Stanlow and Shell Haven (*Financial Times* 1992c; Higgs 1994). Mobil Oil has followed a similar pattern, moving craftsmen to staff status during 1992 (IDS 1992b).

Developments such as these have not been confined to the oil companies within this sector. At Tioxide, a pigments manufacturer in the North-East, recognition was withdrawn from ASTMS for technicians in 1980. Intentionally or not, this cleared the way for the company to transfer manual workers to staff status and eliminate collective bargaining. In 1987 manual workers at Tioxide's plant at Grimsby voted to give up collective bargaining in exchange for a staff status package which included generously enhanced pension rights. However, derecognition was not extended to the company's neighbouring plant at Greatham owing to resistance from the unions and the workforce there. Even so, as new production processes have been developed at Greatham, newly joining employees have been hired on staff status terms and conditions. Thus the long-term commitment to the removal of collective bargining remains (Tioxide 1988; Malloch 1992).

Over time, management in the petro-chemicals sector appears to have become more willing to act more openly and aggressively in order to effect a transition away from collective bargaining to managerially determined terms and conditions of employment. This development has taken place in the context of job reductions and, increasingly, the possibility of contracting out certain operations. In the case of Fawley in the early 1970s, Ahlstrand found that

Once management had detailed the terms and conditions of staff status and presented these to each member of the group, management withdrew from any further active solicitation and left it to the individual members to put pressure on the union hierarchy. It was therefore the workers themselves who, in the end, approached full-time officials to request a move to staff terms (1990: 163).

Ahlstrand notes that this reflected management's desire not to be seen as promoting deunionization. Nevertheless, some efforts at persuasion were seemingly made, since an internal TGWU memo is quoted which expressed concern at the 'continuing pressure' being put on warehousemen to move to staff status (1990: 162–3). By 1982, however, Fawley management were acting more openly in their attempts to extend staff status to the boilermakers' group. The boilermakers' position in the earnings hierarchy at the plant depended on a relatively high level of overtime work compared with other groups. Management made clear its determination to drive down overtime hours and signalled that acceptance of staff status was the only way in which the boilermakers would be able to maintain their earnings (1990: 165).

At BP, derecognition and the move to staff status at Barry was said by management to have followed demands from the workers to be transferred onto staff contracts which were presented to management in 1983 (IRS 1986). Management arranged meetings of small groups of employees on each shift, including shop stewards, to explain the package. This was followed by a ballot of the workforce in November 1984 at which a two-thirds majority in favour of acceptance was required for the scheme to be implemented. Sixty-eight per cent voted in favour of the management proposal.

At Tioxide, management set up a staff status committee, which included shop stewards, to develop a staff status proposal. The outcomes of each meeting were communicated to every employee. As at Esso, this led to workers putting pressure on shop stewards to accept the management proposal. At the same time, management determinedly excluded full-time officers from any discussion and prevented them from meeting with members on-site, since it was from this quarter, rather than the shop stewards, that opposition was anticipated. A ballot of employees, requiring a simple majority vote, resulted in 76 per cent voting in favour of staff status, according to management sources. (IDS 1987; Tioxide 1988).

Some other companies have acted more coercively. During 1986–7 Scottish Agricultural Industries at Leith—a fertilizer manufacturer part-owned by ICI—presented a set of proposals for changes in working patterns and a move to staff status terms and conditions including the derecognition of the AEU, EETPU, and GMB. Subsequently new contracts of employment were sent to individual employees at the same time as voluntary redundancy terms were offered in order to reduce the workforce by 20 per cent (Scottish Agricultural Industries 1988).

At Monsanto chemicals at Ruabon, management targeted individual areas within the plant, got 60 per cent of workers within that area to sign staff status contracts, and then declared them staff contract areas. Those refusing to accept such contracts were transferred to other areas of the plant. Two particular areas which were considered to be crucial to the plant's operation, namely the effluent plant and the boiler-house, were simply declared to be staff status areas. As at Tioxide, enhanced pension entitlements were seen by the unions to be a strong incentive to a relatively aged workforce to give up collective representation. Meanwhile, the unions were threatened with the contracting out of work unless staff contracts were accepted. A proposal from the TGWU that the workforce be balloted on staff status was rejected by management on the grounds that a number of employees had already agreed to the change (TGWU 1988).

More recently, the TGWU has alleged that in seeking to gain acceptance of staff status contracts over the last two or three years, oil companies have made general use of coercive tactics. In written evidence to the House of Commons Select Committee on the Future of Trade Unions, the TGWU referred to the derecognitions by BP at Baglan Bay and Llandarcy, Esso at Fawley, Mobil at Coryton and Birkenhead, and Shell at Stanlow and Shell Haven during 1992–3. It drew the Committee's attention to what it alleged were examples of 'extreme pressure' put on individual employees to give up collective representation. In one instance, according to the union, attempts by management to gain voluntary acceptance of staff status were rejected by the membership. Consequently management began to impose the changes, interviewing each employee 'and presenting them with contracts for staff-status and no negotiating rights. All our members were told by management in the interviews that if they did not sign new contracts within 24 hours any job offer would be withdrawn' (Higgs 1994: 3).

The TGWU also asserts that recent cases of derecognition in the oil industry have shared four 'common elements', namely the announcement of redundancies or the threat that certain jobs such as drivers' would be contracted out, notice of termination of union agreements, selection for redundancy based on individual assessment of employees, and strong signals that 'post-redundancy only those employees who are prepared to sign individual contracts will be employed'. This commonality of approach, argues the union, reflects a strategy agreed between the companies at regular meetings where 'union derecognition is an agenda item' (Higgs 1994: 2).

There are also signs that some other large companies outside the petroleum and chemicals sector may be following a similar gradualist path to derecognition. In 1986 Cable and Wireless sought to introduce individualized pay for managerial and technical staff. In 1987 it terminated pay bargaining for these employees and in 1991 withdrew formal recognition from the unions MSF and USDAW. USDAW was also derecognized as a representative of cable layers at London Mercury, a company owned by Cable and Wireless (*Financial Times* 1986, 1991).

In the light of these developments one cannot discount the possibility that what appears to be a grade- or plant-specific derecognition having only a marginal impact on union representation may in fact be the first step in a long-term attack on union recognition throughout the organization. While clear examples of this may still be limited and concentrated in particular industries, there are signs that they are beginning to be emulated more widely. It is also possible that, through the pressures of competition or, conversely, through cooperation between large employers in industries where inter-organizational competition is organized and controlled, derecognition initiatives, once initiated by one or two key players, may begin to permeate other industries.

At the same time, however, there is only limited evidence to suggest that derecognitions so far have been the culmination of other forms of partial exclusion such as the introduction of performance-related pay and Employee Involvement initiatives. Our survey of union officers yielded usable data concerning innovations on personnel policies prior to derecognition in forty cases, overwhelmingly in the private sector. Of these, sixteen had introduced elements of performance-related pay, thirteen had introduced team briefing, twelve had set up quality control circles or TQM initiatives, and seven had employee share ownership or profit-sharing schemes. Only one organization, Rowntree Mackintosh, where USDAW had its bargaining rights removed in respect of chargehands, had all of these elements in place, and this reflects the particular employment philosophy of the organization. Only four others had three of the elements, nine just two, and sixteen only one, this being predominantly performance-related pay. Ten of the organizations had introduced none of these prior to derecognition. Retail distribution and miscellaneous private services predominated among this group. On this basis there is little to suggest that moves towards human resource management are a precursor of union derecognition. This gives support to Smith and Morton's contention that such initiatives are seen as alternatives to derecognition, at least in the medium term.

5. Conclusions: Patterns of Derecognition and Possible Union Response

The findings presented above mean that it is very difficult to assess the significance of derecognition simply in terms of the form it takes at a particular point in time. Thus Claydon (1989) argued that the predominance of grade-specific derecognition indicated an opportunist approach aimed at the margins of the unionized workforce. Subsequent developments suggest that now such a conclusion might be misleading. Successive grade-specific derecognitions at British Telecom and British Rail, as well as grade- and plant-specific derecognitions in oil companies, have in fact been aimed at paring away union representation over time rather than eliminating it at a stroke.

As a result of the analysis presented here it is possible to define two general approaches to derecognition. The first can be seen as 'reactive' in the sense that it represents a management response to a weakening of union power brought about largely by changes in the organization's industrial relations environment rather than resulting from purposive management action. Such derecognitions may be general, or they may be grade-specific, plant-specific, or a combination of both. While derecognition may be reactive, this does not necessarily imply an absence of management strategy in other employment matters. Some of the cases of derecognition in engineering following the termination of the national engineering agreement appear to have been of this type. In these cases, it seems that the unions' claim to a share in job control derived from the status conferred upon them by the national agreement, rather than from significant organizational power or managerial legitimacy in the workplace. With the ending of the agreement, employers who chose to derecognize could do so with little difficulty.

The second approach to derecognition can be labelled 'purposive', reflecting a long-term effort by management to eliminate unionized industrial relations. Such efforts may begin with limited forms of derecognition; in particular, it may be directed at specific groups of workers who are seen as offering least resistance or small groups occupying strategic positions in the production process. In the latter case, the incentive to remove union influence may be strong, and small numbers may mean that the costs of doing so, both financially and in terms of the managerial resources required to substitute for collective bargaining, are sufficiently low in relation to the perceived benefits to make them acceptable to management.

One implication of this distinction is that union representation and collective bargaining is being challenged by derecognition on two fronts. 'Reactive' approaches to derecognition seem most likely to be adopted at the margins of the unionized workforce. Of course, as union density falls and union power becomes increasingly circumscribed, the margin shifts inwards. It is here that the 'synergy' between government policy and managerial action is most obvious. Recognition is gradually eroded as 'soft' organization is washed away. However, bands of 'hard' organization set limits to this erosion and prevent it from becoming complete, within as well as across organizations. Purposive derecognition, on the other hand, is a hollowing-out of unionized industrial relations at the centre as the hard core of union organization is itself undermined. This raises the possibility of an implosion of unionized industrial relations as exemplified in the petro-chemicals sector. It would seem that it is this form of derecognition which is most likely to be confined to organizations possessing large financial and managerial resources.

There seem to be grounds for thinking that purposive derecognition might become more widespread, since the circumstances which encourage it and make it practicable appear to be spreading. Workforces have shrunk, small core groups of key workers exercising discretion in their tasks are becoming more common. This may make it easier for employers to develop divide-and-rule strategies with which to attack collective bargaining on a step-by-step basis. Moreover, 'enterprise-confined' union organization, resulting from the collapse of multi-employer bargaining and legal restraints on solidary action, have weakened unions' ability to resist such challenges.

While it might seem banal to say that the extent of derecognition will depend crucially on the quality of union organization and its response to these threats, there is room for discussion of what responses might be most effective and on what basis they can be mounted. Metcalf has said that 'in the current legal climate if an employer decides to derecognize, the union is almost impotent' (1991: 25). He goes on to argue that unions may be able to stave off derecognition in two ways; by agreeing to negotiate locally when employers decide to end national bargaining, and by moving towards single-table bargaining and a cooperative industrial relations stance (1991: 25). This argument recalls the issue raised at the end of the third section of this chapter, namely whether a decline in union power is more or less likely to encourage more widespread derecognition. If, as Purcell (1991) has argued, it is the strength of British trade-unionism that has limited the extent of derecognition and, according to Smith and Morton, encouraged 'partial exclusion' as an alternative to it, we should expect a weakening of trade union power to result in wider derecognition, since the costs of overcoming resistance are reduced. On the other hand, it is possible that weaker or more cooperative trade unions reduce the incentive to derecognize, this being the outcome suggested by Metcalf. The evidence from WIRS3 and CLIRS, which found derecognition to be associated with low and/or declining membership density within organizations, indicates that it is the first hypothesis which should be supported. This contention is strengthened when we consider what is meant by a 'cooperative industrial relations stance' on the part of trade unions.

The term 'cooperative industrial relations stance' begs the question of what 'cooperation' means. Who is calling the tune here and what does a more cooperative stance imply for unions' ability to continue to represent their members' interests and retain their loyalty? In the current climate, 'coopera-tion' can surely be read as unions conceding control over key elements of the employment relationship to management, i.e. a weakening of their bargaining position. There is very little evidence that trade unions have been successful in developing a new, cooperative bargaining agenda involving the extension of union influence to new areas of decision-making in exchange for relaxing controls in traditional areas (Millward *et al.* 1992: 255; Claydon and Green 1994). Therefore, a more cooperative stance by unions may help to pave the way for derecognition rather than avert it. This possibility is clearly illustrated in Ahlstrand's study of Fawley (Ahlstrand 1990). Ahlstrand shows how, during the early 1980s, Fawley management moved to end collective bargaining for the boilermakers, who had been seen as 'the most militant and recalcitrant group on the site' (1990: 64). A key step along this road was the maintenance enabling agreement concluded with the union in 1982. In signing this agree-ment the maintenance stewards effectively 'sold away two significant control dimensions; control over (1) overtime administration and allocation and (2) contractor usage' (1990: 169). Ahlstrand argues that the loss of these controls reduced union influence on earnings and thereby undermined members' 'faith in the ability of union representation to deliver anything of value or substance to their members . . . [and] made it increasingly difficult for the stewards to command loyalty from their membership' (1990: 169). He goes on to say that this 'paved the way for worker acceptance of the "devil's bargain"—the relinquishing of collective bargaining rights in return for an "individual" staff status employment contract' (1990: 169–70). Evidence from other petroleum and chemical companies where derecognition has occurred suggests that a long history of cooperative industrial relations did not save the unions once management came to consider moving away from collective bargaining. Indeed, as Claydon (1989) suggested, plant-focused loyalties among a long-serving workforce contributed to the workers' decision to surrender collective bargaining in exchange for staff status.

On the evidence, therefore, Metcalf's dictum represents dubious advice. It is possible that cooperation might prevent management from considering dere-cognition in the first place, although it will only be one of several influences which might influence the direction of management thought and action. It is far less likely that it will lead to management turning aside from derecognition should it already have commenced on that course. Finally, it is worth noting that of the eleven cases of unsuccessfully attempted derecognition reported by respondents to our questionnaire to union officials, nine were dropped following industrial action or the threat of it. The ability to maintain effective workplace organization, not only in terms of membership but also willingness to act, would seem to be more productive of success in resistance to derecogni-tion than policies of appeasement. While cooperative industrial relations may in some circumstances reduce the incentive for managers to attempt derecog-nition, unions ignore their traditional sources of power at their peril. The seemingly intractable issue facing trade unions, however, is precisely how to maintain these traditional sources of power in the face of the movement towards union exclusion which has increasingly come to define the 'new industrial relations'.

REFERENCES

ACAS (1988), *Annual Report 1987* (London: ACAS).
——— (1992), *Annual Report 1991* (London: ACAS).
Ahlstrand, B. (1990), *The Quest for Productivity: A Case Study of Fawley after Flanders* (Cambridge: Cambridge University Press).
Bain, G.S., and Price, R. (1993), 'Union Growth, Dimensions, Determinants and Destiny', in G.S. Bain (ed.), *Industrial Relations in Britain* (Oxford: Blackwell).
Beardwell, I. (1992), 'The "New Industrial Relations"? A Review of the Debate', *Human Resource Management Journal* 2/2: 1–7.
Brown, W. (1993), 'The Contraction of Collective Bargaining in Britain', *British Journal of Industrial Relations*, 31/2: 189–200.
——— and Sisson, K. (1984), 'Current Trends and Future Possibilities', in M. Poole, W. Brown, J. Rubery, K. Sisson, R. Tarling, and F. Wilkinson, *Industrial Relations in the Future: Trends and Possibilities over the Next Decade*, (London: Routledge and Kegan Paul), 11–38.
Claydon, T. (1989), 'Union Derecognition in Britain during the 1980s', *British Journal of Industrial Relations*, 27/2: 214–23.
——— and Green, F. (1994), 'Can Trade Unions Improve Training in Britain?' *Personnel Review*, 23/1: 37–51.
Dunn, S. (1993), 'From Donovan to . . . Wherever', *British Journal of Industrial Relations*, 31/2: 169–83.
Financial Times (1984), *Financial Times* (6 Dec.).
——— (1986), *Financial Times* (12 Nov.).
——— (1988), *Financial Times* (1 Sept.).
——— (1991), *Financial Times* (15 Mar.).
——— (1992a), *Financial Times* (14 Feb.).
——— (1992b), *Financial Times* (18 Feb.).
——— (1992c), *Financial Times* (10 Dec.).
——— (1994), *Financial Times* (13 Jan.).
Flanders, A. (1964), The Fawley Productivity Agreements: A Case Study of Management and Collective Bargaining (London: Faber).
Fox, A. (1974), *Beyond Contract: Work, Power and Trust Relations* (London: Faber).
Gilbert, R. (1993), 'Workplace Industrial Relations 25 years after Donovan: An Employer View', *British Journal of Industrial Relations*, 31/2: 235–53.
Gregg, P., and Machin, S. (1991), 'Changes in Union Status, Increased Competition and Wage Growth during the 1980s', *British Journal of Industrial Relations*, 29/4: 603–11.
——— and Yates, A. (1991), 'Changes in Wage-Setting Arrangements and Union Presence in the 1980s' *British Journal of Industrial Relations*, 29/3: 361–76.
Higgs, F. (1994), *Transport and General Workers Union Supplementary Submission on Union Recognition and Collective Bargaining Rights (Companies in the Oil Industry)*

Evidence to the House of Commons Select Commitee Enquiry on the Future of Trade Unions, 6 Jan.

IDS (1987), *IDS Report,* 498: 4–5.

——— (1991), *IDS Report,* 606: 5.

——— (1992*a*), *IDS Report,* 627: 8.

——— (1992*b*), *IDS Report,* 630: 5.

——— (1993*a*), *IDS Report,* 646: 4.

——— (1993*b*), *IDS Report,* 645: 2.

IRS (1986), 'BP Chemicals at Barry: A Move to Staff Status', *Industrial Relations Review and Report* 362: 9–11.

——— (1993), 'Local Bargaining in the NHS: A Survey of First- and Second-Wave Trusts', *Industrial Relations Review and Report,* 537: 7–16.

Labour Research Department (1988*a*), 'New Wave Union Busting', *Labour Research,* 77 (Apr.): 13–15.

——— (1988*b*), 'Undermining Collective Bargaining', *Labour Research,* 77 (Dec.): 18–19.

Malloch, H. (1992), 'Management Values and Change: The Case of Tioxide UK', in B. Towers, (ed.), *The Handbook of Human Resource Management* (Oxford: Blackwell), 340–59.

Marginson, P., Armstrong, P., Edwards, P., and Purcell, J. (1993), 'Decentralisation, Collectivism and Individualism: Evidence from the 1992 Company Level Industrial Relations Survey', British Universities Industrial Relations Association Conference, University of York, July.

Metcalf, D. (1991), 'British Unions: Dissolution or Resurgence?', *Oxford Review of Economic Policy,* 7/1: 18–32.

Millward, A. (1994), *The New Industrial Relations?* (London: PSI).

——— Stevens, M., Smart, D., and Hawes, W. R. (1992), *Workplace Industrial Relations in Transition: The ED/ESRC/PSI/ACAS Surveys* (Aldershot: Dartmouth).

Poole, M. (1994), 'A Framework for Analysis and an Appraisal of Main Developments', in M. Poole, W. Brown, J. Rubery, K. Sisson, R. Tarling, and F. Wilkinson, *Industrial Relations in the Future,* (London: Routledge & Kegan Paul), 39–94.

——— (1986), *Towards a New Industrial Democracy: Workers' Participation in Industry* (London: Routledge).

——— and Mansfield, R. (1993), 'Patterns of Continuity and Change in Managerial Attitudes and Behaviour in Industrial Relations', *British Journal of Industrial Relations* 31/1: 11–35.

Purcell, J. (1991), 'The Rediscovery of the Managerial Prerogative', *Oxford Review of Economic Policy,* 7/1: 33–59.

——— (1993), 'The End of Institutional Industrial Relations', *Political Quarterly,* 64/1: 6–23.

——— and Sisson, K. (1983), 'Strategies and Practice in the Management of Industrial Relations', in G.S. Bain (ed.), *Industrial Relations in Britain* (Oxford: Blackwell), 95–134.

Scottish Agricultural Industries (1988), Interview with Deputy Works Manager, 18 July.

Smith, P., and Morton, G. (1990), 'A Change of Heart: Union Exclusion in the Provincial Newspaper Sector', *Work, Employment and Society,* 4: 105–24.

——— ——— (1993), 'Union Exclusion and the Decollectivisation of Industrial Relations in Contemporary Britain', *British Journal of Industrial Relations,* 3/1: 97–114.

———— ———— (1994), 'Union Exclusion in Britain: Next Steps', *Industrial Relations Journal*, 25/1.

Streeck, W. (1987), 'The Uncertainties of Management in the Management of Uncertainty; Employers, Labour and Industrial Adjustment in the 1980s', *Work, Employment and Society* 1/3.

TGWU (1988), Interview with District Officer, Wrexham, 14 July.

Tioxide (1988), Interview with Managing Director, Tioxide Pigments Division, 6 June; Interview with Personnel Director, Tioxide Ltd., Grimsby, 13 June.

TUC (1988), *Trades Union Congress Report* (London: TUC).

8

THE NEW NEW UNIONISM

Edmund Heery

1. Introduction

Twenty years ago Coates and Topham published *The New Unionism* (1974). They argued in the book that the established forms and policies of trade unions were increasingly irrelevant to the needs of British workers and that, in consequence, a new unionism was emerging. This, they claimed, was based on the mobilization and direct participation of rank and file union members and was oriented towards challenging management control, both in the workplace and beyond. Coates and Topham's book was openly prescriptive in intent and was subtitled *The Case for Workers' Control.* Other, less didactic analyses of trade unions in the 1970s, however, shared their view that the labour movement was shedding old baggage and changing rapidly both in terms of its internal structures and relationships and in the face it showed to other actors on the industrial relations stage (cf. Crouch 1979; Hyman 1983; Terry 1983; Undy *et al.* 1981).

In the 1990s it has become increasingly common to argue that the unionism of the 1970s, celebrated by Coates and Topham, is itself constraining and must in its turn give way to a new 'new unionism'. Brown (1985: 169–73) has argued that 'the acceleration of the shop steward bandwagon' left workers fragmented and exposed when faced with tightening product markets and newly assertive managers in the 1980s; Kelly and Heery (1994) have argued that decentralization in unions has made it harder to mount coordinated recruitment campaigns and extend union organization to growing sectors of the economy; while Willman *et al.* (1993: 17–19) have demonstrated a marked deterioration in union finances between 1970 and 1979 and have concluded bluntly that 'the British trade union movement cannot afford another decade like the 1970s'. Willman *et al.* also demonstrate that in response to their difficulties many unions initiated a successful reform of their finances in the 1980s. The purpose

Thanks to Alan Grant, Tim Morris, Marc Thompson, Steve Williams, and Phil Wyatt for providing information and to John Kelly and Huw Morris for commenting on an earlier draft.

of this chapter is to identify other areas where the developments of the 1970s have been reversed or supplemented by new initiatives.

The focus of examination is on the internal structure and processes of trade unions and the 'new unionism' of the 1970s is contrasted with the new 'new unionism' of the 1990s along three dimensions: first, the approach that unions have adopted to servicing their members and the associated beliefs about members' interests which underpin the servicing relationship; second, the forms of union government and the procedures which exist for ensuring democratic control and accountability within unions; and third, the system of union management and the policies and procedures that unions rely upon to ensure the effective use of their human, financial, and physical resources.

The comparison is based, in the first instance, on case studies of the TGWU in the 1970s and the GMB in the 1990s, as these have been widely identified as exemplary unions in the respective decades. Both have been the focus of interest from within and beyond the labour movement and have been said to exemplify more general trends. To demonstrate this latter point, survey and other information, drawn from a broader set of unions, is used to indicate that the comparison has a wider validity. Finally, use is made of contemporaneous writing about unions to demonstrate that concrete developments in the two periods have found an echo in ideologies circulating around the trade union movement. The comparison between the two forms of new unionism is followed by an attempt to account for the movement from one to the other and to explain, in particular, why unions like the GMB have become more managerial in the way they conduct their affairs. The chapter concludes with a more abstract consideration of metaphors of historical change and their relevance to and implications for the study of change in trade unions.

2. The New Unionism of the 1970s

One of the purposes of Coates and Topham's book was to celebrate the TGWU under Jack Jones and offer it as a model to be followed across the trade union movement (1974: 83–6, 179–91). What they liked about Jones and his allies in the TGWU was their commitment 'to the concept of democratic trade union-ism, under rank and file control' (1974: 190). And in the late 1960s and early 1970s the TGWU did take a decisive step towards what can be called a participative servicing relationship with its members. Before, the union had been officer-dominated and a professional servicing relationship obtained, in which full-time officers acted as professional representatives on behalf of a largely passive body of clients-members (Undy *et al.* 1981: 277). Under Jones, in contrast, the union leadership both endorsed and encouraged participation by members in union decision-making and activities and promoted self-reliance, such that policy objectives, workplace organization, collective bar-gaining, and representation rested increasingly in the hands of members themselves and their shop stewards. The function of union officers in this new servicing relationship was to facilitate 'self-activity' among members by education, training, and tutelage in the norms of union activism. Jack Jones himself described the objective as follows:

I am working for a system where not a few trade union officials control the situation but a dedicated, well-trained and intelligent body of trades union members is represented by hundreds of thousands of lay representatives—every one of whom is capable of helping to resolve industrial problems and assisting in collective bargaining and the conclusion of agreements (quoted in Taylor 1978: 133).

To achieve this vision Jones instituted a series of reforms in the government of the TGWU (Undy *et al.* 1981: 91–100, 262–78). One thrust was directed at reducing the power of national trade groups, the base of the union's old guard, by widening the prerogatives of Jones himself as General Secretary and by introducing or strengthening district and regional levels of government. Another thrust was directed at extending lay participation in the process of job regulation. This was done, in the first instance, by encouraging the appointment of shop stewards, while other significant initiatives included advocating or complying with the decentralization of collective bargaining, promoting greater lay participation in negotiation teams and encouraging the spread of reference-back procedures, such that collective agreements were ratified by a test of member opinion. There was also greater tolerance of unofficial strike action which represented an effective decentralization of the strike decision.

Accompanying these changes in the structures of decision-making were changes in union management (Undy *et al.* 1981: 94, 99–100, 264–7). The most striking development was a switch from officer to lay representation. At a time when the union was rapidly expanding its membership and number of shop stewards, the size of the officer workforce fell. In financial terms this represented a switch from resourcing the union's activities directly towards reliance on both the unpaid efforts of volunteers and employer subsidy through the medium of facilities agreements. At the same time the union's internal financial system was decentralized, as regions were given greater responsibility for financial and administrative decisions, such as the hiring of office staff and the purchase of office equipment. The system of employee resourcing for officers was also changed and Jones enforced tight control over appointments to ensure that the strategy of participative unionism was implemented and the culture of the organization changed. National officers who were not supportive of the movement towards activist participation were encouraged to resign and a record of shop-floor activism became essential for appointment as a District Officer. A final set of changes occurred in the union's systems of training and communication. Training courses for shop stewards were expanded and a series of pamphlets and guides for activists were produced through the 1970s which were designed both to reinforce the leadership's strategy and promote organizational self-reliance and adversarial collective bargaining among the union's stewards.

These developments earned the TGWU the sobriquet of the 'shop stewards' union' but they found an echo in many other parts of the trade union movement. Increased reliance on shop steward representation at the workplace, for instance, was a general phenomenon. Batstone (1988: 77–80) estimates that the number of stewards increased by '50 per cent or more' between 1966 and the late 1970s as a result both of increasing steward density in well-organized industries like engineering and the spread of steward organization to public and private services. These years also witnessed the development of more sophisticated shop steward organization, as indicated by a growth in steward hierarchy, the establishment of shop steward committees, increased time-off for union activity, and improved facilities (Terry 1983: 69–71). The arguable result, particularly in larger workplaces, was steward organization which was more independent of the external union and better able to achieve self-reliance (Batstone 1988: 103; Brown 1981: 70).

This shift towards participative unionism was reinforced by constitutional and administrative changes within unions. While the TGWU was distinctive in the extensiveness of its constitutional reform, other unions changed their rule books to facilitate the establishment or spread of shop steward organization and to promote greater accountability of officers to delegate conferences (Beaumont 1992: 55; Hyman 1983: 41–4; Seifert 1992: 295; Undy et al. 1981: 119–26, 310–13). Changes were particularly widespread in the structure of decision-making in job regulation where Undy and his colleagues (1981: 310) note 'a greater dispersal of decision-making' both in the sense that responsibilities for bargaining moved down the union hierarchy and that at each level there was greater participation by lay representatives. Not all unions participated in this trend, with some like UCATT and EETPU seeking to reinforce leadership control, but they conclude that dispersal was the dominant 'pattern of change'. A final change in union government had less to do with the content of formal structures and more to do with the way in which they were operated. In several unions, including CPSA, NALGO, NUT and UCATT, the late 1960s and 1970s saw the growth of 'rank and file' opposition movements, committed to a programme of militant confrontation with employers and the expansion of activist democracy, while in other less factionalized unions, such as GMWU, NUPE, and the TGWU itself, lay conferences and executives became more assertive and more prepared to challenge national officers (England 1981).

Running alongside shifts in formal structures of decision-making were changes in union management. While the TGWU was again distinctive in reducing the size of its officer workforce, other unions failed to increase the numbers of officers employed proportionate to their increase in membership with the effect that the number of members per officer increased across the trade union movement (Brown 1980: 143; Undy et al. 1981: 311). The appointment of officers supportive of greater lay participation was also seen in other unions and the issue of employee resourcing assumed greater prominence in policy-making with several union conferences debating officer election and remuneration (Kelly 1988: 148). Another general trend was towards increased reliance on employer subsidy of union activities and an associated expansion of shop steward training and education, the bulk of which was provided by the TUC. Moreover, to support this latter development, both the TUC and individual unions increased their employment of specialist training and education officers and the TUC expanded training in educational methods for union field officers to support their role as facilitators of lay participation. A further change in the role of full-time officers arose from the greater emphasis on accountability to members and shop stewards. There are indications that this trend weakened hierarchical relations within unions, endowing even appointed officers with a democratic legitimation for contesting management control of their activities (Kelly and Heery 1994).

Both reflecting and influencing these concrete developments in union servicing was a distinctive 'rank and filist' current in union ideology, of which Coates and Topham's book was a representative (cf. Cliff 1970; Fairbrother 1984; Lane 1974; Roberts 1973). At the heart of this ideology were a series of claims about workers' interests and the organizational forms which were appropriate to their realization. The first claim was that representation through shop stewards and direct action by workers themselves were more effective means of improving pay and conditions and contesting management control than reliance on professional full-time officers. The second was a conviction that workplace activism was universally applicable and capable of transfer from its traditional engineering heartland to virtually any work environment. The third was that active involvement in unions had intrinsic as well as instrumental value to workers, which fed demands for the democratization of union decision-making over and above other union aims. Democratization itself was typically held to reside in reducing the discretionary powers of representatives through mandating and recall and in reliance on specifically collective forms of decision-making, such as mass meetings, workplace and branch meetings, and block votes. Fourth was a belief that union activism could serve as a basis for a wider transformation of industry and society, essentially through its capacity to generate changes in worker beliefs, attitudes, aspirations, and skills. In reformist versions of the ideology union democracy provided a platform for the construction of industrial democracy and the appetites and abilities acquired by involvement in union government would be deployed in the governance of industry. In revolutionary versions, in contrast, the emphasis was more upon the generation of an oppositional class-consciousness through activism and the significance of workplace organization as a 'prefigurative form' which would reach fruition in the transition to socialism. These beliefs may only have had currency among a minority of trade-unionists in the 1970s but they influenced several prominent union leaders and a large number of activists and were successful in setting the agenda for a great deal of debate within and about trade unions for more than a decade (Joyce *et al.* 1988: 238–56; Kelly 1988; Seifert 1984; Undy *et al.* 1981: 278).

3. The New Unionism of the 1990s

The GMB

Under John Edmonds the GMB has also sought to develop a self-consciously new unionism, though one suited to the very different environment of the 1990s. An important strand in its new agenda has been an attempt to make the union more responsibe to its members and potential members, not just through the operation of democratic machinery, but by directly researching workers' aspirations and designing union services in the light of findings. This represents a movement towards what can be called a managerial servicing relationship, as there is an emphasis on the union operating proactively and seeking to discover what will attract workers to the GMB and retain them in membership and then harnessing its internal resources to ensure appropriate services are delivered. A better managed, more consumer-responsive unionism, in the view of Edmonds and his supporters, is essential if the GMB is to cope with the primary problem with which it is faced, a sustained and continuing decline in union membership. Edmonds himself has identified the thinking behind the GMB's new unionism as follows:

By the middle of the 1980s . . . the trade unions had some difficulty putting together a prospectus or a pitch which would appeal to people in growing sectors of employment. We had a marketing problem. People were asking the 'what can you do for me?' question . . . The unions were dealing with too narrow a range of issues and these were not the ones which employees regarded as most important to them. This was highlighted by surveys we did with MORI. The main thrust of the New Agenda was to identify what we should be doing to represent people according to *their* priorities (Storey *et al.* 1993: 67).

The development of managerial unionism in the GMB can be seen in a number of steps taken by the union since Edmonds became General Secretary in 1986. The first step, as the quotation indicates, has been to directly research what employees want at work and want from their union. Such research has taken two forms. On the one hand the GMB has used projections of changing workforce structure to identify target groups for recruitment activity, and on the other it has commissioned opinion poll and market research to identify employee concerns and aspirations. Much of this latter research has been directed at specific groups, such as women or young workers or workers in new service industries whom the GMB is anxious to recruit. The second step has been to try and develop new services designed to attract and retain targeted workers in the union. A number of these services are designed for consumption by the individual employee and represent a movement towards 'associate unionism', in which discount and advisory services are offered to employees in addition to or in lieu of collective bargaining. The main thrust, however, has been towards changing the collective bargaining agenda to make it more directly relevant to workers' needs. In 1990 the GMB adopted its New Agenda, which sought to broaden the subject-matter of collective bargaining in the light of market research which indicated that 'job security, the opportunity to develop your abilities, flexible work arrangements, and jobs that allow workers to use their initiative and earn promotion all count highly with working people' (GMB 1993: 9). Subsequently the union has tried to make a priority of equal rights, health promotion, flexible hours, and training entitlements in negotiations, out of a belief that these issues have high salience for particular groups of members.

A third step has been to diminish some of the costs of union membership. In part this has been done by changing the union's image so that it is less alienating, particularly to employees who have not been union members before. The GMB's white-collar section, for instance, has been renamed the APEX Partnership after market research indicated that female clerical employees did not want to join an organization with 'union' in its name. The GMB's emphasis on developing a partnership with employers and seeking to develop cooperative industrial relations is also partly designed to reassure prospective members that they will not be involved in industrial action (Edmonds 1988). Finally, the union intends to revise its scale of subscription charges in conjunction with a revision of benefit levels to provide attractive subscription–benefit packages to a range of membership groups, including the low-paid and part-time service sector workers (Willman *et al.* 1993: 152).

These revisions to member servicing have been accompanied by two other steps. One has been to improve the promotion of union services. A new logo has been commissioned, leaflets outlining the union's mission statement distributed to all members, the journal *GMB Direct* revamped, and a series of magazines launched which are targeted at particular membership categories. These adopt the styles of popular women's and youth magazines and include *Working Women; issue,* for younger members; *Community,* for public services; *Threads,* for clothing and textiles; and *Team,* for members in the food and leisure sector (Labour Research Department 1993). The union has also engaged in a number of high profile, integrated campaigns, such as the FLARE campaign for workers' rights, which are intended to operate in the manner of an advertising campaign, raising the profile of the union and attracting particular groups of employees into membership.

The other additional step has been the introduction of control mechanisms to gauge the success of servicing initiatives. The union has begun monitoring collective bargaining claims to ensure that items from the New Agenda are included and has surveyed members to measure satisfaction with individual benefits and estimate the degree to which services are meeting workers' needs. In addition, new procedures have been put in place to measure the union's success in recruitment and the types of worker which are joining and leaving the GMB (Chee and Brown 1990).

Innovation in the servicing relationship in the GMB has been accompanied by innovation in the formal structures of union government. The association is only partly deliberate, however, as some of the most significant changes in union government have arisen from legislation rather than the implementation of a coherent union strategy. As a result of the Trade Union Act 1984 and the Employment Act 1988 the GMB has had to overhaul its procedures of government (Smith *et al.* 1993). The major change has been the replacement of the indirect election of lay representatives to the union's governing Central Executive Council (CEC) and the ex-officio position of Regional Secretaries as CEC members with the election of all CEC officers by individual-member ballot. While this change may have been required by legislation it clearly accords with the emphasis in managerial unionism on direct communication with the membership and Edmonds has sought, so far unsuccessfully, to secure the extension of individual-member ballots to the election of annual conference and regional councils.

Other changes in government have flown more directly from the union's approach to member servicing. Reflecting the concern to differentiate member servicing, a trade-group structure has been developed on top of the existing regional structure and GMB members are now allocated to one of a series of 'product-based' divisions (Technical Crafts, APEX Partnership, Food and Leisure, Clothing and Textiles, Public Services, Energy and Utilities, Process Industries and Construction, Furniture, Timber, and Allied). Another form of differentiation which has been incorporated in changes in union government is that based on gender (GMB 1993: 8; SERTUC 1989). In 1987 the union adopted the principle of positive discrimination in respect of its women members and introduced ten reserved seats for women on the CEC. This decision was followed by the introduction of reserved seats on GMB Regional Councils in 1990 and the GMB has also supplemented its traditional position of National Women's Officer with regional and branch equality officers. Finally, in order to 'encourage recruitment and involvement of young workers' the GMB has tried to create 'the most active young members structure in the UK trade union movement' (GMB 1993: 8).

Developments in the internal management of the GMB have been equally marked. In the field of employee resourcing there has been a review of recruitment procedures with the aim of attracting more women into Organizer positions (GMB 1991), officers have been redeployed to allow more time for recruitment and to give a clearer industrial perspective to their work, and there has been a strengthening of specialist functions and greater use of external consultants. In the field of employee development the union has adopted an objective of trebling the number of GMB postholders receiving training, and particular priority has been attached to equal rights training and training in management techniques for senior officers (GMB 1993). Finally, in employee relations the main developments have been the greater use of involvement and communication techniques, to promote officer and activist support for the New Agenda, and the adoption of a series of measures intended to clarify the responsibilities of officers and ensure closer management control. Prime among the latter has been a new job description for Organizers.

Complementing these changes in the union's personnel management system have been a series of further changes affecting other areas of management (GMB 1993; Willman *et al.* 1993: 150–2). The union has developed a mission statement, identified 'key performance areas', and developed a three-year action programme which set priority tasks and targets for 1992–5. Supporting this venture in performance management have been a new financial system designed to 'tighten links between expenditure and objectives' and new information systems to permit the central tracking of membership and expenditure. Summarizing these developments, Willman *et al.* (1993: 151) have concluded that the GMB 'has been at the forefront of attempts to use accepted management techniques in the administration of union affairs'.

The TUC and Other Unions

While the GMB may be distinctive in its embrace of managerialism, other unions have followed the same route. A perception that unions have drifted out of touch with their constituency has been widespread among union leaders (Kessler and Bayless 1992: 150–1) and Edmonds has not been alone in identifying needs for unions to become more responsive and to market their services more effectively. Roger Lyons, General Secretary of MSF, has written that:

[W]e . . . need to see members as our customers. As sophisticated users of services, people will make choices depending on what impresses them about a particular company or product and what is in it for them. They have become used to high standards and have expectations based on those standards. It is in this framework, of consumer choice, that unions increasingly have to stake their claim to recruitment. We need to reassess what people really want from a union and what will make them join (Lyons 1993).

Lyons goes on to report that his union has been carrying out market research to identify members' needs. This reflects a general trend. The TUC has issued advice to its members on commissioning or conducting surveys of members and a large proportion of unions have made use of this technique, including ANSA, ATL, AUT, BGSU, BIFU, COHSE, IPMS, IRSF, ISTC, LGU, NATFHE, NUPE, NUT, TGWU, TSSA, and USDAW (Chee and Brown 1990; Heery and Warhurst 1994; Labour Research Department 1991*b*, and 1993). The depth and significance of this research activity may not be great in many cases and most unions fall well short of the development of a fully fledged marketing strategy but a fairly generalized shift towards greater use of consumer information is apparent.

There has also been a general movement to make union servicing more attractive. The initiative which has attracted most attention has been the promotion of new individual member services, such as discounts, financial benefits, and advice (cf. Kessler and Bayliss 1992; Sapper 1991). Alongside services intended for consumption by individual members, however, have been two other types of change. First, unions have attempted to change the collective bargaining agenda to increase the relevance of membership to employees. A fairly widespread initiative attempts to negotiate improvements in the conditions of part-time employees, reflecting their growing importance in the labour force (Labour Research Department 1989; TUC 1991). Second, unions representing professional employees, such as ATL, AUT, and NUT, have sought to give greater priority to representing the professional interests of their members out of a belief that such a representative strategy will prove more effective in the longer term than one narrowly focused on pay and conditions and that it is more in tune with the aspirations of their members (AUT 1993).

An additional reason for unions like the NUT accentuating their role as representatives of professional interests, arises from a belief that resort to industrial action in the 1980s alienated teachers from the union and led to a loss of membership. Other unions, including APAP, ATL, AUCL, EETPU, MPO, and PAT, have deliberately stressed their lack of militancy in an attempt to diminish both the psychological and potential economic costs to employees of taking out membership. A considerable number of unions have also sought to reduce barriers to membership by instituting changes in the administration of union subscriptions. This has been done either by making trade-unionism more affordable via sliding-scale subscriptions or by reducing the visibility of increases in dues through indexation. (Willman *et al.* 1993: 205; Morris and Willman 1993).

Improvements in the promotion of trade-unionism have also been fairly widespread. More appealing titles and logos have been adopted by a number of unions (e.g. MSF, NUT, UNISON) and there has been a general attempt to improve the readability of union publications (Labour Research Department 1993). In a number of cases (ATL, IPMS, RMT, TGWU, TUC) these initiatives have been extended to embrace the provision of free helplines, more accessible advisory services, and the establishment of new local offices adjacent to concentrations of membership (Maksymiw *et al.* 1990: 52–3; TGWU 1992). There has also been a growth in the use of video and advertising both by individual unions and the TUC, and the launch by most large unions of promotional campaigns, targeted at members, prospective members, or the general public. In 1994 the TUC itself was 're-launched' as 'a campaigning organization' (TUC 1993*a*: 12).

Evidence of unions attempting to gauge the effectiveness of member servicing is less apparent, though there are some indications that a concern with generating and using management information is growing. A feature of several opinion surveys commissioned by unions, for instance, has been to assess member satisfaction with new services or with channels of communication. There has also been a general improvement in the quality of membership information as a result of the legislative impulse to computerize membership records, which can and has been used to analyse the flow of workers in and out of unions (Rees and Owens 1993). According to Bain *et al.* (1993), much recruitment activity by unions is poorly managed but sophistication is growing and about a third of unions monitor the success of recruitment initiatives.

In the field of union government, the need for the GMB to revise its constitution has been experienced across the trade union movement, though the extent of reform has varied according to the degree to which existing rules complied with Conservative legislation (Smith *et al.* 1993: 368–70). The result has been the consolidation across the trade union movement of a 'parliamentary' form of democracy based on individual-member ballots. One effect of the spread of individual balloting, particularly for leadership elections, has been the strengthening of the position of General Secretaries *vis-à-vis* activist-dominated conferences and intermediate levels of government (Kessler and Bayliss 1992: 149–50; Smith *et al.* 1993: 379). Other developments pointing to the centralization of control in the hands of senior officials include proposals to reduce the size and frequency of governing conferences in several unions, the withdrawal of financial decisions from scrutiny by conferences, and the introduction of new controls on strike activity (Hearn 1993; Martin 1992; Willman *et al.* 1993). Parallel initiatives can be seen in the TUC, where proposals exist for an extensive pruning of the structure of representative committees (TUC 1993*a*).

The attempt in the GMB to provide for the expression of more differentiated membership interests in formal structures of decision-making can also be seen in other unions. Newly established UNISON has adopted a divisional structure and several unions operating in the public sector or privatized utilities have been driven down a similar path as a result of changes in the structure of collective bargaining. UNISON is also committed to the principle of proportionality in the composition of all committees, conferences, meetings, and delegations reflecting a general trend across the labour movement to increase the representation of women in decision-making structures (SERTUC 1989). An associated development in several unions, including UNISON, has been the introduction of representative structures for minorities constituted on the basis of disability, ethnicity, age, and sexual orientation (Labour Research Department 1991*a*). Moreover, women's and minority groups have become increasingly assertive in recent years and a significant change in trade union politics has been the emergence of pressure groups, like the Pay Equity Project, the Trade Union Disability Alliance, and Lesbian and Gay Employment Rights.

Evidence of greater managerialism in union administration is also available. The best publicized developments have occurred within the TUC, where the past decade has seen a number of strategic planning initiatives. The reports of the Special Review Body into trade union organization (TUC 1988; 1989), for instance, embody the assumptions of rational business planning, in that they contain a review of environmental change, propose new services designed to match changing markets, and contain proposals for updating communications, marketing, and personnel management to support these new initiatives. More recently the review of the TUC's own role has resulted in the formulation of a mission statement and the adoption of a form of performance management (TUC 1993*a*).

A number of individual unions have also gone down this business planning route. ATL and the TGWU have commissioned consultants to review their organizations and the TGWU, MSF, and UNISON have developed mission statements and strategic plans (Maksymiw *et al.* 1990; TGWU 1992). While integrated planning initiatives of this kind may be confined to a minority of unions, there is evidence of a more general attempt to plan specific union activities. Bain *et al.'s* (1993) survey of recruitment initiatives indicates a growth in the use of specific campaigns and there has been a growth in the use of other planned campaigns to influence public opinion, retain political funds, or minimize the adverse effect of the Government's anti-check-off legislation. The spread of more sophisticated budgeting systems within unions, noted by Willman *et al.* (1993), is also indicative of greater weight being attached to business planning.

Innovation in union management can also be seen in the management of specific resources. With regard to personnel management, for example, there has been both a strengthening of specialist functions, such as computing, public relations, equal rights, and finance, which support the managerial servicing relationship, and widespread if rather limited attempts to appoint more women and members of ethnic minorities to officer posts in order to reflect differentiation among union members (Kelly and Heery 1994). There has also been a major initiative on the part of the TUC to improve officer training. Partly this is directed at securing a more professional workforce by formulating clear occupational standards of competence with supporting training modules; partly it is intended to restructure officer attitudes and priorities to increase sensitivity to the requirements of particular groups of union members, such as women, ethnic minorities, and gays and lesbians; and partly it is intended to endow senior officers with managerial skills (TUC 1993*b*). To secure the latter objective the TUC has established a training partnership on 'Strategic Management in Trade Unions' with Cranfield University. This emphasis on the role of senior officers as union managers has also led in a number of unions to a strengthening of the line management relationship and the use of performance appraisal and even performance-related pay to guide the work of front-line organizers (Kelly and Heery 1994).

Running alongside these developments in personnel management have been changes in the management of other resources. There is some evidence of a rationalization of union offices, largely driven by a need to reduce costs, but also by a desire to concentrate employees and improve their accessibility to members (TGWU 1993). Office procedures and the management of information have also been upgraded by the computerization of membership records and the wider use of information technology (Rees and Owens 1993). And finally, there has been a reform of union finances, which has improved the financial performance of a number of unions despite falling membership (Willman *et al.* 1993).

Managerialism within unions has been reflected in a growing interest in union management among those who write about them. One manifestation of this has been a renewed focus on the activities of union officers and on the formal structures and policies of unions, which has partly displaced the focus of the 1970s on the workplace and shop stewards (cf. Kelly and Heery 1994; Mason and Bain 1991; Sapper 1991; Willman *et al.* 1993). Another manifestation has been the emergence of studies which analyse union activities using concepts drawn from management disciplines, such as marketing and corporate strategy (cf. Chee and Brown 1990; Willman 1989; Willman and Cave 1994). A third manifestation has been a number of publications which argue explicitly for unions to adopt a new consumerism in relation to members, a new managerialism in their internal administration, and a new realism in relations with employers (cf. Bassett 1986; Bassett and Cave 1993*a*, 1993*b*; Lloyd 1986). The most trenchant statement of this view has come from Bassett and Cave. They have argued that unions should model themselves on private sector service organizations, like the AA, and promote carefully researched packages of member services to individual employees. Unions should shed their old collectivist baggage, including collective bargaining, they argue, and endorse the new consumerist individualism. Such views have naturally been contested in the labour movement but they nevertheless represent a significant and novel current in trade union ideology.

Summary

The new unionism of the 1990s has consisted of a partly fortuitous and partly deliberate combination of three elements. At its heart is a managerial servicing relationship, in which unions seek to research members' needs and design and promote attractive servicing packages in response. This relationship rests on the assumption that members are largely instrumental in their orientation to unions and behave as reactive consumers who can be attracted or alienated from unions by the quality of service which is provided. It also rests on the assumption that members possess differentiated needs, which require a customizing of union servicing both for different industrial and occupational groups and for groups whose identities are formed outside employment but which are work-mediated, such as women, ethnic minorities, the disabled, and gays and lesbians (Murray 1994). A final assumption is that employees possess interests which extend beyond the workplace, but which can nevertheless be addressed by trade unions. This has led on the one hand to the provision of discount and advisory services which are consumed by the individual member away from work, while on the other it has led to an attempt to broaden the representative strategy of unions and address environmental and public policy issues (Edmonds 1986).

These themes are reproduced in the other elements of the new unionism. Union government has been reformed to afford greater scope for the expression of individual member opinion through secret ballots, while representative structures have been divisionalized to accommodate differentiation in members' aspirations. Union management has also experienced reform with the growth of experiments in business planning and the albeit halting development of new skills and systems to enable union head offices to track member opinion, design and deliver appropriate servicing, and monitor union success. A final theme which connects all of these developments is a trend towards centralization of decision-making, largely at the expense of union activists and officers at intermediate levels of union organization.

While the changes which constitute the new new unionism can be clearly identified and are manifest in a range of unions there are limits to the extent and depth of innovation. New approaches to servicing members, to governing unions and managing union resources have been seized upon enthusiastically in some quarters, but in others change has been marginal. Different unions have also accentuated different elements of the new unionism: the representation of gender interests in UNISON versus the promotion of individual member services in the AEEU. Moreover, new initiatives have largely originated among senior union leaders and specialist advisers and like any strategy have been contested and negotiated as they have passed down the organization. In the GMB powerful Regional Secretaries have imposed a brake on several of the initiatives proposed by John Edmonds and the annual conference has repudiated elements of reform intended to centralize decision-making. Partly as a consequence of such resistance new elements in trade-unionism exist alongside forms established earlier, with the result that most unions display hybrid approaches to member servicing, government, and administration. The GMB retains a strong commitment to participative unionism, for example, and continues to be heavily dependent on the work of its shop stewards. This has led the union to minimize the possible contradiction between participative and newer approaches to member servicing. It has sought to integrate its stewards within a national union framework through increased training and communication, while attempts to encourage women and members of minorities to seek representative positions are an attempt to create a new activist tier more supportive of the leadership's New Agenda.

4. Explaining the New New Unionism

The new unionism of the 1990s has emerged against a background of union decline both in membership and in influence. Not all unions have experienced a reduction in membership or a diminution in their bargaining power or even influence over government but the perception of crisis has been pervasive across the trade union movement in recent years. It is this perception which has formed the background to changes in union servicing, government, and internal management. However, it is possible to go beyond the statement that most unions face a more hostile operating environment and try and identify specific factors which have generated particular responses to change. In what follows, therefore, four types of pressure on unions are considered as originators of the changes within unions described above. They are: coercive pressures emanating from government and employers, consumer pressures emanating from the unions' 'membership market', competitive pressures deriving either from other unions or from employers, and the process of mimesis, the modelling of union organization on other organizational forms because the latter are available, actively promoted in the 'organizational field' in which unions operate and widely endorsed (DiMaggio and Powell 1991: 69–70).

It has frequently been claimed that structures and relationships within unions are determined by external pressure exerted by employers and government (Bramble 1993; Hyman 1989*b*: 78–85). The need to reach an accommodation with other powerful actors in industrial relations, it is argued, encourages union leaders to centralize decision-making and enforce internal discipline over union members. Coercive pressures of this kind undeniably have helped generate the new new unionism. Trade unions have acquiesced in the government's legal regulation of their internal systems of government and in several cases have centralized decision-making in order to minimize the risks to their funds from civil action initiated either by employers or by their own members (Smith *et al.* 1993). The divisionalization of union government has also been shaped in some cases by a prior divisionalization of the public services, utilities, and firms in which unions have members.

Beyond changes to the formal structure of union government, however, the influence of coercive pressure is less easy to identify. It is the case that the legislative requirement to maintain a record of members' names and addresses has stimulated improvement in union information and communication systems but there is less certainty that pressures from government and employers have shaped the content of policies which unions have sought to promote using new techniques. In some unions, like the EETPU, the launching of new services for members has been combined with an attempt to coax employers into new-style recognition agreements. In other cases, though, new unionism has been allied with policies which challenge management prerogative. Examples are the use of surveys of union members' attitudes to contest management initiatives, such as the introduction of performance-related pay, or to extend the collective bargaining agenda to new issues, such as training and participation (Heery and Warhurst 1994; Storey *et al.* 1993). The attempt by white-collar unions, like AUT and NUT, to broaden their representative strategy to embrace professional issues also challenges the 'new managerialism' in the public services, notwithstanding its association with a withdrawal from militancy. What these cases suggest is that new approaches to member servicing in unions enjoy an essentially contingent relationship with policies towards employers and cannot be viewed as a functional response on the part of union leaders to coercive pressure.

John Edmonds and other advocates of the new new unionism have presented it as demand-driven, a rational and necessary response on the part of unions to pressure from their consumers. In one sense this is incontrovertible. Aggregate union membership and the membership of many individual unions has fallen and the structure of the unions' membership market has changed with the growth in service, non-manual, and atypical employment (Waddington 1992). However, in a second more precise sense there is less evidence that the innovations described above are demand-driven. The belief that they are has two components: that employees have deliberately rejected unions and that simultaneously they have acquired a new set of differentiated interests which unions perforce must represent. Regarding the first proposition, available research indicates that the most powerful influences on union membership are 'the structural contexts' in which people are employed rather than their 'individual preferences' (Gallie 1989: 27). Declining union membership is primarily the result of these changing contexts rather than alienation from unions, and in fact opinion polls and the British Social Attitudes survey suggest that popular support for unions has grown rather than diminished over the past decade (Edwards and Bain 1988: 313–14; Millward, 1990: 28–30).

The second proposition also finds little support in available evidence. Research on union joining indicates that employees' motivations are often instrumental but that that instrumentality is typically of a traditional nature. Workers continue to join unions or believe unions to be of value because they secure better pay, working conditions, and job security, provide protection from arbitrary management, offer representation in disciplinary and grievance cases, and provide legal assistance in the event of injury at work (Gallie 1989; Guest and Dewe 1988; Kerr 1992; Millward 1990; Sapper 1991). Demand for new services, such as financial advice and discounts, which have been a prominent feature of the new unionism, does not seem particularly high outside areas like nursing and teaching where indemnity insurance has traditionally been valued (Blyton and Turnbull 1994: 126; Kerr, 1992; Sapper 1991). Moreover, while surveys indicate some differentiation of members' interests on lines of gender, they also suggest that there is a large degree of overlap in what men and women want from unions and that differences within the sexes, influenced by variable labour-market situations, are as extensive as those between (Kelly 1990: 37). The formation of pressure groups within unions to promote the interests of women and minorities perhaps provides alternative evidence of a growing segmentation in the membership market, but equally it can be viewed as a change on the supply side, in the ideology and politics of trade unions themselves.

A third possible explanation of recent changes in union servicing, government, and management is that they have been generated by competitive pressures amongst trade unions themselves and from employers. The fight to retain a share of a declining pool of membership has served as a trigger for innovation in a number of cases. Several TUC-affiliated unions, including NATFHE, NUT, and UNISON, have either reviewed their approach to member servicing or altered their formal structures of government in the wake of intensified competition from non-affiliated rivals. Competition from MPO, for example, has led UNISON to initiate new services for its management membership, while its adoption of a service-based structure is partly designed to counter the strong occupational identities articulated by rivals like the RCN. Innovation has also been encouraged by competition for merger partners. The introduction of a divisional structure by the GMB has been motivated in part by a desire to attract smaller unions into merger and facilitate their integration. Not all unions which have reviewed and updated their approach to member servicing or divisionalized their structures, however, have been engaged in competition for members, either directly or through merger. The civil service unions, for instance, have displayed several of the features of the new unionism but are relatively sheltered from competition.

As well as competing with each other, unions can be drawn into competition with employers, and an additional source of innovation could be the spread of human resource management with its promise of intensified worker commitment to the firm. It has been suggested that the spread of human resource management could reduce employee demand for union protection and there has certainly been some concern among trade unions at the use of new management techniques to displace the union role (Guest 1989: 44; Heaton and Linn 1989). However, the evidence of acute competition to unions from this source is again limited. Serious application of the human resource management model is restricted to a minority of firms in Britain and evidence on the effects of a variety of management techniques associated with human resource management indicates that they are often unsuccessful in changing 'us and them' attitudes among workers (Sisson 1993; Kelly and Kelly 1991). The NCU, whose members at British Telecom have been subject to a battery of new management techniques and the Project Sovereign programme of culture change, recently discovered through a commissioned survey that 'employees were five times as likely to trust information given to them by their union than that provided by the employer' (Norman 1993: 123).

A fourth possible source of the new new unionism is mimesis, or the more or less deliberate imitation of organizational forms found elsewhere. Among advocates of the 'new institutionalism in organizational analysis' (Powell and DiMaggio 1991: 1) mimesis has been offered as an explanation of isomorphism in organizations, the fact that often there is a striking homogeneity in institutional forms across any given organizational field. Bassett and Cave's admonition to unions to act like the AA is an attempt to encourage precisely this kind of isomorphic transfer, while the use of the language of 'new wave' management by union leaders in several of the quotations above suggests that contemporary business practice is being accepted as a desirable model. In this, the unions are not alone as a wide range of organizations including charities, other voluntary agencies, public services, and political parties have sought to remodel themselves in recent years on the lines of the 'excellent firm'. The themes of customer-responsiveness and the efficacy of professional management have been ubiquitous.

It is also probable that mimicry has been mixed with an element of coercion, as unions have assumed business norms and practices to demonstrate to employers that they too are well managed and worth doing business with. An anecdote can illustrate this pressure. A large number of unions in recent years have commissioned surveys from consultants and market research organizations. A researcher at the Institute of Employment Studies, which has been used by several unions, reported that his organization was commissioned rather than a labour movement body, because research findings would be treated more seriously by managers and government departments, who were themselves used to commissioning consultants' reports. The need to influence managers to secure union objectives, therefore, can lead to the adoption of the language, techniques, and organizational forms which managers recognize and value (DiMaggio and Powell 1991: 68).

Mimesis may also account for the spread of new forms between unions and indeed between national union movements. What is striking about many of the elements of the new new unionism in Britain is that they echo developments in the United States (cf. Clark and Gray 1991; Dunlop 1990). The reports of the TUC's Special Review Body are modelled on the AFL–CIO's earlier report, *The Changing Situation of Workers and Their Unions*, and several TUC initiatives, including the promotion of individual member services and the launching of 'Union Yes' publicity campaigns, are direct imports from the USA. Among British unions the pressure to imitate has also probably been supplemented by the pressure of competition, though competition for status and prestige rather than directly for members. One of the GMB's key objectives is 'to ensure that the GMB is the best known and best respected union in Britain' (GMB 1993) and the launch of new services, of recruitment and other campaigns, and the updating of communications and corporate image seem partly directed to this end. Moreover, where one union acquires status and prominence through changing its approach to member servicing then there is likely to be pressure on others to follow. These again can be illustrated by an anecdote. A UNISON full-time officer described how under John Edmonds her GMB colleagues had begun to arrive at joint negotiation sessions with professionally produced and very impressive looking briefing documents. These, she alleged, were not consulted during negotiations, but rather had a symbolic purpose and had most effect on officers from other unions who wanted the same type of support. Once managerial unionism has been established, therefore, it can diffuse as other unions mimic innovators, leading to the situation described above, in which a large number of unions, of different sizes and structures, with differing occupational bases and trends in membership and even different ideologies, are making use of the same repertoire of organizational techniques.[1]

The new new unionism should be viewed as the product of a combination of forces. In part it has been forced upon unions by other industrial relations actors, in part it represents an adaptation to consumer and competitive pressures, and in part it originates in the absorption of currently fashionable approaches to organization and their diffusion across the labour movement. Recognition of this last factor implies qualification of the others. Accounts of change in trade unions have tended either to present change as a functional accommodation to external pressure or a rational adaptation to environmental change. Where innovation is mimetic, however, it may be neither functional nor rational. According to DiMaggio and Powell (1991: 69), mimetic behaviour is likely 'when an organization faces a problem with ambiguous causes or unclear solutions'. This is precisely the situation facing British unions. The rational response to the key problem of membership decline which many of them face is uncertain and this has led, whether deliberately or not, to imitation; to the adoption of institutional forms which are used elsewhere, which possess high legitimacy, and which are promoted by opinion-formers and consultants. Innovations such as new member services, or attitude surveys, or management development for general secretaries may prove effective over time but effects are not causes and changes of this kind are as much conventional as functional.

5. Conclusion: Time's Arrow, Time's Cycle

Stephen Jay Gould (1988; 1991) has argued that theoretical controversies in the historical sciences originate in competing metaphors of the historical process. He terms these 'time's arrow' and 'time's cycle' and differentiates them in terms of the way they order historical data. Each comes in two versions and each of these can generate very different models of historical

---

[1] The concept of 'mimetic isomorphism' has been developed to explain why large numbers of organizations, facing seemingly dissimilar environments, display the same characteristics. The focus is on accounting for uniformity, rather than the normal social science concern with describing and explaining variation. It may be, however, that organizations have a differential capacity to imitate. Among unions one could hypothesize that a tendency to innovate and absorb organizational practices from outside will be a function of the openness of a union. Mimesis, that is, is likely to occur where union officers are appointed, particularly from outside; where the union's membership straddles organizational, industrial, and occupational boundaries; where the union is part of an established network, such as the TUC; where officers and activists are trained outside their own organization; and where the union employs and accords relatively high status to specialists, who will typically be locked into occupational networks extending beyond their own organization and even the trade union movement. Reversing the perspective, one would expect to see relatively limited adoption of the new new unionism, apart from those elements required by law, among enterprise and occupational unions, non-TUC unions, unions which elect their officers or recruit from their own membership, and unions with small and peripheral specialist departments.

change. Although Gould's argument has been developed for the natural sciences of geology and palaeontology it is equally applicable to the social sciences, including industrial relations, and each version of his two metaphors can and has been used to generate very different theories of change in trade unions. In what follows the metaphors are described, examples are given of their application in industrial relations, and the implications of each for theorizing the transition from the old to the new new unionism are explained. There is also an attempt to evaluate each metaphor and assess its utility. As will be seen, the conclusion echoes Gould's own preference for the second version of time's arrow in which historical change is cumulative but directionless and driven by contingency rather than the unfolding of an essential purpose.

In the first version of time's cycle historical data simply express an imma-nent and unchanging reality. An example from industrial relations is the Leninist theory of trade-unionism in which the essential features of unions are given by their location in capitalist societies and the particular histories of individual unions reveal the limitations of unionism *per se* to generate significant social change. Clearly the utility of this metaphor is limited if one's purpose is to elucidate change in trade unions. It nevertheless has value in highlighting possible limitations to change or the fact that institutional development within trade unions is constrained by certain fixed elements in the trade union form (cf. Dunn 1990: 23; Blyton and Turnbull 1994: 11). It has been argued above, for example, that a managerial servicing relationship has lain at the heart of innovation in trade unions in the 1990s. The logical conclusions of such a relationship are that union policies should be selected solely by consumer preference while unions should withdraw from those segments of the membership market where it is not possible to service members cost-effectively. Neither conclusion is likely, however, because unions are value-driven organizations and typically formulate and pursue their policies on 'non-economic grounds' (Willman *et al.* 1993: 213). The status of unions as voluntary and not-for-profit organizations, therefore, imposes a constraint on the lengths to which recent reforms can be pushed. To use Hyman's (1991: 637) phrase the dominant trend may be towards business unionism but it is 'business unionism with a social conscience'.

In the second version of time's cycle, there is again an emphasis on stability and the enduring quality of natural and social forms, but historical data are conceived of as repeating sequences of events. History in this case runs to a biological rhythm in which structures experience decline, renewal, and decline once more. There are many theories in industrial relations which are rooted in this metaphor, though they tend to fall into two types. In the first are theories which account for union behaviour in terms of adaptation to an external cycle. Examples include theories of union membership or strike activity which accord primacy to the effects of cyclical factors, such as inflation, trends in real wages, and unemployment. In the second, a cyclical pattern in union behaviour originates in an internal contradiction or conflict between groups within unions. An example in this case is provided by the frequent claim that 'unions are characterized by a set of dual pressures towards control and constraint [of their members], on the one hand, and resistance [to employers], on the other' (Fairbrother 1990: 171; cf. Fairbrother and Waddington 1990; Hyman 1989*a*). The logical conclusion of this claim is that union behaviour will be characterized by alternate phases of mobilization and quiescence, depending on which moment is dominant in the contradictory relation between unions and their members.

The value of this second version of time's cycle is that it provides a useful counter to crude attempts to extrapolate into the future from the current situation facing trade unions (Crouch 1990; Kelly 1990). However, there are problems associated with both internal and external cyclical theories. A problem with the latter is that cyclical effects may only be generated within more fundamental institutional constraints and may cease to operate if those underlying constraints are altered (Price 1991). In the late 1980s, for instance, declining unemployment and rising inflation might have been expected to generate an increase in union membership, but this failed to occur (Kelly and Richardson 1989: 148). Arguably, the reason why such cyclical factors had failed to operate in the way they had done before, was that the economic and political changes of the early 1980s had shifted the rules of the industrial relations game. According to Dunn (1993: 181; cf. Millward 1994: 119–20), the 1980s witnessed a 'de-incorporation' of management thinking, such that resistance to union organizing and even derecognition of unions became accepted policy options for a growing proportion of employers. The effect of this shift has been to make it harder for unions to attract and retain members and to nullify the influence of cyclical economic pressures which previously served as effective stimulants of union growth.

The problem with internal theories of cyclical change is that they tend to conflate dissimilar phenomena. A cyclical interpretation of the emergence of a more managerial approach to member servicing, for example, would suggest that this represents the re-establishment of bureaucratic control within unions after the period of member mobilization in the 1970s. It represents a return, in other words, to a phase of leadership dominance and member passivity. However, there are marked differences in the approach to member servicing currently being developed by unions and the approach which obtained in the 1950s and early 1960s before the shop steward decade got under way. In the earlier phase a professional servicing relationship was dominant, in which a professional cadre of full-time officers acted on behalf of a largely passive body of members or clients, who required expert representatives to define, interpret, and advance their interests. This is very different from the model of member servicing proposed by John Edmonds, for whom the union member is a reactive consumer, whose interests must be continually tracked and responded to by the well-managed union organization. Both approaches are distinguishable from participative unionism, where member autonomy and self-servicing are the goal, but they are also distinct from each other. The flaw in theories of trade-unionism which are rooted in the metaphor of time's cycle is that they are blind to this significant difference.

The other great metaphor of historical change is time's arrow. Gould labels the first version of this metaphor 'time's directional arrow', essentially because historical data are conceived of as non-repetitive and ordered in a discernible and meaningful sequence. Change is cumulative and occurs in a clear direction, and in most versions, takes place through the gradual evolution of new forms. Theories which originate in this metaphor, therefore, typically make bold claims about the sweep of history and their adherents are usually confident that current developments can be extrapolated into the future. Examples of time's directional arrow in industrial relations are manifold. Perhaps the best example are the writings of the Oxford School, with their implicit view that trade unions and collective bargaining are the natural precipitation of a maturing capitalist democracy (Dunn 1990: 24). More recent versions tend to follow one of two routes. In the first, change in trade unions, or even their extinction, is viewed as the product of deep-seated, structural changes in the economy. The emergence of 'post-industrialism', or 'disorganized capitalism', or 'post-Fordism', or whatever label is used to denote change in the industrial and occupational structure is identified as both the cause of trade-unionism's crisis and the source of new needs among employees which unions must strive to represent. In the second version, change in trade unions is occasioned not so much by changes in the material infrastructure of society, as in values. For this idealist version of time's directional arrow the source of trade-unionism's crisis is the 'new individualism', which requires that unions should shed their traditional collectivism and target advisory, training, and negotiation services at the individual union consumer (Bassett and Cave 1993a).

The value of this account of change in trade unions has lain in its challenge to the rather complacent 'nothing much has changed' school in industrial relations. Its main deficiency is its view of history as a gradual unfolding, either of ideas or of structural developments within the economy. What is striking about the recent history of British trade unions is its discontinuity and the fact that over a short span of twenty-five years the trade union movement has experienced rapid swings in its fortunes and equally rapid shifts in policy-making and styles of organization. Trends in aggregate union membership bear this out. Unions grew rapidly between 1969 and 1979 and have declined equally precipitously since. This fluctuation in union fortunes, moreover, occurred against a background of relatively steady change in industrial and occupational structure and of reasonably stable values within British society (Kelly 1990). It can also be argued that recent developments in the government and management of unions represent not so much a functional adaptation to the logic of history as an uncertain borrowing from other types of organization, precisely because the causes of and solutions to unions' problems are complex and obscure.

Gould's own work in evolutionary biology is characterized by three main claims. First, that evolution displays a pattern of 'punctuated equilibrium', in which periods of stability or gradual change are suddenly overturned by catastrophe, which redirects the process down a new and unforeseen route. An example is the sudden extinction of dinosaurs, probably as the result of an asteroid impact, which enabled the evolution of large mammals. Second, that chance or contingency plays a large part in determining which life-forms survive and flourish and which yield to extinction. It is often not the fittest who survive in life's race, according to Gould, but the luckiest, who happened to be in the right place when catastrophe struck or to have had the good fortune to inherit some characteristic from their ancestors which enabled survival in a changed environment. Third, that life-forms are often only imperfectly adapted to their environments, one reason being that structures inherited from the past must be put to new uses in new environments to which they are not ideally suited. One of Gould's favourite examples here is back pain in humans which, though it may be exacerbated by poor ergonomics, essentially originates in the fact that our spines are inherited from creatures which walked on all fours.

These claims are rooted in the metaphor of time's arrow as history is seen as a cumulative process of continual and often surprising innovation. Time's arrow in Gould's account, however, is directionless: change is often sudden, unpredictable, and catastrophic and historical data are the product of contingency, of chance cause and chance inheritance.[2] Very similar views of historical change can be seen in a broad range of industrial relations writings. Thus, Kelly's (1988: 295) restatement of Marxist theory ends with the proposition that the generation of class consciousness is dependent on the contingent response of the ruling élite to waves of industrial militancy. Other writers have sought to explain variation in national patterns of industrial relations and the structure and character of national trade union movements in terms of the variable impact of and response to catastrophic events originating outside the industrial relations system, such as wars and global recession (cf. Gallie 1983; Price 1991; Sisson 1987). Increasingly in comparative industrial relations use has been made of the concept of 'historical compromise'. The term refers to key turning-points in industrial relations history, when, in response to national crisis, government, employers, and unions reached an accord which set the institutional pattern of industrial relations in individual nation states for a considerable period of time. These

---

[2] Contingency in the form of a dinosaur-obsessed 4-year-old led to my own discovery of Gould's work. On a trip to the Natural History Museum in South Kensington I found one of his collections of essays in the bookshop and was hooked. Reading Gould I was struck by the parallels between many of the debates in palaeontology he described and very similar controversies in industrial relations. Since social Darwinism there has been an understandable reluctance on the part of social scientists to borrow from natural historians, but the contemporary concerns of the latter with models and metaphors of change provide a potentially useful quarry of ideas. However, the parallel should not be overdrawn. Patrick, now 7, is still keen on dinosaurs but displays no interest in trade unions and we are yet to visit the Labour History Museum.

chance inheritances from the past, it is argued, determine union membership levels, union structure and ideology, strike patterns, and the forms of union interaction with governments and employers to the present day.

The metaphor of time's directionless arrow suggests four propositions should guide analysis of recent change in trade unions: first, that change is discontinuous with periods of rapid innovation giving way to stability; second, that change is cumulative, with inheritances from the past both limiting current developments and being bent to new purposes; third, that change is driven by contingency or unique combinations of events which have turned trade unions down unpredicted routes; and fourth, that change may be non-functional, so that recent developments in unions do not represent an optimal or complete adaptation to present circumstances. Each of these propositions underlies the account of transition from the old to the new new unionism set out above.

Thus, evidence has been presented to support the view that there have been two significant waves of innovation in unions in the past three decades, which have both represented a sharp break with pre-existing approaches to member servicing, union government, and union management. Each innovation, however, has occurred on the site of existing institutional forms (cf. Dunlop 1990). It was pointed out above, for instance, that change in the GMB has been resisted because new patterns of union government cut across the established system of semi-autonomous Regions. More generally, there is evidence that attempts by union leaders to deploy full-time officers and lay activists within integrated recruitment campaigns have been met with resistance. The decentralization of decision-making and officer accountability, which occurred in several unions in the 1970s, has acted as a constraint on new attempts to direct unions from the centre in the 1990s (Kelly and Heery 1994). There is also evidence, however, of union leaders seeking to integrate elements of participative unionism with a more managerial approach to member servicing, so that a kind of hybrid unionism is emerging. The attempts within the GMB to expand shop steward training, to integrate stewards and lay officials more fully in national policy initiatives, and to alter the gender and ethnic make-up of the union's activist tier all provide examples.

In explaining the emergence of the new new unionism resort has not been made to the effect of catastrophe, though perhaps the election of Margaret Thatcher in 1979 deserves that description. Rather, innovation in unions has been seen as the product of a unique combination of forces which have pushed or encouraged unions to change their approach to member servicing or reform systems of government and internal management. The explanation offered, that is, is conjunctural (cf. Blyton and Turnbull 1994: 110–11) and as such differs both from cyclical and directional interpretations of change, while also matching Gould's requirement of contingency. Finally, the claim that much recent change in unions has occurred through mimesis or the absorption of institutional forms found elsewhere accords with the argument on imperfect adaptation. The new new unionism has been forced on unions by external pressures to a degree, but it has also arisen from competition for prestige among unions and union leaders, from attempts by union managers, specialists, and factions to accumulate power and influence, and from the simple fact that trade-unionism is not a closed world and that those who work within it are capable of imitating the language, techniques, and organizational forms found beyond its walls.

REFERENCES

AUT (1993), *Promoting Professionalism: The Way Forward on Pay and Conditions* (London: AUT).

Bain, P., Mason, B., and Snape, E. (1993), 'Trade Union Recruitment: A National and Local Level Assessment', paper presented to Cardiff Business School Conference, Unions on the Brink? The Future of the Trade Union Movement.

Bassett, P. (1986), *Strike Free: New Industrial Relations in Britain* (London: Macmillan).

———— and Cave, A. (1993*a*), *All for One: The Future of the Unions* (Fabian Pamphlet, 559; London: Fabian Society).

———— ———— (1993*b*), 'Time to Take the Unions to Market', *New Statesman and Society* (Sept.), 16–17.

Batstone, E. (1988), *The Reform of Workplace Industrial Relations: Theory, Myth and Evidence* (Oxford: Clarendon Press).

Beaumont, P. B. (1992), *Public Sector Industrial Relations* (London: Routledge).

Blyton, P., and Turnbull, P. (1994), *The Dynamics of Employee Relations* (Basingstoke: Macmillan).

Bramble, T. (1993), 'Trade Union Organization and Workplace Industrial Relations in the Vehicle Industry 1963–1991', *Journal of Industrial Relations*, 34/1: 39–61.

Brown, W. (1980), 'The Structure of Pay Bargaining in Britain', in F. Blackaby (ed.), *The Future of Pay Bargaining* (London: Heinemann), 129–47.

———— (1981) (ed.), *The Changing Contours of British Industrial Relations* (Oxford: Basil Blackwell).

———— (1985), 'The Effect of Recent Changes in the World Economy on British Industrial Relations', in H. Juris, M. Thompson, and W. Daniels (eds.), *Industrial Relations in a Decade of Economic Change* (Madison, Wisc.: Industrial Relations Research Association).

Chee, H., and Brown, R. (1990), *Marketing Trade Unions* (Bradford: Horton Publishing).

Clark, P. F., and Gray, L. S. (1991), 'Union Administration', in G. Strauss, D. G. Gallagher, and J. Fiorito (eds.), *The State of the Unions* (Madison, Wisc.: Industrial Relations Research Association).

Cliff, T. (1970), *The Employers' Offensive* (London: Pluto Press).

Coates, K., and Topham, T. (1974), *The New Unionism: The Case for Workers' Control* (Harmondsworth: Penguin).

Crouch, C. (1979), *The Politics of Industrial Relations* (Glasgow: Fontana).

———— (1990), 'Afterword', in G. Baglioni and C. Crouch (eds.), *European Industrial Relations: The Challenge of Flexibility* (London: Sage).

DiMaggio, P. J., and Powell, W. W. (1991), 'The Iron Cage Revisited: Institutional Isomorphism and Collective Rationality', in Powell and DiMaggio (1991).

Dunlop, J. T. (1990), *The Management of Labor Organizations: Decision Making with Historical Constraints* (Lexington, Mass.: Lexington Books/DC Heath and Company).

Dunn, S. (1990), 'Root Metaphor in the Old and New Industrial Relations', *British Journal of Industrial Relations*, 28/1: 1–31.

——— (1993), 'From Donovan to . . . Wherever', *British Journal of Industrial Relations*, 31/2: 169–87.

Edmonds, J. (1986), 'Uniting the Fragments', *New Socialist* (June), 18–19.

——— (1988), 'Goodbye to Confrontation', *New Socialist* (Mar.), 12–15.

Edwards, P. K., and Bain, G. S. (1988), 'Why Are Trade Unions Becoming More Popular? Unions and Public Opinion in Britain', *British Journal of Industrial Relations*, 26/3: 311–26.

England, J. (1981), 'Shop Stewards in Transport House', *Industrial Relations Journal*, 12/5: 16–29.

Fairbrother, P. (1984), *All Those in Favour: The Politics of Union Democracy* (London: Pluto Press).

——— (1990), 'The Contours of Local Trade Unionism in a Period of Restructuring', in P. Fosh and E. Heery (eds.), *Trade Unions and Their Members: Studies in Union Democracy and Organization* (Basingstoke: Macmillan).

——— and Waddington, J. (1990), 'The Politics of Trade Unionism: Evidence, Policy and Theory', *Capital and Class*, 41: 15–56.

Gallie, D. (1983), *Social Inequality and Class Radicalism in France and Britain* (Cambridge: Cambridge University Press).

——— (1989), *Trade Union Allegiance and Decline in British Urban Labour Markets* (Oxford: Nuffield College).

GMB (1991), *Women Organisers: Special Report to Congress '91* (London: GMB).

——— (1993), *The Future of Trade Unions: GMB Submission to the House of Commons Employment Committee: October 1993* (London: GMB).

Gould, S. J. (1988), *Time's Arrow, Time's Cycle: Myth and Metaphor in the Discovery of Geological Time* (Harmondsworth: Penguin).

——— (1991), *Wonderful Life: The Burgess Shale and the Nature of History* (Harmondsworth: Penguin).

Guest, D. (1989), 'Human Resource Management: Its Implications for Industrial Relations and Trade Unions', in J. Storey (ed.), *New Perspectives on Human Resource Management* (London: Routledge).

——— and Dewe, P. (1988), 'Why Do Workers Belong to Trade Unions? A Social Psychological Study in the UK Electronics Industry', *British Journal of Industrial Relations*, 26/2: 178–201.

Hartley, J. (1992), 'Joining a Trade Union', in J. Hartley and G. M. Stephenson (eds.), *Employment Relations: The Psychology of Influence and Control at Work* (Oxford: Blackwell).

Hearn, S. (1993), 'Trade Union Finances 1975–1990 and The Unions' Response to Financial Decline', BA Business Studies Dissertation, Kingston University.

Heaton, N., and Linn, I. (1989), *Fighting Back: A Report on The Shop Steward Response to New Management Techniques in TGWU Region 10* (Barnsley, Northern College and TGWU Region 10).

Heery, E., and Warhurst, J. (1994), *Performance Related Pay and Trade Unions: Impact and Response* (Kingston: Kingston University Business School).

Hyman, R. (1983), 'Trade Unions: Structure, Policies and Politics', in G. S. Bain (ed.), *Industrial Relations in Britain* (Oxford: Basil Blackwell).

—— (1989*a*), *The Political Economy of Industrial Relations: Theory and Practice in a Cold Climate* (Basingstoke: Macmillan).

—— (1989*b*), *Strikes* (4th edn., Basingstoke: Macmillan).

—— (1991), 'European Unions: Towards 2000', *Work Employment and Society*, 5/4: 621–39.

Joyce, P., Corrigan, P., and Hayes, M. (1988), *Striking Out: Trade Unionism in Social Work* (London: Macmillan).

Kelly, J. (1988), *Trade Unions and Socialist Politics* (London: Verso).

—— (1990), 'British Trade Unionism 1979–1989: Change, Continuity and Contradictions', *Work Employment and Society* (special issue), 29–65.

—— and Heery, E. (1994), *Working for the Union: British Trade Union Officers* (Cambridge: Cambridge University Press).

—— and Kelly, C. (1991), ' "Them and Us": Social Psychology and "the New Industrial Relations" ', *British Journal of Industrial Relations*, 29/1: 25–48.

—— and Richardson, R. (1989), 'Annual Review Article 1988', *British Journal of Industrial Relations*, 27/1: 133–54.

Kerr, Alan (1992), 'Why Public Sector Workers Join Unions: An Attitude Survey of Workers in the Health Service and Local Government', *Employee Relations*, 14/2: 39–54.

Kessler, S., and Bayliss, F. (1992), *Contemporary British Industrial Relations* (Basingstoke: Macmillan).

Labour Research Department (1989), 'Unions and Part-timers—Do They Mix?', *Labour Research*, 78/3: 19–22.

—— (1991*a*), 'Sexuality a Union Issue?', *Labour Research*, 80/6: 10–12.

—— (1991*b*), 'Are Members Safe in Union Hands?', *Labour Research*, 80/9: 13–14.

—— (1993), 'Union Journals', *Labour Research*, 82/8: 10–12.

Lane, T. (1974), *The Union Makes Us Strong* (London: Arrow).

Lloyd, J. (1986), 'Trade Union Policy: Consumerism over Politics?', *Manpower Policy and Practice* (Summer), 36–40.

Lyons, R. (1993), 'Modern Times', *Tribune* (21 May).

Maksymiw, W., Eaton, J., and Gill, C. (1990), *The British Trade Union Directory* (Harlow: Longman).

Martin, R. (1992), *Bargaining Power* (Oxford: Clarendon Press).

Mason, B., and Bain, P. (1991), 'Trade Union Recruitment Strategies: Facing the 1990s', *Industrial Relations Journal*, 22/1: 36–45.

Millward, N. (1990), 'The State of the Unions', in R. Jowell, S. Witherspoon, and L. Brook (eds.), *British Social Attitudes: The 7th Report* (Aldershot: Gower).

—— (1994), *The New Industrial Relations?* (London: PSI).

—— and Stevens, M., Smart, D., and Hawes, W. R. (1992), *Workplace Industrial Relations in Transition* (Aldershot: Dartmouth).

Morris, T., and Willman, P. (1993), 'The Union of the Future and the Future of the Unions', paper presented to Cardiff Business School Conference, Unions on the Brink? The Future of the Trade Union Movement.

Murray, G. (1994), 'Structure and Identity: The Impact of Union Structure in Comparative Perspective', *Employee Relations*, 16/2: 24–40.

Norman, D. (1993), 'Trade Unions and New Management Techniques', in C. Gouch and D. Marquand (eds.), *Ethics and Markets: Cooperation and Competition within Capitalist Economies* (*Political Quarterly*, special issue; Oxford: Blackwell).

Powell, W. W., and DiMaggio, P. J. (1991), *The New Institutionalism in Organizational Analysis* (Chicago: University of Chicago Press).

Price, R. (1991), 'The Comparative Analysis of Union Growth', in R. J. Adams (ed.), *Comparative Industrial Relations: Contemporary Research and Theory* (London: HarperCollins Academic).

Rees, T., and Owens, D. (1993), 'The Computerisation of Trade Union Membership Records', *Work Employment and Society*, 7/1: 121–33.

Roberts, E. (1973), *Workers' Control* (London: George Allen & Unwin Ltd.).

Sapper, S. (1991), 'Do Members' Services Packages Influence Trade Union Recruitment?', *Industrial Relations Journal*, 22/4: 309–16.

Seifert, R. (1992), *Industrial Relations in the NHS* (London: Chapman & Hall).

—— (1984), 'Some Aspects of Factional Opposition: Rank and File and the National Union of Teachers', *British Journal of Industrial Relations*, 22/3: 372–90.

SERTUC (1989), *Still Moving Towards Equality* (London: SERTUC).

Sisson, K. (1987), *The Management of Collective Bargaining: An International Comparison* (Oxford: Basil Blackwell).

—— (1993), 'In Search of HRM', *British Journal of Industrial Relations*, 31/2: 201–10.

Smith, P., Fosh, P., Martin, R., Morris, H., and Undy, R. (1993), 'Ballots and Union Government in the 1980s', *British Journal of Industrial Relations*, 31/3: 365–82.

Storey, J., Bacon, N., Edmonds, J., and Wyatt, P. (1993), 'The "New Agenda" and Human Resource Management: A Roundtable Discussion with John Edmonds', *Human Resource Management Journal*, 4/1: 63–70.

Taylor, R. (1978), *The Fifth Estate: Britain's Unions in the 1970s* (London: Routledge & Kegan Paul).

Terry, M. (1983), 'Shop Steward Development and Management Strategies', in G. S. Bain (ed.), *Industrial Relations in Britain* (Oxford: Basil Blackwell).

TGWU (1993), *One Union T&G* (London: TGWU).

TUC (1988), *Meeting the Challenge: First Report of the Special Review Body* (London: TUC).

—— (1989), *Organising for the 1990s: The SRB's Second Report* (London: TUC).

—— (1991), *Collective Bargaining Strategy for the 1990s* (London: TUC).

—— (1993a), *The Future of the TUC* (London: TUC).

—— (1993b), *Trade Union Standards and Qualifications* (London: TUC).

Undy, R., Ellis, V., McCarthy, W. E. J., and Halmos, A. M. (1981), *Change in Trade Unions: The Development of UK Unions Since the 1960s* (London: Hutchinson).

Waddington, J. (1992), 'Trade Union Membership in Britain, 1980–1987: Unemployment and Restructuring', *British Journal of Industrial Relations*, 30/2: 287–324.

Willman, P. (1989), 'The Logic of "Market Share Trade Unionism": Is Membership Decline Inevitable?', *Industrial Relations Journal*, 20/4: 260–70.

—— and Cave, A. (1994), 'The Union of the Future: Super-Unions or Joint Ventures?', *British Journal of Industrial Relations*, 32/3: 395–412.

—— Morris, T., and Aston, B. (1993), *Union Business: Trade Union Organization and Financial Reform in the Thatcher Years* (Cambridge: Cambridge University Press).

9

JAPANIZATION AND NEW INDUSTRIAL RELATIONS

David Grant

1. Introduction

By the end of January 1993 there were 167 Japanese manufacturers in the UK employing a total of 50,315 local workers (AJEI 1992; JETRO 1993).[1] These companies are portrayed as being in the vanguard of employers who have implemented new industrial relations practices in the UK (Bassett 1986; Wickens 1987; White and Trevor 1983; Trevor 1988; IRS 1990; Roberts 1988; Gleave and Oliver 1990; Reitsperger 1986a; Garrahan and Stewart 1992). So as to survive both the direct challenge of Japanese competitors and the economic climate of the 1980s and 1990s Japanese management techniques have also been widely adopted among UK companies. In the sense that Japanese management techniques are representative of new industrial relations practices this further embellishes the argument that they are a key characteristic of new industrial relations in the UK.

In this chapter a theoretical link (described as an overlap) between the issues of Japanization and new industrial relations is explored. This is followed by an examination of the management practices in operation at a Japanese transplant in the UK consumer electronics sector. Finally, the implications of the case study results for Japanization and the wider debate concerning new industrial relations are considered.

I am particularly grateful to Cliff Oswick and Patrick Barber for their helpful comments on earlier drafts of this chapter. The research upon which the chapter is based formed part of an ESRC-funded Ph.D. at the Department of Industrial Relations and Personnel Management, LSE.

[1] If joint ventures with local companies and Research and Development operations are included in this calculation then the figures rise to 207 establishments, employing 60,341 locals.

2. Japanization and New Industrial Relations: A Theoretical Overlap

Oliver and Wilkinson (1992: 1) suggest that the concept of 'Japanization' in the UK operates at the two levels described in the above introduction: it can be used to describe either the actual 'process and impact' of Japanese inward investment or to describe the 'attempts of British companies to emulate Japanese practices'. However, a more refined definition of Japanization is presented by Ackroyd *et al.* (1988: 11–13) who identify three types. The first of these is 'direct' Japanization. This refers to the arrival in Britain of Japanese firms who bring Japanese practices with them.

The second type of Japanization identified by Ackroyd and his colleagues is that of 'mediated' Japanization. They use it to describe the emulation of Japanese practices by non-Japanese firms and divide it into two subcategories. The first, 'mediated Japanization 1', applies to British companies who have adopted Japanese practices in the belief that if Japanese companies enjoy higher standards of business performance than their Western counterparts, then copying their practices should result in a correspondingly better business performance. The argument is simply that the Japanese are doing something right and that British indigenous industry is doing something wrong, so it is of value to copy the Japanese method. 'Mediated Japanization 2' discusses the use of Japanese practices by emulating companies, as a tool to force through changes in production methods and working practices. The workforce is persuaded that the only way the company can survive in the face of strong competition is to adopt Japanese practices as soon as possible. Ackroyd *et al.* argue that in fact what management are doing is implementing Japanese management practices not because they see them as Japanese, but because they represent the sort of changes that they may have wished to put into place for some time. They take the UK car industry as an example of this approach, citing Marsden *et al.*'s work concerning Ford's attempt to introduce its 'After Japan' campaign. Marsden and his colleagues argued that 'increasing the flexibility of workers has less to do with imitating Japan than with the need to improve productivity and maintain production levels with much reduced workforces and with the effects of the changing technology' (Marsden *et al.* 1985: 117).

Ackroyd *et al.*'s final type of Japanization is that of 'full' or 'permeated'. In this instance Britain could be seen to mirror Japan's economic and social structure: State and private sector emulating Japanese approaches to Research and Development, education and training, investment and marketing.

Binding these definitions of Japanization together is the explicit belief that, in the context of manufacturing industry, it offers an alternative production system to traditional Western methods and is one that incorporates a very distinctive brand of employee relations. Several pieces of work on Japanization go on to argue that when transplanted to the UK, Japanese production methods owe a great deal of their success to these employee relations practices. The practices aim to encourage certain employee attitudes and behaviour which improve the individual's work performance and therefore the performance of the company overall (Turnbull 1986, 1988; Wickens 1987; Bassett 1986; White and Trevor 1983; Oliver and Wilkinson 1992; Jenner and Trevor 1985; Reitsperger 1985, 1986*b*).

White and Trevor's study of Japanese transplants in the UK captures this perception perfectly, arguing that their employee relations practices aim to foster

a stable workforce with a high level of commitment to the company: extremely co-operative in accepting change, extremely unwilling to enter into strikes or any other forms of conflict, and generally putting the company's interests level with or even ahead of its own. The outcome is a high and rising level of productivity, and an altogether easier climate in which management can plan for changes in products and processes (1983: 5).

At one level, this particular quote can be seen as representative of discussion concerning the definition and concept of Japanization and its attendant employee relations. At a second level it highlights an overlap of Japanization with the issue of new industrial relations in the UK. The overlap is demonstrated by the importance it attaches to the issue of committed and cooperative workforces who identify with the interests of their employing Japanese transplants or emulators. This directly relates to the definition of new industrial relations used in this chapter.

In the context of British industrial relations a key feature of new industrial relations is management's attempt to use employee relations practices that attack and reduce attitudes among employees that are best encapsulated by the popular expression 'them and us'. A social psychological definition of 'them and us' is given by Kelly and Kelly (1991). They argue that it stems from a perception that there exists a clear division between management and workers and that these two groups have conflicting interests (see also Guest *et al.* 1993). Here, it is argued that employee relations practices at Japanese transplants in the UK are in line with a strategy of reducing 'them and us' attitudes among employees and are therefore highly salient to the issue of new industrial relations.

Kelly and Kelly's theoretical framework is based on the argument that reductions in the division between management and workers may be induced by certain employee relations practices that use any one, or a combination, of three mechanisms (see Fig. 9.1). They refer to these practices as 'new industrial relations initiatives'. These are defined as initiatives that focus on altering employee attitudes through the use of financial participation, new forms of job design, influence in decision-making, and communications (1991: 27–33).

The first of Kelly and Kelly's three mechanisms to attitude change concerns intergroup contact. An increase in contact between the two groups of

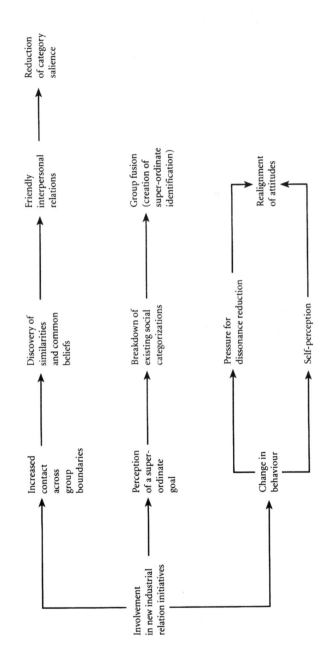

FIG. 9.1. Three possible routes to attitude change

Source: Kelly and Kelly (1991: 33)

management and workers will result in a reduction of the importance of group membership and the development of interpersonal relationships. The two groups begin to find common interests and realize that the negative perceptions they hold of each other are inaccurate (Allen 1986; Allen and Stephenson 1983, 1985). Consequently, a more cooperative and productive relationship emerges at the workplace (Hewstone and Brown 1986). Attempts to build such a relationship are apparent at Japanese transplants in the UK. Hence, the company handbook distributed to all new employees at one Japanese firm, contains a welcoming address from the Japanese managing director in which he describes intergroup contact in terms of a partnership, emphasizing that it 'depends on mutual co-operation and understanding, and is a contract where each partner is prepared to make a positive contribution to the overall success of the venture' (Oki 1990: 1).

The second mechanism is the creation of superordinate goals. A superordinate goal may be defined as one which supersedes the sectional goals of opposing parties and which cannot be achieved unless they cooperate with each other (Sherif 1966). In effect, a unitarist outlook is adopted whereby the interests of the worker and the company merge into one based on the profitability or success of the company. Japanese companies in the UK are keen to foster superordinate goals. The company handbook at one such transplant states that all staff, whether management or employees, should follow the philosophy that 'we are one' (Hitachi 1990: 4). The handbook distributed to employees at another stresses that its joint representative body, where management and employees discuss matters of common interest, should 'Work as a team' and that it 'has responsibility for reviewing the performance and plans of the Company and recommending to the Company polices, practices and procedures which will be to the *mutual benefit* of the Company and its staff' (author's emphasis) (Pioneer 1991: 8).

The third mechanism is based on the possibility of altering worker attitudes by changes in behaviour at the workplace. At one Japanese transplant the company handbook tells employees that management will seek to use participative and cooperative practices in order to promote a 'positive and harmonious relationship between the Company and all members of staff' (Pioneer 1991: 7). Such an approach conflicts with old traditional worker perceptions of the management–worker relationship being adversarial. This conflict leads to a state of dissonance which is resolved by altering attitudes so that they are aligned with the new behavioural requirements (Cooper and Fazio 1984).

Kelly and Kelly's work draws on a series of studies of new industrial relations practices to identify what are described as 'obstacles to attitudinal change' (1991: 33–9). These contribute to the failure of new industrial relations practices to capitalize on any of the three mechanisms for attitude change. The overlap between the issues of Japanization and new industrial relations means that they can also be assumed to apply to employee relations practices implemented at Japanese manufacturers in the UK. In summary, the four obstacles are:

1. A lack of choice for workers over participation in new industrial relations schemes. Do workers have any say in the decision to adopt any new industrial relations practices that they are to be subject to and can they opt out after introduction?
2. A lack of institutional support whereby management fail to show or maintain interest in new industrial relations practices because they either provide unprofitable results or threaten their own power and expertise. The practices therefore lose impetus.
3. A possible lack of trust between workers and management about the operation of new industrial relations schemes. For example, do management establish a record of allowing employees genuine participation in making decisions that may affect them?
4. An inequality of status and outcomes so that the benefits of the new industrial relations practices are perceived to favour one group of participants more than the other.

So far, a theoretical overlap between Japanization and new industrial relations has been identified. It has also been argued that employee relations practices in use at Japanese transplants facilitate the successful operation of their production methods. However, the relationship between employee relations practices and production methods in operation at Japanese transplants is more complex than this.

Take Wood's analysis of Japanization. In it he notes that: 'The distinctiveness of Japanese methods is not simply that a particular set of practices are followed, but that they are devised and adopted in such a way that they are *integrated and mutually supportive* of each other' (1992: 584; author's emphasis). One must then consider the nature of the link between employee relations practices at Japanese transplants in the UK and the production methods that they are designed to support. This is exactly what Oliver and Wilkinson do where they discuss a theory of 'dependency relations' (1992: 68–88) and then apply it to the management of these companies. They describe the production systems at Japanese transplants as comprising three basic sets of characteristics. For a transplant to perform successfully it is essential that these three sets of characteristics integrate. Accordingly, Oliver and Wilkinson argue: 'If there is a "secret" to Japan's success, we suggest that it lies in the *synergy* generated by a whole system, and not, as some have suggested, in the specific parts of that system' (1992: 43; author's emphasis).

The first set of Oliver and Wilkinson's characteristics is described as an internal dependency and relates to employee relations practices. These include the harmonization of terms and conditions of work which aim to break down distinctions between blue- and white-collar workers and management and employees; rigorous selection procedures; induction for all employees; participation techniques such as quality circles; employee flexibility coupled with training programmes so that workers may, at management's request, carry out any task that is in their trained ability; communications structures such as morning briefings; and performance-related appraisal (for more detailed discussion of the use of these practices at Japanese transplants see e.g. Wilkinson and Oliver 1992; White and Trevor 1983; Gleave and Oliver 1990; Wickens 1987; Trevor 1988; IRS 1990; Jenner and Trevor 1985; Reitsperger 1985, 1986*b*).

Where transplants are unionized, their approach to employee relations will have generally led to their signing of new-style agreements with a single union. These agreements are based on a spirit and intention which seeks to move industrial relations from a conflictual process to one based on cooperation and trust. In this context, new style agreements can be seen as attempting to facilitate reductions in 'them and us' (Grant 1993; 1994).

New-style agreements incorporate a number of key components. The union accepts that flexibility and single status are features of the workplace. It also becomes involved in detailed participative arrangements designed to enhance employee influence over management decisions. Joint representative bodies, often called advisory boards, are able to discuss any issue either management or employee representatives wish to raise such as management strategy, investment policy, and business performance. They are also a forum in which to discuss industrial relations issues and conduct collective bargaining. Decisions are supposed to be reached on a consensual basis and though not binding on either management or the union they are expected to adhere to them since they have participated in their formulation. Some new-style agreements may also include a no-strike procedure. These forbid strikes and lock-outs at any stage of the bargaining and grievance procedures, and use some form of morally binding arbitration for solving irreconcilable differences (for more detailed discussion of these agreements and their use at Japanese transplants see Wilkinson, Morris, and Mundy 1993; Bassett 1986; Burrows 1986; Gregory 1986; Rico 1987; IRS 1989; Reitsperger 1986*a*; IDS 1987; Pegge 1986; Grant 1993, 1994).

The second and third sets of characteristics discussed by Oliver and Wilkinson relate to production methods. The second set, which is again an internal dependency, concerns 'just-in-time' management. Examinations of Japanese production methods invariably acknowledge that 'just-in-time' management is a central feature (Wood 1992; Piore and Sabel 1984; Schonberger 1986; Womack *et al.* 1990). Specific definitions of 'just-in-time' vary, but essentially it comprises a package of techniques that marshal both human and non-human resources during the manufacturing process so that they contribute to the production of high quality, competitively priced products with the minimum of wastage. It is also seen as being highly vulnerable to disruption caused by labour disputes, machinery or technical faults, or late delivery of components (Voss 1987; Voss and Robinson 1987; Shingo 1982; Mondon 1981, 1983). Facets of just-in-time include manufacturing techniques reliant on new technology (Bratton 1992; Krafcik 1988; Kenney and Florida 1988; Cusumano 1985; MacDuffie and Krafcik 1990). Just-in-time management can also be seen as a process based on the effective design and organization of the work area, the use of quality control mechanisms such as self-checking and batch sampling, and team-working (Tailby and Turnbull 1987, Turnbull 1988; Ohno 1988; Wood 1989; Slaughter 1987; Jurgens and Stromel 1986). The third set of characteristics concerns the external dependency of supplier relations. In line with the aims of just-in-time, a premium is set on a close relationship with suppliers that encourages quality components delivered at the right time and right price (Nishiguchi 1990; Sako 1992; MacBeth 1987; Trevor and Christie 1988).

The employee relations practices at Japanese transplants can therefore be seen as one part of a production system, interacting with other production-related management practices. Such interaction has important implications for any study of new industrial relations in the context of its attempts to reduce 'them and us'. If the Japanese production system is *synergistic* to the extent that its employee relations and other production methods are *mutually supportive* then it follows that what affects 'them and us' attitudes is not only the effective operation of employee relations practices, but also the effectiveness of the production methods in use. This contradicts the assumption that there is a simpler relationship between the employee relations practices that new industrial relations strategies encompass, and an organization's production methods: one where the reduction of 'them and us' through effective employee relations leads to the successful utilization of production methods. This in turn benefits production performance.

That good employee relations practices can impact on the successful performance of the production system is not actually disputed here, but it is only part of the story. In this chapter considerable emphasis is placed on the extent to which production methods in use also affect the ability of a new industrial relations strategy to reduce 'them and us'. In short, production methods will act as an intervening variable where a Japanese transplant (or for that matter a non-Japanese manufacturing company) seeks to create a work environment conducive to reductions in 'them and us' through the operation of employee relations practices. Fig. 9.2 therefore features Kelly and Kelly's three routes to attitude change in amended form. It shows that 'them and us' attitudes are not only affected by how well employee relations practices are operating: they will also be affected by employee perceptions of the performance of the production methods in operation at the company. Both the employee relations practices and the production methods in use at a Japanese transplant can either impede or bolster the effectiveness of a new industrial relations strategy to reduce 'them and us'.

3. The Research Methodology and Background

The remainder of this chapter examines the attempts of a Japanese manufacturing transplant in the UK to affect 'them and us' attitudes and behaviour

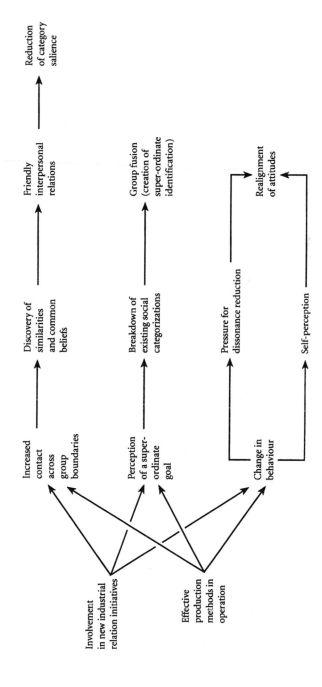

FIG. 9.2. Three possible routes to attitude change incorporating production methods as an additional variable

Source: amended from Kelly and Kelly (1991: 33)

among its employees. The company can be described as representative of 'direct Japanization'. What occurred there illustrates the impact of both employee relations practices and production methods on 'them and us' attitudes and behaviour. Hereon the Company is referred to using the alias of RENCO.

RENCO is in the UK consumer electronics sector. It is, to use Woodward's (1980) classification, a 'large batch' manufacturer, producing different models of the same product on assembly lines. At the time this study was carried out the manufacturing site was divided into three work areas: a main assembly area, a press–weld area, and a subassembly area. The company had a total workforce of 230 people.

All employees at RENCO had gone through an intensive selection procedure incorporating a detailed application form and three interview stages. This sought to identify candidates who would be most receptive to a work environment conducive to reductions in 'them and us'. The work environment offered a package of employee relations practices which included harmonized terms and conditions of employment, flexibility, training, and communications structures such as daily employee briefings. The Company also encouraged workers to participate in production-related issues by coming forward with suggestions about how to improve production and quality.

RENCO's employee relations included a new-style agreement with the then electricians' union, the EETPU.[2] Eighty-four per cent of non-management employees were union members. The agreement featured a no-strike clause and a commitment to enhanced employee participation via a Company Advisory Board. As was the usual practice where the EETPU negotiated a new-style agreement with an employer, the workforce at RENCO had been balloted on whether they accepted the terms of the agreement. They had voted in favour by a substantial margin.

The Personnel Manager at RENCO explained that the 'successful reduction of "them and us"' would enable it to 'lock in' employees. They would not wish to leave because the Company offered a structure of employee relations that made them feel they had helped make it successful. On this basis everyone, irrespective of whether they were management or employees, would come to feel a 'sense of ownership' of the Company. Employee motivation to work and a commitment to stay with RENCO was to be based on them feeling that this is 'our company' (Grant 1993: 278–80).

The Company had commenced manufacturing operations eighteen months prior to the study. The production methods in use there were 'just-in-time'-oriented. Accordingly, RENCO was reliant on its suppliers delivering quality components and by the date requested. Some new technology (robotics and semi-automatic production machinery) was used in the press–weld and subassembly areas. The Company had also put in place a number of quality

---

[2] In 1993 the EETPU merged with the engineers' union to form the AEEU.

control mechanisms including self-checking and batch sampling. Workers were organized into teams.

The following research methodologies were applied at the Company:

1. A workforce questionnaire which included Likert scaled and other questions.[3]
2. Structured interviews with (*a*) a sample of employees as a follow-up to the questionnaire, (*b*) management, and (*c*) shop stewards and full-time officials.
3. A two-month period of observation at the workplace.[4]

These methodologies sought to show how not only employee relations but also production methods in operation at RENCO impacted on 'them and us' attitudes and behaviour among the workforce. In doing so, they were to demonstrate whether any of Kelly and Kelly's three routes to attitude change were successfully in operation at the workplace, or whether they had been blocked by obstacles to attitude change.

4. Japanization and New Industrial Relations in Practice

One hundred and eighty employees at RENCO (up to, but not including, supervisors) were defined as non-managerial. They were invited to fill in the workforce questionnaire. One hundred and forty-four responses were received representing a response rate of 77.3 per cent. Responses to questions were measured on a six-point scale from 'agree very strongly' to 'disagree very strongly'. Means, standard deviations, and percentage scores for these responses are shown in Table 9.1.

Questions concerning employee relations at the Company elicited a number of unfavourable responses. Nearly 80 per cent of respondents disagreed to some extent that communication between workers and management was good at the Company while 67.3 per cent were in some agreement that there was no point in complaining about anything. Fifty-five per cent of respondents were dissatisfied with the way in which the Company treated its workers.

Respondents also expressed dissatisfaction with the union's performance at RENCO. A percentage of 60.4 agreed to some extent that it lacked influence over management decisions, 67.9 per cent that it was weakened by the no-strike clause in the new-style agreement it had signed with the Company, and 65.8 per cent that it was 'too co-operative with management'.

---

[3] The questionnaire incorporated questions from the following sources: Clay Hamner and Smith's (1978) Work Attitude Model; Hackman and Oldham's (1975) Job Diagnostic Survey; and Dewe *et al.*'s (1998) study of Employee Share Option Schemes.

[4] Observation was akin to an 'observer continuous diary' advocated by Thurley and Wirdenius (1973). This involved shadowing supervisors and maintaining a record of the actions and events surrounding them.

Table 9.1 Workforce attitudes at RENCO

Statement	Mean	Std dev	Agree very strongly	Agree fairly strongly	Agree a little	Disagree a little	Disagree fairly strongly	Disagree very strongly
This firm is good to its workers.	3.97	1.33	1.4	9.0	34.6	20.8	14.8	19.4
I am very satisfied with my job.	3.61	1.41	4.9	18.1	28.5	21.4	13.9	13.2
This is a friendly place to work.	2.63	1.30	18.8	31.2	34.0	6.9	2.8	6.3
There is a good team spirit in my work area.	2.93	1.60	19.4	27.8	25.7	8.3	5.6	13.2
I can influence management decisions that affect the work I do	4.44	1.56	6.3	5.6	14.6	14.4	18.1	41.0
I frequently get ideas about how to improve the way I do my job.	2.64	1.18	16.0	30.6	37.4	9.7	2.1	4.2
Morale is good here.	4.66	1.46	2.1	6.9	16.7	15.2	15.3	43.8
It is worth complaining here.	4.40	1.75	9.0	9.8	13.9	11.1	11.8	44.4
Management here are interested if I have an idea that might improve the way I do my job.	3.84	1.79	15.3	9.7	18.8	16.0	12.5	27.7
My job gives me freedom to get on with my work in my own way.	3.76	1.53	10.4	10.4	20.1	27.8	14.6	16.7
The job I do has responsibility attached to it.	2.76	1.73	34.0	17.4	19.4	9.0	8.4	11.8
If a problem comes up in my work area the workers there usually try and sort it out themselves.	2.36	1.24	29.2	28.4	26.4	10.4	4.2	1.4
Communications between workers and management are good here.	4.74	1.48	3.5	7.6	9.0	17.4	16.7	45.8
It would take a lot for me to leave this firm.	4.25	1.74	8.3	15.3	8.3	16.7	13.9	37.5
It bothers me if I do not do my job well.	1.52	1.05	70.1	19.4	4.9	1.4	2.1	2.1
There is variety in my job.	3.55	1.74	20.1	6.3	22.2	20.2	11.8	19.4

RENCO gives its workers enough information about its present and future plans.	4.08	1.60	6.9	13.2	13.2	26.4	11.8	28.5
The union here is good at taking up our individual grievances.	3.86	1.48	5.6	9.0	34.7	16.0	13.9	20.8
The union here influences some of the management decisions that affect the work I do.	4.03	1.35	2.1	9.0	28.5	25.7	13.9	20.8
I feel loyalty towards the union here.	3.90	1.57	6.7	9.6	32.6	16.3	8.1	26.7
Having a 'No Strike' agreement at RENCO does not weaken the union.	4.06	1.59	9.1	9.8	13.2	28.0	13.3	26.6
The union here is not too co-operative with management.	4.17	1.47	3.5	11.2	19.5	21.7	18.2	25.9

Notes: n = 144.
Some of these questions are presented in reverse format to those on the original questionnaire.

Table 9.2 Expectations of the union at RENCO

I expect the union to concentrate on:	Mean score (1–99)	Overall rank ordered position	Item expressed as an expectation of the union %	Item expressed as a first- or second-rank ordered choice %	
				1	2
Increasing my wages	26.0	1	71.3	34.6	26.7
Giving me job security	38.7	2	56.9	27.4	17.6
Improving work conditions	53.3	3	40.2	2.9	26.5
Giving me an opportunity to participate in making some of the decisions that affect how the company is run	73.5	6	16.7	1.0	6.9
Working with management to try and find solutions to problems	72.7	5	17.6	2.9	5.8
Not letting management gain any advantage over the workforce	71.0	4	19.6	3.9	7.8
Something else	99.0	7	0	0	0

Notes: n = 102.

To calculate mean scores the rank scores allocated by a respondent to each item were added together and then divided by the total number of respondents. (Where a respondent identified one or more expectations, but did not rank order them, an average rank score was calculated for the expectation cited.)

Perceptions of the union's performance at the Company contradicted employee expectations of it. Seventy-one per cent of questionnaire respondents at RENCO had joined the EETPU. They were presented with a list of six things they might expect the union to focus on and were asked to state in order of preference which two they considered to be the most important (Table 9.2). The four reasons most cited by respondents identified a belief in union membership as an investment based on both collective interests (e.g. 'not letting management gain any advantage over the workforce'), and individual interests (e.g. 'it will give me job security'). The fifth-placed and less traditional expectation (which was more in line with the spirit and intention of new-style agreements) was the hope that the union would 'work with management to try and find solutions to problems'. A desire for greater participation in the Company's decision-making process received little response. These results suggest that many union members expected it to play a traditional representational role, one that necessitated an adversarial and low-trust relationship with management. This conflicted with the principles behind the new-style agreement the union had signed with RENCO.

Questionnaire responses also suggested that employee relations at RENCO discouraged respondents' participation in production-related issues (Table 9.1). While 84 per cent of respondents agreed to some extent that they 'frequently' had ideas about how to improve the way they did their jobs,

56.2 per cent of them said they believed management would not be interested if they approached them with such an idea. In addition, over two-thirds of respondents expressed some dissatisfaction with the amount of information the Company passed to employees about its present and future plans and nearly three-quarters of them disagreed that they could influence management decisions concerning work-related issues.

Respondents had mixed perceptions about the organization and management of production methods at RENCO (Table 9.1). There were positive responses to questions about problem-solving in teams (83.9 per cent of respondents) and engendering team spirit (72.8 per cent), though it appeared from subsequent interviews that these responses were more a reflection of friendliness of co-workers than endorsement of the actual practice of teamwork. This may also explain why nearly three-quarters of questionnaire respondents gave a positive answer when asked whether RENCO was a friendly place to work. The level of job responsibility felt by respondents was high at 70.8 per cent, but their responses to other questions about the design and content of jobs at the Company indicated areas of dissatisfaction. Only 51.5 per cent demonstrated a degree of job satisfaction and less than half agreed that there was any autonomy or variety in their jobs.

It would be tempting to assume that some of the questionnaire results so far reported point to the importation of these attitudes into the Company, i.e. responses were influenced by the respondent's previous work experiences and the media. While these factors may have had some influence they were certainly not the sole cause. It appears that duration of employment at RENCO had an effect.

T-tests were conducted which compared the responses of the thirty-three (22.9 per cent) respondents who had been employed at RENCO since it commenced production with the responses of those subsequently employed (Table 9.3). As has already been shown, employees at RENCO had poor perceptions of employee relations and a number of issues related to the organization and management of production methods (Table 9.1). The key point is that length of exposure to the Company's work environment had accentuated a number of these perceptions. Those employed at the Company's outset indicated the lower levels of job satisfaction and were least satisfied with levels of job autonomy, management–worker communications, and aspects of the union's performance.

The questionnaire results indicate workforce dissatisfaction with both employee relations and a number of issues related to the organization and management of production methods at RENCO. Explanations for these responses became apparent during observation and interviews carried out at the Company.

Much of the dissatisfaction with employee relations at RENCO can be attributed to the management structure in place at the Company. Because of its size, it employed local as well as Japanese management. It therefore had what the research terms a 'dual management structure'. Most of the senior

Table 9.3. T-Tests: those employed at RENCO when it first commenced production v those subsequently employed

Statement	Mean		SD		T-SCORE
	Original employees (n = 33)	Subsequent employees (n = 117)	Original employees (n = 33)	Subsequent employees (n = 117)	
This firm is good to its workers.	4.42	3.82	1.20	1.39	2.43*
I am very satisfied with my job.	4.45	3.36	1.12	1.38	4.65***
This is a friendly place to work.	2.18	2.75	1.42	1.23	−2.10*
There is a good team spirit in my work area.	3.03	2.89	1.68	1.58	0.42
I can influence management decisions that affect the work I do.	3.13	3.69	1.78	1.48	−1.65
I frequently get ideas about how to improve the way I do my job.	2.90	2.55	1.46	1.06	1.28
Morale is good here.	4.72	4.12	1.04	1.48	2.20*
It is worth complaining here.	3.76	3.30	1.88	1.71	1.26
Management here are interested if I have an idea that might improve the way I do my job.	3.34	2.70	1.72	1.78	1.85
My job gives me freedom to get on with my work in my own way.	3.31	2.60	1.48	1.51	2.42*
The job I do has responsibility attached to it.	1.46	1.85	1.64	1.74	−1.19
If a problem comes up in my work area the workers there usually try and sort it out themselves.	2.51	2.31	1.37	1.15	0.76
Communications between workers and management are good here.	4.19	3.61	1.31	1.50	−2.15*
It would take a lot for me to leave this firm.	3.70	3.12	1.64	1.75	1.75
It bothers me if I do not do my job well.	1.37	1.57	0.96	1.07	1.04

There is variety in my job.	2.64	2.54	1.71	1.74	0.31
RENCO gives its workers enough information about its present and future plans.	3.61	2.93	1.54	1.58	2.21*
The union here is good at taking up our individual grievances.	4.24	3.74	1.54	1.44	1.64
The union here influences some of the management decisions that affect the work I do.	4.21	3.97	1.45	1.31	0.85
I feel loyalty towards the union here.	4.21	3.79	1.64	1.54	1.29
Having a 'No Strike' agreement at RENCO does not weaken the union.	3.28	3.00	1.62	1.59	0.85
The union here is not too cooperative with management.	3.64	3.04	1.02	1.55	2.59**

Notes: n = 144
* P = <0.05
** P = <0.01
*** P = <0.001

Six-point scale: 1 = Agree very strongly, 6 = Disagree very strongly

Some of these questions are presented in reverse format to those on the original questionnaire.

management positions were occupied by Japanese managers, while the majority of middle management positions were occupied by local managers. One outcome of this structure was that employee relations at RENCO was predominantly the remit of local management. They were involved in most of the day-to-day interaction with employees and shop stewards at the Company. Japanese management appeared content to let this happen because, as one of them explained, they felt that they lacked the knowledge and confidence to deal with UK trade-unionism. Their remoteness from industrial relations matters meant that during the study they never directly interfered in, questioned, or criticized the methods used by local management to maintain control and discipline of employees.

The style in which local management operated employee relations was low-trust and adversarial. It was therefore not conducive to reductions in 'them and us' at the workplace. Their approach to practices designed to foster communications and participation over production-related issues reflected this and was seen by employees as unenthusiastic, if not hostile. For example, an operator from the assembly area complained that: 'When we first came here we had a morning meeting every day. I think we're still supposed to, but we don't any more. That sums up management's interest in telling us what's going on. They assume we're too thick to understand or not interested.' Similarly, another operator explained that he secretly kept a cache of screws under his work bench. He was not meant to have these screws (they were purchased for another job) but he had taken them from stores anyway. These, unlike the ones he was supposed to be issued with, screwed easily into the product. This made his job less taxing, but also meant that he could work more quickly and therefore not disrupt the flow of line. Often whole boxes of the normal issue screws had inferior threads. He claimed he had told his manager this and had suggested that the Company order the more reliable screw, but that the manager had shown no interest: 'All I got was "I see what you mean" and he just walked off!'

Local management were also accused of applying rules related to the regimentation of the work environment in a harsh, unfair style. One particular rule was that workers should not talk to each other in the work areas and workers complained that it was enforced using an excessive number of verbal and written warnings. Several employees argued that this type of behaviour was indicative of RENCO's local management exhibiting what they saw as traditional British management attitudes. 'They're not looking for co-operation,' observed one. 'They believe that bawling you out and using threats is more effective and far quicker.'

The style in which local management operated employee relations at the Company had a further implication. It rendered the union ineffective so that many of its members believed the union to be weak and/or too cooperative. In the union's defence, a steward explained why this sentiment was only half-correct:

Weak yes, but too co-operative no. Management won't let us be co-operative. Depending on the issue, I've tried suggesting that rather than go into a disciplinary procedure they should let me have a quiet chat with the individual to warn him or her that they're being watched. But they just call me in to the disciplinary as the rep and that's that. Our relations are very formal. The idea that we are supposed to help the place run better just doesn't cross management's minds. They just see us as the other side. We do our best, but with management having that sort of attitude we rarely get a fair hearing. Workers see what's going on and think that because we're not allowed to organize a strike we're weak.

Poor perceptions of the union's performance at RENCO may have been exacerbated by events surrounding the most recent pay discussions. What happened illustrates the sort of difficulties the union encountered when dealing with local management.

Local management conducted the pay discussions which took place at the Company's Advisory Board. Their first offer was rejected by the workforce in a ballot. This was despite a recommendation from stewards who sat on the Board that the workforce accept it because it was all the Company could afford.

After three months of talks a revised and more complex package was assembled. This did not improve on the basic rate of pay previously offered because management remained adamant that the Company could not afford such an increase. Instead, it offered additional payments and benefits related to sick pay and skills accrued. These were to pay for themselves by improving the Company's performance.

Once again, stewards accepted in good faith that the offer was all the Company could afford, and along with management set about persuading the workforce to accept it. They encountered considerable difficulty. Many workers found it hard to understand the package and asked why management could find extra money to fund the additional payments and benefits, but not an increase in basic pay.

Management realized that the offer was likely to be rejected. Their reactions to this showed that they were not interested in the spirit of trust and cooperation supposed to underlie the Company's new-style agreement. They simply called in the local full-time official and the senior steward and made an increased offer on the basic rate of pay for all shop-floor workers. There were no additional payments and benefits attached.

Shop-floor workers were delighted and accepted this offer, but as the basis of the deal sank in they became aware that they, the Advisory Board, and the union had been misled. For many, the events showed that management could not be trusted and therefore the Advisory Board was an ineffective body. In the words of one operator: 'For weeks now management have been telling them on the board that they can't afford any more and then when they realize they can't get what they want they suddenly find the extra money!'

These events were a blow to the union's credibility and furthered the already low-trust relationship between management and stewards. As a steward explained: 'Anything we bring back from the advisory board, they're [the employees] going to be deeply suspicious of now. We've been made to look like management mouthpieces.' She also noted: 'We're [the union] not going to believe anything they tell us on the board anyway.' This was a poor portent for future employee relations at the Company.

In summary, even where institutional processes which could be termed new industrial relations practices were in operation at the Company (such as its new-style agreement or communications and participation techniques), their success at influencing 'them and us' attitudes among the workforce appeared to be hampered by the style in which local management attempted to maintain control and discipline of the workplace. This was a style which could best be termed as traditional British industrial relations: low-trust and adversarial.

As reported above, the questionnaire results indicated employee dissatisfaction with a number of issues related to the organization and management of production methods at RENCO. These responses as with those identifying dissatisfaction with employee relations at the Company could be attributed to problems resulting from the dual management structure in place there: in particular, problems of poor communications and interaction between Japanese and local management. This meant that while UK managers were expected to organize and manage production methods at the Company using Japanese practices they received little support and guidance as to how to go about doing so.

Poor communications and interaction between Japanese and local management was reinforced by a hierarchical structure which excluded local management from much of the decision-making process. An Executive Management Committee (EMC) existed which several local managers described as 'the inner cabinet'. All eight of its members with the exception of the UK Personnel Manager were Japanese. Key policies were formulated and decisions taken in this committee, but even the Personnel Manager was sceptical as to his role. 'I'm pretty sure that a lot of late night meetings go on before anything arrives for discussion there,' he remarked. 'The result is usually a foregone conclusion.'

Other local managers expressed concern about inadequate local management representation on the EMC and the lack of proper consultation over production-related decisions that it took. One of them explained: 'What we have here is an élite of Japanese. We do not have any meaningful input into the decision-making process. They make a decision at the EMC and then it suddenly arrives as a memo or is brought up at a production meeting for us to implement.'

It has to be remembered that at 18 months old RENCO was relatively new, still trying to establish a consistent manufacturing performance. It would be understandable that the Company should encounter production problems during its start-up period, but the poor communications and interaction between the Japanese and local management exacerbated them. This was apparent in a number of ways. Two examples concern the repair and maintenance of production machinery and the quality of components supplied to the Company.

Taking the first example, production at RENCO was frequently disrupted by machinery faults. Insufficient spares were carried while the UK maintenance technicians had a poor reputation among operators who viewed them as being poorly skilled. The local manager responsible for repairs and maintenance argued that the technicians' poor reputation was because 'We can't get anything from the maintenance manuals since they're all written in Japanese! Our only real training is done by watching the Japanese work on machinery that is unfamiliar to us.'

These problems led to lengthy machine shutdowns and a reliance on Japanese management to repair them when they had the time. For instance, a semi-automatic weld line was particularly prone to breakdown and this necessitated a reversion to manual welding while it was being repaired. The frequency of this disruption impacted on employee attitudes and behaviour. They complained about the 'stop-start' nature of work that it caused and criticized management for their incompetence at failing to remedy the problem. Moreover, several argued during interviews that workers felt disinclined to put extra effort into their work since they felt that the gains were regularly offset by machinery breakdowns.

Employee attitudes and behaviour were also affected by the quality of components delivered to RENCO. The Company was supposed to have a buyer–supplier relationship that was 'just-in-time'-oriented. Though not as developed as buyer–supplier relationships operated in Japan, this nevertheless required that external suppliers delivered consistently high quality components. The local manager in charge of procurement had not operated a 'just-in-time'-oriented supply system before and complained that his Japanese colleagues had given him no real guidance or support about how to do so. As a result, the Company frequently received poor quality components and in the assembly area, which was particularly reliant on the supply of a large number of components, there were regular disruptions to production. The severity of these disruptions could be such that, as on one occasion during the period of observation at the Company, production was held up for three days while a faulty component batch was reworked and the Company waited for a replacement batch to be delivered.

Nearly three-quarters of questionnaire respondents agreed that morale was low at RENCO (see Table 9.1) and the Personnel Manager believed that much of this was due to the disruptions to production. As he saw it: 'They affect worker morale. Without a continuous flow of production, workers know we can't deliver the success that we constantly promise.' His concern reflected the fact that what amounted to a vicious circle had emerged at the Company. Fig. 9.3 summarizes this vicious circle and incorporates the issue of poor quality components as an example. It shows that, although RENCO placed great emphasis on quality, workers believed management were actually uninterested in the issue. They were perceived as allowing the workforce to be supplied with poor quality components which often disrupted production. Employees were supposed to take responsibility for the quality of products by self-checking.

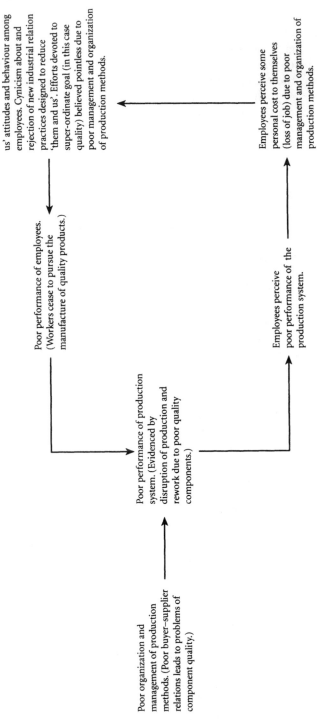

FIG. 9.3. How poor management and organization of production methods at RENCO led to the emergence of a vicious circle (with special reference to the issue of quality)

However, several explained that they saw little point in self-checking when they doubted the quality of the components used to build the product. As one pointed out: 'Why bother to self-check when you know you're going to see the thing back on the line as rework anyway?' This further contributed to the Company's poor performance: hence the emergence of a vicious circle.

Fuelling this vicious circle was the feeling among many employees that the poor performance of the Company's production system had resulted in some personal cost to themselves. They expressed doubts and cynicism about the superordinate goal of both management and workers working together to make the Company successful. Further, they had no confidence in management's ability to manage the company successfully and were especially critical of local management with which they had the most contact. An operator summed up these feelings:

As far as I can see there's no respect for management's ability to manage here any more. The British management just don't know what they're doing. A lot of them don't even seem to care about what's going on. Everyone can see that. If they're no good then they won't get any respect and I don't see how they can expect people to work for the good of the Company.

Other workers saw the personal cost in more dramatic terms, believing that their initial expectations of job security at RENCO were now under serious threat. Two other well-known and successful Japanese companies operated in the same locality (companies X and Y) and RENCO's employees could not help but make comparisons, so that as one operator put it:

I thought the chance of a permanent job in a Japanese factory would be great. They look after their workers differently and they know how to make a place run. You have only got to look at how well X and Y have done. That was before I came here. Now I can't see how we'll still be open in a year's time when nothing's going out of the door.

Loyalty to the Company was undermined by these perceptions and may have contributed to 68.1 per cent of questionnaire respondents being in some disagreement with the statement 'It would take a lot for me to leave this firm' (see Table 9.1).

To summarize, management were being blamed for RENCO's poor production performance and this was to the detriment of any attempt to reduce 'them and us' attitudes and behaviour among its workforce. Had employee expectations of well-organized and -managed production methods been met, then the Company's attempts to reduce 'them and us' might have been more favourably received.

5. Conclusions and Implications

Earlier, it was argued that there was a theoretical overlap between Japanization and new industrial relations. The use of Japanese employee relations practices in the UK were shown to be in line with a strategy of reducing 'them and us' using Kelly and Kelly's (1991) three routes to attitude change (see Fig. 9.1). In addition, it was argued that it was not only Japanese employee relations practices which facilitated reductions in 'them and us' but also the use of Japanese production methods.

The RENCO case study does not demonstrate the extent to which employee relations affected 'them and us' more than production methods or vice versa. However, when we consider Kelly and Kelly's three routes to attitude change in relation to the Company's experience, it becomes apparent how a combination of both employee relations and production methods there created a work environment that was not conducive to reductions in 'them and us' attitudes among employees. First, increased inter-group contact as a result of the Company's employee relations practices and production methods did little to improve 'them and us'. Secondly, the Company's attempt to create a superordinate goal was rejected by workers. Thirdly, workers saw no real evidence of changes in management behaviour in respect of their handling of employee relations and did not see them as able or willing to alter their behaviour so as to successfully operate Japanese production methods.

The failure of RENCO's employee relations and production methods to successfully impact on 'them and us' is attributable to their encountering a number of obstacles to attitude change. These were similar to the four discussed by Kelly and Kelly (1991).

The first of these obstacles was that there was a possible lack of choice for workers participating in, and subject to, both the employee relations practices and production methods in use at RENCO. When RENCO first commenced manufacturing, workers had been willing parties to many of the employee relations practices and production methods that management had put in place. They believed, and had been persuaded by management, that these were indicative of the importance management attached to reductions in 'them and us' and would contribute to the successful performance of the Company. Workers perceived that their willingness to work under the Company's employee relations and production methods was their contribution towards a superordinate goal of everybody, workers and management alike, working to make RENCO successful.

By the time the study was conducted workers had become hostile towards employee relations at the Company and in particular towards the new-style agreement it had signed with the EETPU. Just after the Company had commenced production, and once it had finished negotiating the agreement, workers had been balloted on whether to accept it. They had done so by a large majority. A criticism of new-style agreements is that they might benefit productivity not because they engender conflict-free industrial relations, but because management can use them purely as a means to try and reduce the ability of the union and its members to disrupt production and control the workplace (Garrahan 1986; TUC 1988). Given the style in which local management operated employee relations at RENCO, this appears to have been what subsequently transpired even if it was not their original intention. On this basis, workers were willing parties to the agreement as it was described by management and union representatives who were canvassing their support at the time of the ballot, but unwilling parties to the agreement once they saw it put into practice.

A similar situation had evolved concerning production methods in operation at RENCO. Workers believed them to be poorly organized and managed. Their willing participation in production methods designed to ensure high standards of production had given way to resentment, cynicism, and a lack of commitment. For example, they no longer bothered to self-check for quality.

The second obstacle at RENCO relates to a lack of institutional support among management for its employee relations practices and production methods. Management at the Company argued that its employee relations were fundamental to its strategy of reducing 'them and us'. Similarly, they understood the need for the successful organization and management of Japanese production methods in use there. Yet 'Strategic rhetoric' among senior management was not translated into 'operational reality' (Grant 1993). The necessary institutional support to ensure these management practices were properly implemented and sustained was not in evidence. Local management operated employee relations in a style that discouraged reductions in 'them and us' attitudes and behaviour. Moreover, the lack of communications and interaction between local and Japanese management meant that local management received little advice or direction about how to operate the Japanese production methods in use at the Company. Production methods were therefore poorly managed and production suffered accordingly. Workers lost confidence in management and this also impacted on their 'them and us' attitudes and behaviour.

The third obstacle concerns the basic lack of trust that existed between management and workers at RENCO. It can be linked to what was described as the traditional style in which local management operated employee relations. Control of the workplace and management's relationship with employees and the EETPU exhibited low-trust, adversarial characteristics and this was inconsistent with a strategy to reduce 'them and us' attitudes and behaviour.

Problems with the management and organization of production methods in use at RENCO also led to a lack of workforce trust in management. This stemmed from management being perceived as failing to play their part in the pursuit of a crucial superordinate goal, where in return for the workforce working towards the success of the Company, management would manage production successfully.

The fourth and final obstacle to securing changes in 'them and us' attitudes and behaviour at RENCO concerns inequality of status and outcomes. It has already been explained how workers believed that management at RENCO were not fulfilling their role in the pursuit of a superordinate goal. While this led to a lack of trust in management's ability to manage, it also meant that workers began to see an inequality of status and outcomes. They could see no reward for themselves in return for their working hard since their efforts were undermined by the inadequate organization and management of the production methods in use at the Company. Instead, many feared that the poor performance of the production system would be at some personal cost to themselves in that some or all of the workforce would lose their jobs. In this situation workers believed that their working hard in the interests of the Company had become pointless. They therefore performed poorly and this further contributed to the Company's poor performance, hence the emergence of a vicious circle such as that ascribed to the main assembly area.

The workforce at RENCO also perceived an inequality of status and outcomes owing to employee relations and in particular the new-style agreement in operation at the Company. The EETPU's members had what can only be described as very traditional expectations of the role the union should play, for example to increase wages, to improve terms and conditions of work, and to protect them from possible management exploitation. The research shows that where management do not adhere to the 'spirit and intention' behind the agreement then union members may become dissatisfied with their union's performance. Members at RENCO blamed this poor performance on the provisions of the new-style agreement in operation there. For example, they saw the agreement's no-strike clause as weakening the union and believed that the cooperation the agreement was supposed to engender was one-way; that is to say, cooperation was given by workers and exploited by management to their own advantage. In effect, workers saw the agreement as accentuating rather than closing an inequality of status and outcomes between management and workers.

Though there is evidence that other Japanese transplants in the UK have encountered some or all of the obstacles described above (Grant 1993), the way in which both employee relations and production methods at RENCO affected employee attitudes and behaviour is not necessarily typical at Japanese transplants in the UK. Indeed, the research from which the RENCO case study is drawn found evidence of both employee relations and production methods at Japanese transplants having a positive effect on 'them and us' related attitudes and behaviour (Grant 1993). None the less, the obstacles encountered at RENCO were caused by certain key factors—factors which are not exclusive to RENCO (see Broad 1994a; 1994b) and which have important implications for the issues of both Japanization and the wider debate surrounding new industrial relations in the UK.

In the context of direct Japanization, the RENCO case study highlights two potential weaknesses within dual management structures at Japanese transplants in the UK. First, RENCO showed that the introduction of UK management into a transplant may lead to the operation of employee relations practices by them in a low-trust and adversarial style. This will serve to either exacerbate or maintain existing 'them and us' attitudes and behaviour. Second, a dual management structure may also induce poor communications and interaction between Japanese and local management. If local management are unfamiliar with Japanese production methods this will contribute to the poor organization and management of production methods in use at such companies. The resultant deficiencies of the production system will again encourage 'them and us' attitudes and behaviour among workers which are detrimental to its performance. One solution to these problems, examined by Grant (1993), is the use of detailed selection procedures for both the Japanese managers who are posted to UK transplants and the local managers that they subsequently employ. This enables the identification of managers with the ability to modify and adapt their culturally based management styles to the relatively unusual circumstances they will encounter at a transplant. Tayeb's (1994) work suggests that where Japanese and local managers exhibit these characteristics they are likely to enjoy a high degree of success when implementing Japanese management techniques in the UK.

The implications of the research for those companies attempting to emulate Japanese management practices—what Ackroyd *et al.* (1988) describe as mediated Japanization—are considerable. Emulators could simply import many of the problems encountered by Japanese transplants into their own production systems with all that entails for the performance of the production system and attempts to reduce 'them and us'. UK management at RENCO operated employee relations in a low-trust, adversarial manner and this had a detrimental effect on 'them and us' attitudes and behaviour. It therefore follows that UK emulators need to be prepared to encounter this problem among their own management. Similarly, what happened at RENCO suggests that emulators would also need to take a close look at any Japanese production methods they wish to use and at the ability and commitment of their existing management to organize and manage them.

A further implication of the results is that they raise questions about what sort of role there is for trade unions to play under new industrial relations, especially where they have signed new-style agreements. The RENCO case study showed that members can have very traditional expectations of a union's role and that these expectations conflict with the provisions of a new-style agreement based on cooperation and trust. Where such expectations are frustrated because managers operate the agreement in an adversarial and conflictual style, the members may become dissatisfied with their union's performance. There is some evidence that this situation can lead to a loss of membership for the union (Grant 1993; 1994). Alternatively, and as appeared to be emerging at RENCO, the union may feel compelled to take an increasingly traditional stance in order to maintain support: one where it represents the sectional interests of the workforce with very little regard for the superordinate goal of what is good for the company is good for both management and employees. In short, employees who have a traditional set of expectations of their union and a management who appear unfamiliar with or even hostile to the cooperation and trust the agreements are supposed to encourage appears a recipe for an adversarial management–union relationship.

The experience of RENCO would do little to encourage the adoption of new-style agreements at other 'greenfield' or established plants in the UK. It shows how both management and the union can become focused on issues of control at the workplace rather than any commitment to reductions in 'them and us'. From a management perspective, recognizing a trade union under the terms of a new-style agreement may be problematical. The agreements might fail to induce cooperative industrial relations because they conflict with the union members requiring that, in line with their traditional expectations, unions play a more adversarial role when dealing with management. Moreover, what occurred at RENCO does not suggest that new-style agreements offer trade unions a strategy with which to halt the perceived decline in their influence and power at the workplace since the early 1980s. Instead, it appears to give credence to an argument that the agreements are symptomatic of, and may even contribute to, this decline (for explanations and discussions of declining trade union fortunes see MacInnes 1987; Marsh 1992; Kelly 1987, 1990; Batsone and Gourlay 1986; Beaumont 1990; Kessler and Bayliss 1992; Disney 1990; Freeman and Pelletier 1990; Brown and Wadhwani 1990; Purcell 1991; Metcalf 1989).

Finally, what happened at RENCO shows that not only innovative employee relations practices impact upon 'them and us' at the workplace. The production methods in use and the way in which they are organized and managed are also crucial. In the context of new industrial relations there are a whole new set of issues to be considered in terms of what actually influences attempts to alter employee attitudes and behaviour.

REFERENCES

Ackroyd, S. *et al.* (1988), 'The Japanization of British Industry?', *Industrial Relations Journal,* 19/1.

AJEI (1992), *Japanese Addresses in the UK* (London: AJEI).

Allen, P. T. (1986), 'Contact and Conflict in Industry', in Hewstone and Brown (1986).

——— and Stephenson, G. M. (1983), 'Inter-Group Understanding and Size of Organization', *British Journal of Industrial Relations*, 21: 312–29.

——— (1985), 'The Relationship of Inter-Group Understanding and Inter-Party Friction in Industry', *British Journal of Industrial Relations*, 23: 203–13.

Bassett, P. (1986), *Strike Free: New Industrial Relations in Britain* (London: Macmillan).

Batstone, E., and Gourlay, S. (1986), *Unions Unemployment and Innovation* (Oxford: Basil Blackwell).

Beaumont, P. (1990), *Change in Industrial Relations* (London: Routledge).

Bratton, J. (1992), *Japanization at Work* (London: Macmillan).

Broad, G. (1994*a*), 'Japan in Britain: The Dynamics of Joint Consultation', *Industrial Relations Journal,* 25/1: 26–38.

——— (1994*b*), 'Managerial Limits to Japanization: A Manufacturing Case Study', *Human Resource Management Journal,* 4/3: 41–61.

Brown, W., and Wadhwani, S. (1990), 'The Economic Effects of Industrial Relations Legislation since 1979', *National Institute Economic Review* (Feb.), 57–69.

Burrows, G. (1986), *No Strike Agreements and Pendulum Arbitration* (London: IPM).

Clay Hamner, W., and Smith, F. J. (1978), 'Work Attitudes as Predictors of Unionization Activity', *Journal of Applied Psychology*, 69/3: 415–11.

Cooper, J., and Fazio, R. H. (1984), 'A New Look at Dissonance Theory', *Advances in Experimental Social Psychology*, xvii. 229–66.

Cusumano, M. (1985), *The Japanese Auto Industry: Technology and Management at Toyota and Nissan* (Cambridge, Mass.: Harvard University Press).

Dewe, P., Dunn, S., and Richardson, R. (1988), 'Employee Share Option Schemes: Why Workers are Attracted to Them', *British Journal of Industrial Relations*, 26/1: 1–20.

Disney, R. (1990), 'Explanations of the Decline in Trade Union Density in Britain: An Appraisal', *British Journal of Industrial Relations*, 28/2 (July), 165–78.

Freeman, R., and Pelletier, G. (1990), 'Industrial Relations Legislation and British Union Density', *British Journal of Industrial Relations*, 28/2: 141–64.

Garrahan, P. (1986), 'Nissan in the North East of England', *Capital and Class*, 27: 5–13.

——— and Stewart, P. (1992), *The Nissan Enigma: Flexibility at Work in a Local Economy* (London: Mansell).

Gleave, S., and Oliver, N. (1990), 'Human Resources Management in Japanese Manufacturing Companies in the UK: Five Case Studies', *Journal of General Management*, 16/1: 55–68.

Grant, D. (1993), 'Japanese Manufacturers in the UK Electronics Sector: The Impact of Production Systems on Employee Attitudes and Behaviour', Ph.D. thesis, LSE.

——— (1994), 'New Style Agreements at Japanese Transplants in the UK: The Implications for Trade Union Decline', *Employee Relations*, 16/2.

Gregory, M. (1986), 'The No-Strike Deal in Action', *Personnel Management* (Dec.), 30–5.

Guest, D., Peccei, R., and Thomas, (1993), 'The Impact of Employee Involvement on Organisational Commitment and "Them and Us" Attitudes', *Industrial Relations Journal*, 24/3: 191–200.

Hackman, J. R., and Oldham, G. R. (1975), 'Development of the Job Diagnostic Survey', *Journal of Applied Psychology*, 60/2: 214–32.

Hewstone, M., and Brown, R. (1986), 'Contact is Not Enough: An Intergroup Perspective on the "Contact Hypothesis"', in M. Hewstone and R. Brown (eds.), *Contact and Conflict in Intergroup Encounters* (Oxford: Basil Blackwell).

Hitachi (1990), 'Hitachi and You' (Unpublished employee handbook).

IDS (1987), *No-Strike Clauses and Single-Union Deals* (Study, 44; London: IDS).

IRS (1989), *Single Union Deals* (Study, 442; London: IRS).

——— (1990), *The Japanese in Britain: Employment Policies and Practice* (Study, 470; London: IRS).

Jenner, F., and Trevor, M. (1985), 'Personnel Management in Four UK Electronics Plants', in S. Takamiya and K. Thurley, *Japan's Emerging Multinationals* (Tokyo: University of Tokyo Press).

JETRO (1993), *The 9th Survey of European Operations of Japanese Companies in the Manufacturing Sector* (London: JETRO).

Jurgens, U., and Stromel, H. (1986), *The Communications Structure between Some of the Management and Shop-floor: Comparison of a Japanese and German Plant* (Berlin: International Institute for Comparative Social Research).

Kelly, J. (1987), 'Trade Unions through the Recession', *British Journal of Industrial Relations*, 25/2: 275–82.

—— (1990), 'British Trade Unionism 1979–1989: Change Continuity and Contradictions', *Work Employment and Society* (May), 29–66.

—— and Kelly, C. (1991), 'Them and Us: A Social Psychological Analysis of the New Industrial Relations', *British Journal of Industrial Relations*, 29/1: 25–48.

Kenney, M., and Florida, R. (1988), 'Beyond Mass Production: Production and the Labour Process in Japan', *Politics and Society*, 16/1: 121–58.

Kessler, S., and Bayliss, F. (1992), *Contemporary British Industrial Relations* (London: Macmillan).

Krafcik, J. F. (1988), 'Triumph of the Lean Production System', *Sloan Management Review*, 30/1: 41–52.

MacBeth, D. (1987), 'Supplier Management in Support of JIT Activity: A Research Agenda', *International Journal of Operations and Production Management*, 7/4: 53–63.

MacDuffie, J. P., and Krafcik, J. F. (1990), 'Integrating Technology and Human Resources for High Performance Manufacturing: Evidence from the International Auto Industry', in J. Chelius and J. Dworkin (eds.), *Reflections on the Transformation of Industrial Relations* (Metuchen, NJ: IMLR/Rutgers University).

MacInnes, J. (1987), *Thatcherism at Work* (Milton Keynes: Open University Press).

Marsden, D., Morris, T., Willman, P., and Wood, S. (1985), *The Car Industry* (London: Tavistock).

Marsh, D. (1992), *The New Politics of British Trade Unionism* (London: Macmillan).

Metcalf, D. (1989), 'Water Notes Dry Up: The Impact of Donovan Reform Proposals and Thatcherism at Work on Labour Productivity in British Manufacturing', *British Journal of Industrial Relations*, 27/1: 1–30.

Mondon, Y. (1981), 'What Makes the Toyota Production System Really Tick?' *Industrial Engineering Magazine* (Jan.), 29–46.

—— (1983), *Toyota Production System* (Atlanta: Industrial Engineering and Management Press).

Nishiguchi, T. (1990), 'Strategic Dualism: An Alternative in Industrial Societies', Ph.D. thesis, Nuffield College, Oxford.

Ohno, T. (1988), *Toyota Production System* (Philadelphia: Production Press).

Oki (1990), 'Staff Handbook' (Unpublished employee handbook).

Oliver, N., and Wilkinson, B. (1992), *The Japanization of British Industry* (Oxford: Basil Blackwell).

Pegge, T. (1986), 'Hitachi Two Years On', *Personnel Management* (Oct.), 42–7.

Pioneer (1991), 'Always the Pioneer' (Unpublished employee handbook).

Piore, M., and Sabel, C. (1984), *The Second Industrial Divide* (New York: Basic Books).

Purcell, J. (1991), 'The Rediscovery of Management Prerogative', *Oxford Review of Economic Policy*, 7/1: 33–59.

Reitsperger, W. (1985), 'Personnel Policy and Employee Satisfaction', in M. Takamiya and K. Thurley (eds.), *Japan's Emerging Multinationals* (Tokyo: University of Tokyo Press).

—— (1986a), 'Japanese Management: Coping With British Industrial Relations', *Journal of Management Studies*, 23/1: 72–88.

—— (1986b), 'British Employees: Responding to Japanese Management Philosophies', *Journal of Management Studies*, 23/5: 263–88.

Rico, L. (1987), 'The New Industrial Relations: British Electricians' New-Style Agreements', *Industrial and Labour Relations Review*, 41/1: 63–78.

Roberts, B. (1988), 'A New Era in British Industrial Relations', in *New Departures in Industrial Relations: Developments in the US, the UK, and Canada* (Washington: British-North American Committee).

Sako, M. (1992), *Prices Quality and Trust: Inter Firm Relations in Britain and Japan* (London: Cambridge University Press).

Schonberger, R. (1986), *Japanese Manufacturing Techniques* (New York: Free Press).

Sherif, M. (1966), *Group Conflict and Co-operation*, (London: Routledge & Kegan Paul).

Shingo, S. (1982), *A Study of the Toyota Production System from an Industrial Engineering Viewpoint* (Tokyo: Japan Management Association).

Slaughter, J. (1987), 'The Team Concept in the US Auto Industry', Paper presented to the Cardiff Business School Conference on the Japanization of British Industry, 17–18 Sept.

Tailby, S., and Turnbull, P. (1987), 'Learning to Manage Just-In-Time', *Personnel Management* (Jan.), 16–19.

Tayeb, M. (1994), 'Japanese Managers and British Culture: A Comparative Case Study', *International Journal of Human Resource Management*, 5/1: 145–66.

Thurley, K., and Wirdenius, H. (1973), *Supervision: A Reappraisal* (London: Heinemann).

Trevor, M. (1988), *Toshiba's New British Company* (London: PSI).

—— and Christie, I. (1988), *Manufacturers and Suppliers in Britain and Japan* (London: PPI).

TUC (1988), *Meeting the Challenge: First report of the Special Review Body* (London: TUC).

Turnbull, P. (1986), 'The Japanization of Production and Industrial Relations at Lucas Electrical', *Industrial Relations Journal*, 17/3: 193–206.

—— (1988), 'The Limits to Japanization: Just-in-Time, Labour Relations and the UK Automotive Industry', *New Technology, Work and Employment*, 3/1: 7–20.

Voss, C. (1987) (ed.), *Just-in-Time Manufacture* (London: IFS).

—— and Robinson, S. (1987), 'The Application of Just-in-Time Techniques', *International Journal of Operations and Production Management*, 7/4: 46–52.

White, M., and Trevor, M. (1983), *Under Japanese Management* (London: Heinemann).

Wickens, P. (1987), *The Road to Nissan* (London: Macmillan).

Wilkinson, B., and Oliver, N. (1992), 'Human Resource Management in Japanese Manufacturing Companies in the UK and USA', in B. Towers (ed.), *The Handbook of Human Resource Management* (Oxford: Basil Blackwell).

—— Morris, J., and Munday, M. (1993), 'Japan in Wales: A New IR', *Industrial Relations Journal*, 24/4: 273–83.

Womack, J. P., Jones, D. T., and Roos, D. (1990), *The Machine that Changed the World: The Triumph of Lean Production* (New York: Rawson Macmillan).

Wood, S. (1989), 'The Japanese Management Model: Tacit Skills in Shop Floor Participation', *Work and Occupations*, 16/4: 446–60.

—— (1992), 'Japanization and/or Toyotaism?', *Work Employment and Society*, 5/4: 567–600.

Woodward, J. (1980), *Industrial Organization: Theory and Practice* (Oxford: Oxford University Press).

INDEX

Lightning Source UK Ltd.
Milton Keynes UK
UKOW020502120112

185221UK00001B/85/A